D1610674

The Banshees

Irish Studies

James MacKillop, *Series Editor*

THE

Banshees

A LITERARY HISTORY
OF IRISH AMERICAN
WOMEN WRITERS

Sally Barr Ebest

SYRACUSE UNIVERSITY PRESS

Material from the following publications is used here with permission:

"Ahead of Their Time: Irish American Women Writers, 1945–1960," *After the Flood: Irish America 1945–1960,* James Silas Rogers and Matthew J. O'Brien, eds. (Portland, OR: Irish Academic Press, 2009).

"Evolving Feminisms," *Reconciling Catholicism and Feminism? Personal Reflections on Tradition and Change,* Sally Barr Ebest and Ron Ebest (South Bend: Univ. of Notre Dame Press, 2003).

"Introduction: Writing Green Thoughts," "Mary McCarthy: Too Smart to Be Sentimental," and "Erin McGraw: Expanding the Tradition of Irish American Women Writers," *Too Smart to Be Sentimental,* Sally Barr Ebest and Kathleen McInerney (South Bend: Univ. of Notre Dame Press, 2008).

"'Reluctant Catholics': Contemporary Irish American Women Writers," *The Catholic Church and Unruly Women Writers,* Jeanna Del Rosso, Leigh Eicke, and Ana Kothe, eds. (New York: Palgrave, 2007).

"These Traits also Endure: Irish and Irish-American Women's Novels." *New Hibernia Review* 7.2 (Summer 2003): 55–72.

For a listing of books published and distributed by Syracuse University Press, visit our website at SyracuseUniversityPress.syr.edu.

ISBN: 978-0-8156-3330-3 (cloth)   978-0-8156-5240-3 (e-book)

Library of Congress Cataloging-in-Publication Data

Available on request from the publisher.

Manufactured in the United States of America

To my favorite Irish American women:

Linda Barr Cobbe

Susan Barr Tesh

Mary Barr Goral

April Smith Barr

Andrea Barr Pisano

and our matriarch,

Helen Morris Barr

Sally Barr Ebest is Professor of English and Director of the Gender Studies Program at the University of Missouri-St. Louis. She teaches courses in autobiography; literary, composition, and feminist theory; and, whenever possible, Irish and Irish American women writers. Her publications include *Changing the Way We Teach* (Southern Illinois Univ. Press 2005), *Reconciling Catholicism and Feminism?* (Notre Dame 2003), and *Too Smart to Be Sentimental: Contemporary Irish American Women Writers* (Notre Dame 2008).

Contents

Acknowledgments

In 1998, I fell in love. Although I had jumped through the requisite hoops in graduate school, attended many a conference, and published enough to earn tenure, I had never felt so academically enamored. The site was Charles Fanning's Carbondale Symposium on the Irish Diaspora. For two days, I listened, rapt, to intellectually challenging, interdisciplinary research covering a range of topics. Intimidated but impressed, I longed to be a part of this erudite group.

I was also intrigued. As I listened to papers on Irish American unique-ness, imagination, and immigration, as I learned about writers such as Donn Byrne, Colum McCann, and Frank McCourt, I wondered: Where are the women? While Maureen Murphy discussed depictions of the Irish servant girl and Ellen Skerritt described the Irish in Chicago's Hull House neighbor-hood, no one addressed the works of Irish or Irish American women writers. How could such an impressive array of scholars overlook half the population? I was hooked.

Thus began this scholarly endeavor. For that, I am forever grateful to Charlie Fanning. *The Irish Voice in America* provided an impressive starting point, but Charlie himself was a gracious and informative mentor through-out my research. Jim Rogers was also instrumental. Recognizing the field's gender gap, he published my first essay in *New Hibernia Review*, called on me to review manuscripts on the topic, and invited me to contribute a chap-ter on Irish American women to *After the Flood: Irish America, 1945–1960*. Likewise, Kathleen McInerney, Mary Ann Ryan, Patricia Gott, and Beatrice Jacobson helped raise awareness of Irish American women writers thanks to their contributions to our edited collection, *Too Smart to Be Sentimen-tal*. My colleagues Eamonn Wall, Kathy Gentile, Peter Wolf, and Barbara

Harbach helped promote this work by inviting me to present colloquia for the University of Missouri-St. Louis's Irish Studies Program, Institute for Women's and Gender Studies, English department, and Women in the Arts, respectively. Thanks also to the ACIS regional and national conference planners for accepting my papers at events in Omaha, Milwaukee, Minneapolis, St. Louis, St. Paul, Bloomington/ Normal, DeKalb, Kansas City, Carbondale, Davenport, New Orleans, and Liverpool—and to the UMSL Office of Research, College of Arts & Sciences, and Department of English for funding these trips. This could not have happened without the support and approval of Deans Mark Burkholder and Ron Yasbin and my department chair, Richard Cook.

In fall 2009, support from the University of Missouri-St. Louis Research Board and Joel Glassman, director of UMSL's International Studies Program, funded a semester's research leave to compile the manuscript; in 2013, a second International Studies fellowship underwrote the costs of indexing. As I cranked out the chapters, Nancy Cervetti and Carolyn Brown provided invaluable feedback. Equally important, as I created and rejected various titles, my colleague Drucilla Wall listened and offered a brilliant suggestion: Why not call these writers *The Banshees*? Thanks, Dru.

Finally, none of this would have happened if not for my husband, Ron Ebest. His interest in Irish Studies piqued mine; his research brought me to Charlie's symposium. Our happy hour discussions regarding the lack of research on the confluence of feminism and Catholicism led to our collaboration on *Reconciling Catholicism and Feminism?* Indeed, his tactful persistence convinced a reluctant editor to use that intriguing title. As I delved into early twentieth-century Irish American history, Ron's book, *Private Histories: The Writing of Irish Americans, 1900–1935*, revealed the satirical strengths of Irish American women writers of that period. Not least, his many readings of the *Banshees* manuscript brought a sharp eye, insightful commentary, and wealth of knowledge to the project. His support is the source of my strength.

Thanks to everyone who helped me bring this project to fruition. Their contributions helped introduce the banshees to the field of Irish Studies.

The Banshees

Introduction
The Banshees

Numerous books have been written about American feminism and its influence on education and society. But none have recognized, let alone demonstrated, the key role played by Irish American women writers in exposing women's issues, protecting women's rights, and anticipating, if not effecting, change. Irish American women's writing is particularly appropriate for this approach, for theirs has been a battle against patriarchal bonds on two fronts: society, which has imposed such bonds, and the Catholic Church, which created and reinforced them. By analyzing their work, *The Banshees* addresses this issue while simultaneously expanding the boundaries of the Irish American canon.

Why the banshee? Because Irish American women writers share a good deal in common with the mythical Irish being. Sometimes translated as "scold" or "a scolding woman," the term "banshee"/*bean-si* is a derivation of *badhb*, which can mean "war goddess" or "a dangerous, frightening and aggressive being." One variation, *badb*, is associated with "heroic individuals"; another, *badhbh*, refers to "threatening" females; whereas tales associated with the *si*-woman convey the role of guardian (Lysaght 1986, 37–39, 216).[1] Given these roots it is not surprising that in the 1970s, the banshee was adopted as the symbol of the Irish Women United (IWU), a radical

---

1. For additional information, see Patricia Lysaght, *Banshees*, 1986. Lysaght, the foremost expert on the banshee, devotes at least three chapters to the Irish roots and meanings of the term.

feminist group. The IWU named their journal *Banshee* "not only because the being is feminine, but also because her appearance and behavior do not correspond to conventional male ideas about what a woman should look like and be like" (Lysaght 1986, 243). Although the journal disappeared in 1975, the concept was revitalized for a literary website in 1997 by New Irish authors Emer Martin and Helena Mulkerns. "We chose the name *Banshee*," Mulkerns explains, "because we wanted something strong, loud, female, and Irish" (quoted in Wall 1999, 67).

Like the banshee who delivered messages forewarning imminent death, through their writing Irish American women have repeatedly warned of the death of women's rights. These messages carried the greatest potency at liminal times when feminism was under attack owing to the politics of society, the government, or the church. Similar to the banshee's plaintive lament, Irish American women's writing has been cautionary if not "tutelary" (Lysaght 1986). Moreover, just as the banshee's lament was not heard by everyone, Irish American women—and their writing—have been omitted from "most religious, academic, and popular chronicles" (Dezell 2001, 89).

The American Catholic Church is responsible for women's absence in religious histories. Early works, generally written by and about priests, contained very little information about lay men, but lay women were "invisible" most likely because of what Mary Jo Weaver terms the authors' "invincible ignorance." More recent works, Weaver continues, have simply been guilty of "willful neglect." In Robert Trisco's *Catholics in America 1776–1976* (1976), thirty pictures are of male clerics and only seven of women; the rest are of buildings or political cartoons. Out of 331 pages in James Hennessey's *American Catholics* (1981), information about women amounts to approximately 10 pages, yet that alone represents the largest inclusion among Catholic histories at that time. Ten years later, William Shannon's *The American Irish: A Political and Social Portrait* (1990) devoted only a few paragraphs to women, most often citing their relationships with Irish men or their involvement with the suffrage movement. However, since suffragists were generally upper-class Catholic women, most Irish Americans were left out. Even as late as 2005, Tim Meagher's *Columbia Guide to Irish American History* cited only thirty-six women within over three hundred pages of text. Such oversights are not accidental, nor are they limited to Catholic historians; they simply reflect the fact that throughout much of American history, religion, Catholicism, and women were rarely addressed (Weaver 1985, 11–13).

Since the 1980s, women have been increasingly included in academic studies. Recent years have seen publications devoted to Jewish, Hispanic, Russian, Chinese, African, African American, Italian, Korean, Polish, Asian Pacific, Japanese, Pakistani, Arab, Greek, and Roman women. Studies have focused on lesbians, vampires, lesbian vampires, Islamic, Appalachian, medieval, and Victorian women, to name just a few. In contrast, coverage of Irish women has been scant. When the three-volume 4,000-page *Field Day Anthology of Irish Literature* was published in 1991, female readers were outraged to discover that editor Seamus Deane had "overlooked" the contributions of Irish women. In response, Toni O'Brien Johnson and David Cairn published *Gender in Irish Writing* (1991) and Anne Owens Weekes put out *Unveiling Treasures: The Attic Guide to the Published Works of Irish Women Literary Writers* (1993). In 2002, the *Field Day Anthology* corrected the oversights of its initial publication with a two-volume 3,200-page addition, *Irish Women's Writing and Traditions*. But to date, no similar efforts have been undertaken on behalf of Irish American women.

Within literary studies, *Making the Irish American* lists only (non-Irish) Betty Smith, Mary McCarthy, and Flannery O'Connor (Casey and Rhodes 2006). Although Patricia Monaghan (1993) laments the lack of coverage, her essays tend to focus on Irish American women poets. Charles Fanning, recognized nationally and internationally as the foremost Irish American literary scholar, devoted portions of *The Irish Voice in America* (1991; 2001) to women writers; however, since it covers 250 years, analysis is limited. Likewise, Catriona Maloney and Helen Thompson's *Irish Women Writers Speak Out: Voices from the Field* (2003) features interviews with seventeen contemporary Irish and Irish American women writers, but only six of them are Irish American. While Ron Ebest's *Private Histories: The Writing of Irish Americans, 1900–1935* (2005) addresses detailed attention to women authors of the period, coverage is limited to just three decades. Even the most recent research, such as Christopher Dowd's *The Construction of Irish Identity in American Literature* (2011) includes just one Irish American woman writer:

Margaret Mitchell. As of this writing, the only in-depth study is a collection of twelve critical essays, *Too Smart to Be Sentimental: Contemporary Irish American Women Writers* (Ebest and McInerney 2008). But this work represents at most 10 percent of contemporary Irish American women writers.

Irish American women have been overlooked not only because their writing avoids classic Irish American themes such as camaraderie, drink, violence, and pub life, but also because they refuse to reify saintly mothers or spend much time on priests (Monaghan 1993, 340). Historians and feminist scholars have also ignored Irish American women—historians because they were women and feminists because the women were presumably Catholic (Weaver 1985, 11). Irish American women have been ostracized because of the field's traditional definitions.[2] Eamonn Wall suggests: "If a writer does not write about Irish Americans . . . he or she will be labeled an American writer. The problem for an Irish American writer is that the field of operation is rather small, but if he or she abandons this field, there will no longer be an Irish American novel, *unless the parameters are extended*" (1999, 37, emphasis mine). But Gerda Lerner offers an antidote. In her argument for adding women to historical studies she recommends that the parameters be extended to include "sexuality, reproduction, role indoctrination, [and] female consciousness" as well as women's culture, which might encompass their "occupations, status, experiences, rituals, and consciousness" (quoted in Weaver 1985, 5–15).

The banshees have done just that: they extended the boundaries of the Irish American literary canon by moving inside the bedroom, outside the home, and into the workplace. Perhaps as a result, their works have been overlooked because of their feminist message. Since they arrived in America, the banshees have anticipated, fostered, and protected feminism by exposing domestic violence, fighting prejudice, and refuting political attacks on women's rights.

---

2. As Charles Fanning writes in *The Irish Voice in America*, "writers of Irish background who have chosen not to consider Irish ethnic themes—Flannery O'Connor, for example—will not appear" (4). Similarly, Mary McCarthy merits a single sentence (301).

The Famine Generations

Although the earliest groups of immigrants were primarily male (Fanning 1997, 2), women quickly made themselves heard. A role model for pre-Famine writers, Maria Edgeworth's novel *Castle Rackrent* (1800) was not just the first significant work of Irish fiction; it also made a political statement, for the term "rack-rent" referred to British landowners' practice of raising their tenant farmers' rents too high for tenants to pay, then evicting them and charging interest on any improvements they had made to the property. Originally published in Dublin and London, *Castle Rackrent* was quickly reproduced in America and went through multiple editions between 1814 and 1904. Another model was *The Wild Irish Girl* by Sydney Owenson, Lady Morgan. After its success in London and Dublin, the novel was reprinted five times in New York and Philadelphia. Although part of its popularity was due to a romantic plot, its story of a young English lord banished to Ireland who comes to love the land was not only an indictment of the British; it was also one of the earliest books by a woman to argue for Irish nationalism (Fanning 2001, 13). Still, these works were not typical Irish fare, for they mostly lacked a satiric edge.

The first generation of Irish American writers was more likely to draw on their forebears' tradition of satirical writing to parody and deflate anti-Irish stereotypes. These early emigrants were confident, educated, and articulate; consequently, they had no problem poking fun at their xenophobic neighbors. In 1835, *Six Months in a House of Correction; or, the Narrative of Dorah Mahoney, Who Was Under the Influence of the Protestants about a Year, and an Inmate of the House of Correction in Leverett St., Boston, Mass., Nearly Six Months* was published anonymously to counter Rebecca Reed's anti-Catholic tale *Six Months in a Convent*, which had resulted in a mob burning down a convent (Fanning 1997, 47). "Dorah's" tale is rife with wry one-liners, but the subsequent "Letter to Irish Catholics" is even better. Building on the model of juvenalian satire exemplified by Jonathan Swift's "A Modest Proposal" (1729), the author urges fellow immigrants not to learn to read or write, arguing, "Besides, it is a great trouble and expense to build schools and maintain them, and a great botheration to the brains to pore over books. The Catholic Sentinel and the Jesuit, those two admirably conducted reciptacles [*sic*] of knowledge, contain all that ever was known since the creation of the world" (Anonymous 1835, quoted in Fanning 1997, 60).

This highly literate first generation, who emigrated willingly prior to 1840, was followed by the Famine generation, most of whom were uneducated cottiers and tenant farmers (Fanning 1997, 97). Forced to choose between starvation or emigration, between 1846 and 1875 at least 2,700,000 Irish entered the United States. Half of this number consisted of single women, but by the 1870s female immigrants outnumbered the males—a freedom unique to the Irish (Meagher 2005, 173–74)—and memorialized by the statue of fifteen-year-old Annie Moore, the "first 'official' immigrant to enter the New World through Ellis Island" (Dezell 2001, 58). Miss Moore epitomized the Irish American female immigrant, who was young, single, and traveled alone, with sisters, or with female relations. By the end of the nineteenth century, these women represented over 60 percent of the Irish immigrants (Dezell 2001, 91).

Prior to the Famine, Irish women married, socialized, and worked side-by-side with the men in the fields; however, during the Famine years these opportunities constricted as work disappeared and marriages were postponed. Consequently, Irish women emigrated to escape such subservient positions and regain their financial independence (Nolan 2004, 91–92). They bought their own tickets, traveled unchaperoned, found employment (usually as domestic servants), and then saved their salaries to bring over family members, build churches, attend concerts, support nationalist movements, and pay parochial school tuition for their nieces or nephews (Meagher 2006, 623–24).

On the East Coast, where the majority remained, this influx of emigrants was met with anger, resentment, and palpable anti-Catholicism. According to Christopher Dowd, they were the "hated immigrant group *du jour*" (2011, 12). Coinciding with American concern about national identity, the publication of Darwin's *On the Origin of the Species* (1859), and the rise of Irish nationalism, Irish emigrants were depicted as "violent ape-men bent on political anarchy" (Dowd 2011, 12). Nativists feared the Irish because they were poor, unskilled, and unruly; they hated them because they broke strikes, drank too much, worked jobs no one wanted, and produced too many children (Kenny 2006, 372). By focusing on these social traits and viewing them as "hereditary dispositions," some Americans attempted to reduce the Irish to "fundamentally flawed organisms" who were contaminating society, if not the country (Dowd 2011, 14). Consigned to the lowest stratum of society, this generation constituted the urban poor. Most men took jobs as laborers, whereas three-quarters of the women were hired as domestic servants, a position that ultimately led to their social and economic mobility. This steady work as well as the daily opportunity to observe models of middle- and upper-class culture helped Irish American women grow into solid members of the community and promote their daughters' education and independence (Nolan 2004; Diner 1993).

Nevertheless, this confluence of hardship and negativity yielded three types of novels: nationalistic, evangelistic, and pragmatic (Fanning 1997, 97). Of these, the nationalistic typifies first-stage post-colonial emigrants' efforts to "reclaim the past" (Barry 2009). Mary Meany's 1865 novel, *The Confessors of Connaught; or, The Tenants of a Lord Bishop*, is one example; however, it is also notable for its irate account of a Protestant bishop evicting Catholic women and children into the cold. Another nationalist, Alice Nolan, decried the evictions of Irish tenants and the hanging of an innocent man in *The Byrnes of Glengoulah: A True Tale* (1870). But the most prolific, didactic, and evangelistic writer, as well as the first important Irish American female voice, was Mary Ann Madden Sadlier.

Born in Cootehill, County Cavan, in 1820, at age twenty-four Miss Madden emigrated to Montreal and married James Sadlier. Fourteen years later, the Sadliers and their six children moved to New York. Thanks in part to her husband's publishing company, between 1850 and 1870 Sadlier published over sixty novels, often serialized in popular magazines, praising home and hearth and attacking anti-Catholic rhetoric (Fanning 2001, 114ff). Sadlier's domain was the church. Her purpose, as she set out in her first novel, *Willy Burke; or, The Irish Orphan in America* (1850), was to be "useful to the young sons of my native land, in their arduous struggle with the tempter, whose nefarious design of bearing them from the faith of their fathers, is so artfully concealed under every possible disguise" (3–4). Each novel deals with the difficulty of discovering and resisting a different "tempting disguise" hidden variously in business (*Willy Burke*), domestic service (*Bessy Conway*, 1861), orphanages (*Aunt Honor's Keepsake*, 1866), financial success

(*Old and New; or, Taste vs. Fashion*, 1862), or the big city (*Con O'Regan; or, Immigrant Life in the New World* (1864). Given this focus, it is not surprising that in *Old and New*, Sadlier rejects the suffragist movement and supports the Catholic tradition of women remaining in the home (Fanning 1997, 112). Considering that Sadlier was deeply involved with the family publishing business, this stance was not satiric but unconsciously ironic.

The daughters of the Famine generation were less traumatized than their conservative parents yet still somewhat cautious. After 1875, as they moved into the middle class, their literature either reverted to postcolonial, romantic idealizations of the Auld Sod; continued the moralistic, didactic tradition in what was called the "new realism"; or, among the better writers, moved onto a starker realism that dealt with the lives of common people (Fanning 1997, 177). Regardless of literary style, Irish American women continued to protect their interests. Among the romantics were E. A. Fitzsimons's *The Joint Venture: A Tale in Two Lands* (1878) and Augustine O'Reilly's anthology of similarly themed Catholic tracts, *Strange Memories: Death Bed Scenes, Extraordinary Conversions, Incidents of Travel, etc.* (1880). Examples of the didactic were collected by Eleanor Donnelly in *A Round Table of the Representative American Catholic Novelists, at Which Is Served a Feast of Excellent Stories*, published in 1897 (Fanning 2001, 175). As their titles suggest, these women defended the church.

Katherine E. Conway fell between the first two categories. A journalist and assistant editor of the *Pilot* under John Boyle O'Reilly, Conway covered all the bases. Her first novel, *The Way of the World and Other Ways: A Story of Our Set* (1900), continues the Irish habit of satire; her last publication, *The Woman Who Never Did Wrong and Other Stories* (1909), is considered "uniformly sentimental." Her middle novel and best work, *Lalor's Maples* (1901), splits the difference (Fanning 2001, 166). While it ultimately lapses into sentimentality, Conway's use of the family home as a symbol of Irish Americans' assimilation and ascendancy into the middle class, along with implicit criticism of Mrs. Lalor as a domineering matriarch, mark it as a thematic precursor to realistic twentieth-century Irish American women's novels such as Elizabeth Cullinan's *House of Gold* and Mary Gordon's *The Other Side*.

One of Conway's colleagues on the *Pilot* was Louise Imogen Guiney, whose father came from County Tipperary. Although she was mentored by

Oliver Wendell Holmes and published essays in *Harper's* and the *Atlantic*, Guiney never felt accepted (Fanning 2001, 166). And little wonder. Bostonians viewed the Irish as illiterate peasants and did their best to oust them, forming the American Protective Association, an anti-Catholic, anti-parochial school group; the Immigration Restriction League, which (as its name suggests) tried to halt Irish immigration; the Anti-Saloon League, which tried to shut down Irish businesses; and the Know-Nothings, an anti-Irish Catholic political group (Dowd 2011, 99–100).

Unable to tolerate anti-Catholic sentiment, Guiney left America in 1901 to live in England. Early in her career Guiney's talent was considered second only to the editor O'Reilly's. However, his influence, the anti-Irish nativism she experienced in America, and her visits to Ireland led her to revert to the postcolonial mindset perfected by Yeats, who sought to "regain contact with an earlier, mythical nationalistic Ireland" (Barry 2009, 187). Guiney submerged her talents in American Celticism—unrealistic, sentimental visions of doomed Irish heroes whose lives she explored in *"Monsieur Henri": A Footnote to French History* (1892); a biography of the Irish poet James Clarence Mangan (1897); *Robert Emmet, A Survey of His Rebellion and of His Romance* (1904); and *Blessed Edmund Campion* (1908). Regardless of style, through her writing Guiney defended (or reconstructed) her home country. Similar themes were explored by Anna Scanlan in *Dervorgilla; or, The Downfall of Ireland* (1895), although her argument—that competition over the hand of "a hapless helpless woman" (Fanning 2001, 173) should not be viewed as the cause of the British occupation of Ireland—was admittedly logical.

Yet another journalist, Elizabeth Jane Cochrane, better known as Nellie Bly, stands as a precursor to twentieth-century Irish American women writers. Bly got her start after she wrote a sarcastic response to a sexist article in the *Pittsburgh Dispatch* and signed it "Lonely Orphan Girl." Despite the pseudonym, the editor was so impressed by the strong voice and convincing argument that he assumed a man had written it and invited Bly to interview for a position on the paper. When she appeared he initially refused to hire her because of her sex, but she soon changed his mind. Once on the job, she immediately began churning out stories about the rights of women factory workers—a focus that resulted in her transfer to the women's pages. Bored and discouraged, at age twenty-one she took a position as a foreign correspondent and traveled to Mexico, where she sent home dispatches eventually published as *Six Months in Mexico*. When this work was not sufficient to change her state-side assignments she left Pittsburgh in 1887 and traveled to New York, where she convinced yet another editor to hire her at the *New York World*. Working undercover, she feigned insanity and was committed to the Women's Lunatic Asylum on Blackwell Island. After the *World* secured her release, she published her findings, *Ten Days in a Madhouse*, whose ensuing publicity led to a review of women's commitment policies and better funding for asylums. Bly's next adventure, and the one that contributed to her lasting fame, was to replicate Jules Vernes' fictional journey *Around the World in Eighty Days*. Unchaperoned, she completed the trip in seventy-eight days and famously went on to write about the experience (Kroeger 1995). These early emigrants served as models for future generations of Irish American women writers.

Who Are These Women?

Irish American authors may be defined in a number of ways. The most obvious is by their surnames:

> By Mac and O, you'll always know
> True Irishmen, they say;
> But if they lack
> Both O and Mac
> No Irishmen are they. (Lysaght 1986, 57)

Patricia Lysaght's study lists 180 Irish families protected by the banshee, many of whom dropped the "Mac" or "O" when they emigrated. But other families who moved to Ireland before the seventeenth century and whose names therefore lack the requisite O or Mac are also part of this group. This list includes the following names—Barry, Brady, Brennan, Carey, Corrigan, Cullinane, Daly, Flynn, Gallagher, Manning, Moore, McCarthy, McDermott, O'Brien, and O'Connor—all of whom may be found in this study (Lysaght 1986, 259–80). Their works were selected on the basis of the following criteria:

   • Specific literary genres—the novel and short story—but also popular fiction such as the mystery.

• Novels that trace the development of female experience.

• Novels that look at women's efforts to move beyond "female experience."

• Novels selected on the basis of ethnicity.[3]

In this postmodern era, ethnic identity sometimes involves self-identification. This does not mean that ethnicity is arbitrary: "ancestry, no matter how elastic intermarriage may make the definition, remains the crucial element" (Ebest 2004, 8). Nevertheless, Irish American identity might emerge in part as an expression of desire. Such desire can be seen in the work of Erin McGraw, who legally changed her first name from Susan to Erin to better reflect the influence of her Irish heritage (McGraw 2003), or in the fiction by Mary McCarthy, Mary Gordon, and Eileen Myles, whose works highlight their Irish Catholic heritage. Conversely, the New Irish—emigrants born in Ireland in the 1950s and 1960s who emigrated en masse during the 1980s—tend to view themselves as commuters between Ireland and America rather than as Irish Americans per se. As Helena Mulkerns explains, "The fact that I've been living here for ten years doesn't necessarily mean I get to call myself Irish American" (quoted in Wall 1999, 67). This refusal to self-identify therefore precludes their writing from this study.

The term "Irish American" can be defined by geography as well as birth. Maeve Brennan, for example, was born in Ireland and then moved to America (Bourke 2004), whereas other authors can trace their lineage through their forebears. This ethnic doubleness allows the authors to draw on what Vincent Buckley calls their "source-country," whether that be names, myths, speech, or slant—traits William Kennedy terms a "psychological inheritance" (Quinn 1985, 24, 78). As Irish Americans assimilated into the United States, measuring these traits became more difficult; nevertheless, these writers' literary works remain recognizably Irish. Thematically, they can be identified by the presence of stylistic or cultural language patterns or customs. Many of these traits can be traced to James T. Farrell, whose "regional realis[m] created a solid base of Irish-American fiction" (Fanning

3. This list was adapted from that used by Elaine Showalter in *A Jury of Her Peers*, 2009.

2001, 359). Throughout the twentieth century and into the twenty-first, writers such as Maureen Howard and Elizabeth Cullinan continued this approach as they wrote about women's roles and the impact of the church on their psyche.

After the first generations of emigrants, some writers chose not to self-identify. Nevertheless, they too may be characterized as Irish American if their work contains the following traits: "The dominant mother in her fortress house; the first son marching off to the priesthood; the convent-educated daughter playing the piano in the parlor; parochial schoolmates turning into leaders of the Young Men's Sodality or incorrigible criminals; lives affected by extremes of dissipation, abstinence, profligacy, and piety; lives organized around ideas of religion, family, nationhood for Ireland, hard work, homeownership, the rise to respectability; tableaus of ritual gathering at deathbeds and christenings, weddings and wakes; the gift of humor and invective in public speech joined to an inability to express love and compassion in private; a penchant stylistically for formal experimentation, linguistic exuberance, and satiric modes" (Fanning 2001, 3).

Alice McDermott's family preferred assimilation to self-identification (McDermott 2000). However, her novel *At Weddings and Wakes* not only takes its title from the above definition, but also includes many of its identifying traits. So does her award-winning novel *Charming Billy*, whose plot emanates from Billy's death from alcoholism—an Irish and Irish American trait touched on by Mary McCarthy and running throughout the works of Joyce Carol Oates, Tess Gallagher, and Eileen Myles. Similarly, the works of other "non-identifiers"—Mary McGarry Morris, Jean McGarry, and Tess Gallagher—exhibit clear-cut "regional realism" in their settings; possess explicit names such as Fiona Range and Martha Horgan, Peggy Curran and Joe Keefe, Mr. Gallivan and Bernadine, respectively; and are propelled by plots hinging on fatalism, forgiveness, and redemption. Irish American women writers represent an amalgamation of these traits. In this, they are unique among their race. "Having made the trajectory from rejection to acceptance to success in the United States by 'passing,' many Irish never developed a sense of ethnicity extant their religious identity that wasn't sentimental or superficial" (Dezell 2001, 84). Not so with Irish American women.

Self-deprecation and social anxiety are ubiquitous among these descendants of immigrants (Dezell 2001, 65), often expressed through satire, an Irish habit traceable to Gaelic poets, essayists, and playwrights.[4] In the twentieth century, Mary McCarthy broke tradition by using satire to take on the Catholic Church. Jeanna del Rosso argues that satire "allow[ed] women writers of Catholic literature to demonstrate how the girls in their narratives push the paradoxes of their religion with an irreverence that lessens the severity, although not always the sincerity, of their belief" (149). Addressing issues previously excluded from Catholic girls' lives, topics might include erotic pleasure, egalitarian marriage, homosexuality, engrossing careers, or political activity. Irish American women used their fiction to construct an inner life and assert women's dignity so as to overcome, if not deny, traditional roles. Yet the role of the Catholic Church in women's literature has been widely ignored (Del Rosso 2005).

Stony fathers and distant mothers are almost universal characters; Elizabeth Cullinan and Mary Gordon showcase them well. But Irish American women are also "formidable and tenacious," and they make sure their daughters are too (McGoldrick 1998, 172–73). Whereas early works featured convent-educated daughters, twentieth- and twenty-first-century heroines generally hold college degrees. The Irish maintain "this very nice mix of being intellectual without being pretentious, this love of literature and writing . . . this commitment to thinking" (Dezell 2001, 70), traits that can be observed throughout the works of Maureen Howard, Joyce Carol Oates, and Kathleen Hill. Moreover, as Lisa Carey has shown, female characters are quite often responsible and independent, for they believe they cannot rely on men to take care of them; consequently the mothers may express a sense of martyrdom when they are not accorded the status commensurate with their responsibilities (McGoldrick 1995, 176).

Such attitudes contribute to male characters' ambivalent relationships with their female peers. "From a distance they admire [women's] fire, strength, and martyrdom, but up close they are often tense, scornful, and

---

4. See Vivian Mercier, *The Irish Comic Tradition* (New York: Oxford, 1969), and David Krause, *The Profane Book of Irish Comedy* (Ithaca: Cornell Univ. Press, 1982).

hostile and underneath deeply frightened of their [partner's] power"—characteristics that break down only when mixed with alcohol (McGoldrick 1995, 173). Remarkably, Ann Beattie's male characters have retained these traits over the past four decades. Married couples often appear to live separate lives—when the women deign to tie the knot—for they are still among the latest and most reluctant to marry, traits illustrated early on by Maeve Brennan and most recently by Jacqueline Carey. These innate beliefs stem from how Irish American male and female siblings are raised: the boys are pampered while the girls are forced to be self-sufficient (McGoldrick 1995, 175–76). Nevertheless, relationships between brothers and sisters are often strong, growing into friendships as they mature, although as Diane O'Hehir has demonstrated, bonds between sisters are even stronger.

Mary McCarthy earned the moniker "Contrary Mary" because of her oppositional stances, not least her dismissal of feminism while developing feminist themes in her early novels. In this, McCarthy reflected her Irish roots, for contradiction is a constant among Irish Americans. McCarthy's heroines, like those depicted by Jean McGarry and Mary McGarry Morris, are both persevering and prone to depression, witty but cold, brave yet fatalistic, loyal and thus quick to drop disloyal friends (Dezell 2001, 71). Although the Irish love the drink, drunkenness is followed by guilt and depression. They forgive the male alcoholic but condemn the female (Dezell 2001, 133); they value loyalty then ask why a wife stays with a drunken spouse. Hence the plot of *Charming Billy*. The Irish "bottle up" their grief until it explodes into "alcoholism, addiction, risk-taking, and self-destruction" (Walsh quoted in Dezell 114).

Like feminism and Irishness, women's Catholic fiction can be viewed along a continuum. A novel may be considered Catholic even if it does not make religion its primary focus or include explicitly Catholic themes. Catholicism intersects with a range of other "isms": racism, classism, sexism, and heterosexism—which allows these authors to write from multiple perspectives. Non-Catholics, usually Southern Scots-Irish Protestants such as Carson McCullers, Blanche McCrary Boyd, Dorothy Allison, and Bobbie Ann Mason, may also be considered members of this genre if elements of their fiction include interactions with the religion. Like Judaism, Catholicism is cultural as well as religious. As Jeanna del Rosso notes, "One does not need to practice Catholicism—or even consider oneself Catholic—to experience it" (2005, 17).

The Banshees

To illustrate the growth and contribution of Irish American women's writing, this study is organized chronologically by decade. Each chapter details the progress and setbacks of Irish American women during that period by examining key themes in their novels and memoirs contextualized within a discussion of contemporary feminism, Catholicism, American politics and society, and Irish American history. Chapter 1, "1900-1960: Ahead of Their Time," provides the background. Historically, Irish American women have long constituted the single largest ethnic group of working women. Contrary to popular lore, not all were in low-status occupations; they also comprised the majority of teachers and professional women writers. This chapter examines the factors that helped form and differentiate these women from their peers and predecessors: the Irish American work ethic, education and religion, and an instinctive feminism. In the process, it introduces the foremothers of Irish American women's writing and the themes characterizing their works as well as those that followed. These women laid the groundwork, not just for Irish American fiction, but also for contemporary feminist novels.

Chapter 2, "The 1960s: The Rise of Feminism," juxtaposes the political movements in society and the church with the appearance of the feminist novel. Although women of other ethnicities were writing novels during that decade, Irish Americans stand out not only for their productivity, but also for their distinct characterizations representing women's fights to gain personal identity, independence, and respect not just from their husbands or lovers, but also from the non-Irish American community as well. Manifestly autobiographical, these characters' struggles catch our attention because of their realistic insider's view. Irish American women's writing opened the doors on American marriage and motherhood and put a human face on the women Betty Friedan revealed in *The Feminine Mystique*. At the same time these works are uniquely Irish American, for their stories are inextricably interwoven with the Catholic Church. Hence the themes of guilt and repression, anger and rejection, depression and disappointment.

Chapter 3, "The 1970s: A State of Upheaval," reflects the attitudes and at times the animosity generated by the feminist movement and the church's intransigence. While Americans demonstrated against the war in Vietnam, the feminist movement warred within itself even as Irish American women revolted against the strictures of the church. Assimilation played a major role in these wars. Second generation Irish Americans Elizabeth Cullinan and Maureen Howard conflated Irish and Catholic and thus attacked both, whereas Maeve Brennan, who viewed herself as more Irish than American and thus took the church for granted, left it alone. Third generation Irish Americans Mary Gordon and Elizabeth Savage, more comfortable with their status, took a less jaundiced stance. Feminist issues like women's roles and treatment by the religious hierarchy certainly influenced this decade's authors and their novels; conversely, despite the lack of a strong religious commitment among Southern Protestant Irish Americans, the racism and sexism they observed helped shape their feminism. Perhaps the most striking issue of the decade was sexuality. With Blanche McCrary Boyd's *Nerves*, the 1970s mark the emergence of the Irish American lesbian novel.

Anyone who has read Margaret Atwood's novel *The Handmaid's Tale* will recognize its genesis in *Backlash*, Susan Faludi's account of the Reagan administration's war on women. Similarly, anyone who remembers *Humanae Vitae* will recognize the anger it engendered among its female flock. Chapter 4, "The 1980s: The War against Women," illustrates the effects of the New Right's hypocrisy as well as the church's duplicity on Irish American women's novels of the decade. Irish American women reacted to these assaults with an outpouring of fiction illustrating the ignorance and hypocrisy of Reagan's policies. Three types of novels appeared: lesbian, anti-Catholic, and matrophobic, featuring every possible type of "bad" mother, from crazy or remote to teenage or working.

Chapter 5, "The 1990s: Fin de Siècle," demonstrates the parallels between attitudes and themes in novels at the ends of the nineteenth and twentieth centuries. Any period of pro-marriage propaganda or anti-feminist backlash inevitably yields feminist novels critiquing marriage. This seems particularly true of Irish American women: practically every novel published in the 1990s dwells on unhappy marriages or bitter divorcees. Like their predecessors in the 1890s, these fin de siècle novels break with convention by

fracturing timelines, featuring odd women and androgynous heroines, lesbian and sexually independent women, as well as "hybrid novels" that move
beyond a strictly feminist focus. Such changes underscore "the magnitude
of the societal disruptions associated with the evolution of feminism in this
century" (Gilbert and Gubar 1994, 376).

Chapter 6, "The New Millennium" discusses the impact of 9/11 on
second- and third-wave writers. As Susan Faludi and Barbara Finlay have
documented, gains in women's rights were either ignored—with the hopes
of abolishing women from the workplace—or readily accepted as complete.
This mindset clearly affected the literature of the decade. Some Irish American second-wave feminists defected while others rebelled, but the majority
retreated into the safety of marriage, family, or the church. Luckily, feminism
was protected in historical novels, memoirs, and eco-feminist works as the
authors turned from present to past and from religion to nature. Although
some younger writers took advantage of Irish popularity and post-feminist
attitudes and began churning out formulaic novels for entertainment and
financial gain, new third-wave writers, as well as second-wave feminist novels
published toward the end of 2010, reveal a heartening resurgence. These
novels remind us of women's battles with sexism, sexual abuse, depression,
addiction, and low self esteem, as well as the very obvious need to avoid
complacency.

In sum, despite pressure to desist, Irish American women's novels continue to reflect feminist literary history. Whereas they originally depicted
their milieu, over the course of the twentieth century Irish American women
have increasingly reacted, critiqued, and ultimately helped to shape it. By
comparing the novels published during each decade and following each
author's political trajectory as represented in her fiction, *The Banshees* offers
the first Irish American women's literary history. In the process, it illustrates
these banshees' roles in protecting women's sovereignty, rights, and reputa-
tions via the contemporary feminist novel. Thanks to their efforts feminism,
like the banshee, remains "an intrinsic part of our cultural inheritance"
(Lysaght 1986, 243).

1

1900–1960
Ahead of Their Time

Early on, the word "work" took on for me a gravity, a luster, like
the stone in a monarch's signet ring. "Work" was a word I savored
on my tongue like a cool stone.

—Mary Gordon, *Circling My Mother*

Irish American women writers have been defending their domain since
they set foot in America in 1717. Whether they arrived before, during,
or after the Famine, and regardless of their relegation to the lost generation, midcentury realists, or twentieth-century feminists, their mission has
been consistent: through their writing, they protect their own. From the
beginning, these women wrote to protect their family, their church, and
their nation's reputation via satirical, nationalistic, evangelistic, and romantic
novels (Fanning 2001). However, at the dawn of the twentieth century, this
focus began to change.

Irish American women have always worked. Initially they were nannies
and domestic servants, but as they assimilated they made sure that their
daughters moved up the economic ladder. Some worked in the manufac-
turing sector. But thanks to parochial education—and the nuns and teaching sisters who founded Catholic colleges and universities—through the
first half of the twentieth century, Irish American women dominated the
teaching profession. Moreover, with or without college degrees, the majority of second-generation Irish American women writers began their careers
as journalists. Increasingly, these banshees protected their domain by moving beyond family, church, and nation to expose injustices in government,

society, and the workplace. Through their writing they supported women's right to vote, the legalization of birth control, Irish independence, organized labor, and safety in the workplace.

Certainly their literary heritage, inherent knowledge of English, and membership in the largest single ethnic group gave them an advantage (Fanning 2001). But their dual positions as colonized, second-class citizens of their country and of their religion gave them their political edge. Thanks to their parochial educations, Irish American women grew up with an "inchoate feminism" (Shelley 2006) that can be traced from pious Catholicism to apostasy or ambivalence; from reticence about exposing women's private lives to a willingness to break all taboos, ranging from unhappy wives and unfaithful husbands to adultery, impotence, sexuality, and sexual preference. This chapter not only examines the factors that formed and differentiated these women from their peers and predecessors; it also establishes the themes characterizing their works and those that followed to illustrate how Irish American women laid the groundwork for the contemporary feminist novel.

A Generation Lost, or A New Generation?

Since the first edition of *The Irish Voice in America*, Irish American authors publishing between 1900 and 1935 have been considered "a generation lost" because they seemed less likely to draw on their ethnic heritage than their predecessors. During the early years of the century as Irish emigrants tried to assimilate, one cause for hesitation may have been American reaction to events in Ireland. The Clan na Gael's support for the Kaiser certainly aroused anti-Irish sentiment in the United States, as did the 1916 Easter Rising in Dublin. Effectively marking the beginning of the Irish Revolution, its unhappy conclusion resulting in Ireland's partition and rise of the Troubles did not help. But neither did U.S. postwar immigration laws that cut Irish immigration from 22,000 per year to 1,200.[1] These events, along with the Great Depression, contributed to the literary inhibitions of Irish Americans

---

1. After 9/11, history repeated itself: the establishment of Homeland Security and the Patriot Act resulted in a marked decrease in immigration as well as the belief among Irish immigrants that the United States was anti-Irish.

not yet established within the middle class (Fanning 2001, 239–40). But Ron Ebest's *Private Histories: The Writing of Irish Americans, 1900–1935* argues otherwise. This study illustrates the endurance of family traits (alcoholic father, dominant mother), use of satire, parochial education, neighborhood settings, and traditions like weddings and wakes running throughout Irish American literature of this period—while also tracing their gradual demise thanks to intermarriage (2005, 2–3).

Irish American assimilation was fostered in large part by politically active, highly literate Irish American women. In 1914, the Irish-born feminist Dr. Gertrude Kelly issued a call for "women of Irish blood" to organize an American chapter of Cumann nam Ban (Irish Women's Council) to collect funds for Irish volunteers. A medical doctor and secretary of the Newark Liberal League, Kelly also contributed polemics to the individualist periodical *Liberty*. Termed by the editor Benjamin Tucker "among the finest writers of this or any other country," Kelly's first article argued that prostitution stemmed from women's inability to find gainful employment. In subsequent essays she declared that women were victims of prejudicial stereotypes: "Men . . . have always denied to women the opportunity to think; and, if some women have had courage enough to dare public opinion, and insist upon thinking for themselves, they have been so beaten by that most powerful weapon in society's arsenal, ridicule, that it has effectively prevented the great majority from making any attempt to come out of slavery" (quoted in McElroy, 1).

Following the 1916 Easter Rebellion and the establishment of the Irish Free State in 1921, Kelly was among a group of women comprised of suffragists, professionals, actresses, socialites, and solders' mothers who organized the American Women Pickets for the Enforcement of America's War Aims to picket the British Embassy in Washington, DC. Later that year, this group and the Irish Progressive League organized a strike to protest the arrests of Irish Archbishop Daniel Mannix and Cork Lord Mayor Terence Mac Sweeney. Among the women participating were Kelly, the labor organizer Leonora O'Reilly, the suffragist Hannah Sheehy-Skeffington, and the Celtic actress Eileen Curran. Supported by thousands, the strike halted the loading and unloading of British ships at Manhattan's Chelsea Pier for more than three weeks (Dezell 2001, 97).

Although many were put off by the suffragists' anti-temperance sloganeering, Irish American activists such as Lucy Burns, Alice Paul, and Margaret Foley supported women's suffrage, as did Leonora O'Reilly and Mary Kenney O'Sullivan, who conjoined their activism with support for labor unions (Dezell 2001, 97). Similarly, although her propaganda clearly targeted Irish Catholics, Margaret Higgins Sanger was a key figure in promoting birth control—a term she coined after rejecting "voluntary parenthood," "conscious generation," and the eugenically tinged "race control." Sanger supported her cause by passing out copies of *The Woman Rebel*, a Socialist periodical that helped promote the birth control movement. The first woman to open a family planning clinic, she used the periodical as a forum to argue that the church had "historically sustained an exploitative capitalist system that kept women in bondage." More offensive (although most likely true), she maintained that without birth control, the high birthrate among the working class would weaken their offspring and further open them to exploitation, whereas making birth control available would help liberate the working-class woman. Needless to say, the church hierarchy condemned Sanger along with the women's rights movement and urged good Catholics to participate in neither. In a final irony, Sanger's support for women's sexual freedom alienated the women's movement, although she found supporters among the eugenicists, neo-Malthusians, and Darwinists (Tobin 2003).

As Irish American women moved into the workplace, protecting the domains of family, church, and nation began to seem less important than exposing the injustices perpetrated on their sex. As early as 1892, this group represented "a sizable presence" within the workforce (Nolan 2004, 1). Among their supporters were the Irish American labor activists Leonora Kearney Barry, Mary Harris "Mother" Jones, Mary Kenney O'Sullivan, and Elizabeth Gurley Flynn, who helped ensure union representation for women as well as men (Ruether 2003, 4). Mother Jones, who emigrated as a child from County Cork, was a teacher and a dressmaker before she became involved with the unions, particularly the United Mine Workers (Weaver 1985, 24). Throughout her life she worked to protect the underdogs—blacks, women, children, and the poor—and recounted that story in *The Autobiography of Mother Jones*. Another dressmaker, Mary Kenney, who later married the journalist John O'Sullivan, helped found the Chicago Women's Bindery Union and the Women's Trade Union League. With the support of Jane Adams's Hull House, Kenney formed the Jane Club, a cooperative where poorly paid working women could live together, and later penned an unpublished memoir (see entries for Mary Kenney, Elizabeth Flynn, and Dorothy Day in Simkin).

Despite being dismissed as a "lady tramp" (Weaver 1985, 23), Leonora Barry, a member of the Knights of Labor, rose through the ranks to become a master workwoman in charge of one thousand women and the first female to be elected to the position of General Investigator. In this office she was in charge of a new division—women's work—and helped further the development of unions. A former teacher, she drew on this experience to educate her female workers. Elizabeth Flynn, a co-founder of the American Civil Liberties Union, supported women's rights, among them equal pay, birth control, day care, and suffrage; she also wrote a feminist column for the *Daily Worker* (Simkin). These activists were joined by Kate Mullaney, who organized Irish laundry workers; Lucy Burns, a suffragist and militant activist; and Kate Kennedy, Margaret Haley, and Catharine Goggins, who unionized public school teachers to demand equal pay (Dezell 2001, 95).

This was an important political move, for early on Irish American women comprised the majority of teachers. By 1910, these women, most of them daughters of domestic servants, represented the majority of public elementary school teachers in Providence, Boston, New York, Chicago, and San Francisco (Nolan 2004, 2). By 1939, 70 percent of Chicago's schoolteachers were Irish American women (Nolan 2004, 92). Clearly, teaching was a major entrée into the middle class (McCaffrey 1992, 32). Some of these teachers were also writers. In the early 1900s, Myra Kelly, an elementary school teacher, published three collections of short stories—*Little Citizens, The Humors of School Life* (1904), *Wards of Liberty* (1907), as well as *Little Aliens* (1910)—which drew on these experiences while also emphasizing the difficulties of assimilating (Fanning 2001, 181).

Irish American teachers were members of the 7.1 percent of Catholics residing in the professional class (Schneider 1952, 228–232). They attained this status largely because of their education. As early as 1884, the American Catholic Church directed its parishes to build and run their own schools using teaching nuns. These women, many of them Irish, went on to establish the "most extensive and accessible system of higher education in the country" (Kennelly, quoted in Dezell 2001, 96). In Maryland, Notre Dame Academy for women opened in 1896 (Shelley 2006, 580). By 1900, the Sisters of Notre Dame de Namur had established a girls' industrial school; the Sisters of St. Joseph were teaching typing, bookkeeping, and accounting; and the Sisters of St. Francis were operating a nursing school. By 1918, fourteen parishes had collaborated to open Catholic women's colleges such as Trinity (founded by Sr. Julia McGroarty), the College of St. Catherine (founded by Mother Seraphine Ireland), Manhattanville, and St Mary's. In 1925, the Sisters of St. Joseph Carondelet founded Mt. Saint Mary's College in Los Angeles for daughters of immigrants, most of whom were Irish (Dezell 2001, 177). By 1926, twenty-five Catholic women's colleges had been opened. By 1928, 50 to 66 percent of all Catholic college students attended Catholic colleges and universities (Shelley 2006). Given this degree of support, it is not surprising that Irish American girls were attending school at rates higher than other Americans (Nolan 2004, 81). Moreover, they continued their education: a greater proportion of Irish Americans attended college than did their WASP counterparts (Dezell 2001, 83).

These schools were "pioneers in educating women" (Dezell 2001, 96). The Irish religious provided not only strong role models but also a sense of feminism, especially evident among the Sisters of Mercy and the Sisters of the Good Shepherd (Shelley 2006, 580). Equally important, these women's colleges were academically superior to many of the men's (Gleason 1985, 252). Given this level of attainment, Daniel Patrick Moynihan's statement— that "the performance of Catholic scholars and writers [at midcentury] is particularly galling" (2006, 484)—seems to have overlooked the many accomplishments of its female members.

Long before it was common or fashionable, Irish American women writers resided among the upper-class professionals because they held college degrees. Carson McCullers attended New York University and Columbia University, Mary McCarthy graduated from Vassar, Maeve Brennan attended The Catholic University of America, Elizabeth Cullinan was an alumna of Marymount College, Maureen Howard was a Smithie, and Flannery O'Connor earned an MFA at the University of Iowa. These Irish Americans were among the 15 percent of married American women working outside the home, a figure more significant than it may seem at first glance.

Prior to World War II, American society and government policy openly discriminated against working women: most jobs and relief projects were reserved for men. Married women were expected to stay home, and 85 percent of them did. The 15 percent who worked outside the home were "viewed as selfish, greedy women who took jobs away from male breadwinners" (Hartmann 1982, 16–17). After the war when the influx of returning soldiers displaced the majority of women working in publishing (Friedan 1963), Irish American women retained positions on the major intellectual journals and magazines, writing serialized novels and short stories for women's magazines and occasionally for mainstream outlets.

The most prolific writer during this period was Kathleen Thompson Norris, who turned out over ninety romance novels over the course of her career. Norris could claim an Irish heritage from both sides of the family: her maternal grandfather was the Irish actor Paul Moroney; her paternal grandmother was the Cork native Maria O'Keefe Thompson. As editor for the San Francisco *Call* and later the *Examiner*, Norris began her career exposing the foibles of the nouveau riche Irish in San Francisco. However, after marrying Charles Norris in 1909, she started writing fiction (Fanning 2001, 242). Like Mary Ann Sadlier, Norris's domain was home and hearth (Ebest 2005, 48). Thus it is not surprising that she rejected birth control, working women, and the vote, reiterating those themes in her fiction. Her sentimental first novel, *Mother* (1911), was a huge success. Indeed, her prodigious output, all centered around the same theme, led her to be christened the "grandmother of the American sentimental, domestic novel" (Gale 1999, 506).

Norris's contemporaries conveyed these messages more powerfully. Kate Cleary, who began publishing when she was thirteen, initially wrote short stories for the *Chicago Tribune*. After marrying and while raising six children, she published in *Century*, *Cosmopolitan*, *Harper's*, *Lippincott's*, and *McClure's* magazines, ultimately churning out hundreds of poems, stories, essays, and even a novel, *Like a Gallant Lady* (1897), before her death in 1905 at age forty-two. "The Stepmother" (1901), one of her best stories, recounts the bleak life of Mrs. Carney, a former school teacher whose energy and optimism have been drained by lonely life on the prairie. She makes this point abundantly clear on her deathbed when she warns her step-son, "Don't make [your wife's] life—too hard! Women are not fitted—to bear—as much—as men. They—must—bear—more. Men love women, only—they—don't understand. . . . I hope you'll remember . . . that a woman isn't always—well—or happy—just because she keeps on her—feet—and doesn't—complain" (Cleary 1901, 244).

Margaret Culkin Banning echoed these messages in her works. A 1912 graduate of Vassar, she went on to earn a certificate from the Chicago School of Civics and Philanthropy a year later and was awarded a Russell Sage Research Fellowship in 1914. Writing for *McClure's, Cosmopolitan, Harper's, Redbook,* and the *Saturday Evening Post,* Banning turned out over four hundred articles addressing issues such as alcoholism, body image, sexism, the plight of the single woman, marriage and remarriage (*Harper's*). Over the course of her career she also published thirty-six novels, among them *Country Club People* (1976), *The First Woman* (1935), *Women for Defense* (1942), and *The Women of the Family* (1926). An Irish American Catholic, Banning often addressed issues pertaining to women in the church, particularly marriage and birth control (Vassar College Libraries). Like her contemporaries, Banning was an early advocate for women's rights, often making her point by putting her female characters in nontraditional roles and calling for their participation in World War II. Like Mary McCarthy, although she married four times, Banning kept her own name (Minnesota Author's Biographies).

Katherine "Kate" O'Flaherty Chopin addressed these themes in her novels *At Fault* (1890) and *The Awakening* (1899), and in short stories in *The Atlantic Monthly, Vogue,* and the *Century.* The best-known precursor of second-wave feminist authors, *The Awakening* dealt with formerly taboo topics such as miscegenation, adultery, and unhappy wives, which led to charges of mental illness, not to mention negative reviews. Although Dorothy Anne Dondore praised the novel as ahead of its time in 1930, Father Daniel Rankin's 1932 criticism of it as "exotic in setting, morbid in tone, erotic in motivation" doomed it to obscurity for another two decades. Given its story of an unhappy, adulterous wife who wishes to escape her husband and children and ultimately commits suicide, the reasons for the church's displeasure are obvious. Eventually critics such as Edmund Wilson helped reestablish Chopin's reputation, but Per Seyersted's 1969 critical biography ultimately elevated her status (Kolosky 1996, 5). "Revolting against tradition and authority; with a daring which we can hardly imagine today; with an uncompromising honesty and no trace of sensationalism, she undertook to give the unsparing truth about woman's submerged life" (Seyersted 1980, 198).

Chopin's contemporary, Clara Laughlin, whose parents hailed from Belfast, was a journalist and an editor at *McClure's* magazine. After her father died when she was seventeen, Laughlin went to work writing essays and book reviews, eventually publishing in *Harper's Bazaar* and *Scribner's* magazine (Ebest 2004, 30). Her early novels—*The Evolution of a Girl's Ideal* (1902), *When Joy Begins* (1905), and *Felicity* (1907)—continued the tradition of sentimental romances. However, her fourth novel, *"Just Folks"* (1910), which evolved out of a friendship with a member of Chicago's Hull House neighborhood, not only represented an early foray into realism but also into first-wave feminist critiques of marriage seen in the works of Chopin and Cleary. Laughlin's nonfiction study, *The Work-a-Day Girl: A Study of Some Present Conditions* (1913), based on her experiences as a settlement worker, similarly critiqued women's plight, implicitly reiterating the "almost universal" statement by Irish women, "If I had it to do over again, I'd never marry" (Anthony 1914, 20).

Anne O'Hagan conveyed comparable messages. Although her literary attempts were unsuccessful, her commitment to women's rights shone through her journalistic pieces. In pieces such as "The Shop-Girl and Her Wages" (1913), for example, she exposed the mistreatment of working women. Given the social mores of the times, this commitment was possible in large part because O'Hagan was unmarried. As a result, her activist beliefs were unremitting: in magazine articles she supported women's right to work; exposed the unfair treatment of female schoolteachers; praised women's clubs, businesswomen, and female athletes; and not surprisingly, wrote often in support of women's suffrage. But when questions arose regarding her sexual preference, O'Hagan's Irish literary inheritance was awakened (Ebest 2005).

In a 1907 series of essays for *Harper's Bazaar*, O'Hagan began satirizing the idealization of marriage. After *The Survey* published essays regarding a wife's marital obligations, she asked whether the magazine also proposed reviving the stagecoach; when *Vanity Fair* attacked feminism for its supposedly negative effects on married life, she skewered the notion with a story about Mr. and Mrs. Cave Man; in *Harper's* she ridiculed the treatment of single women, while in *Munsey's* magazine she poked fun at stereotypical romantic depictions of literary heroines. Inadvertently anticipating the actions of second-wave feminists, O'Hagan even criticized her peers. Like the doctor in Charlotte Perkins Gilman's "The Yellow Wallpaper," she considered Gilman an hysteric;[2] like future feminists, she dismissed the next generation as "trivial and ill versed in the contributions of their foremothers." Most ironically, after her own marriage late in life, O'Hagan's work (and unfortunately, her sharp wit) dwindled away (Ebest 2005, 116).

Satire came naturally to Irish American journalists. Ruth McKinney, a daughter of the Irish nationalist Marguerite Flynn McKinney, worked her way up from the Columbus, Ohio *Dispatch* to the *New York Post* in just three years. At that point, she became a freelance writer and began contributing stories to *Harper's Bazaar*, the *New Yorker*, and eventually to *New Masses*, where she took over as editor. Yet these early, serious accomplishments— along with her 1938 exposé of Depression-era factory workers, *Industrial Valley*—were all but forgotten with the publication of her short story collection, *My Sister Eileen* (1938), which quickly went through six reprints, yielded a sequel, and was turned into musical, a Broadway play, a movie, and eventually a sitcom. Unlike the pre-Famine generation, McKinney's satire was not meant to counter anti-Irish slurs; rather, she expressed "amusement over the oafish attempts of the Irish to Americanize themselves" (Ebest 2005, 73–75). In this, she reflected a sense of assimilation characteristic of the third stage of postcolonial writing—a "declaration of cultural independence" (Barry 2009, 189).

During this same period, the Scots-Irish Ellen Glasgow began writing what are now considered feminist novels. Anticipating later French and American feminists, her novels *The Romance of a Plain Man* (1909) and *The Miller of Old Church* (1911) imply that women should begin writing their

---

2. In turn the fictional doctor reflects the feelings of Gilman's real doctor, S. Weir Mitchell. See Nancy Cervetti's biography, *S. Weir Mitchell, 1829–1914: Philadelphia's Literary Physician.*

own stories and thus challenge patriarchal traditions. In *Virginia* (1913), her most successful work, she argues that a woman must search for and establish her own identity. Her 1922 novel, *One Man in His Time*, suggests that females reject the notion of being a "womanly woman" and focus on developing friendships with one another, while *Barren Ground* (1925) implies that self-denial is not a necessary part of a romantic relationship. Further anticipating twenty-first-century gender theory, Glasgow asserted that gender roles should be socially constructed. She expanded on these issues in "Some Literary Woman Myths" (1928) when she attacked the "subservient" role of women vis-à-vis their male colleagues in the publishing world. In 1938, she incorporated some parts of this essay into her novel *She Stooped to Folly*, noting at one point that the derogatory view men took of women could be traced to the Garden of Eden (Matthews 1995).

Glasgow's contemporary, Kathleen Coyle, who was born in Derry, worked as an editor in London, and later emigrated to America, was of a similar mindset (Ulster History Circle). A suffragist, she divorced her husband after four years and took up writing to earn money. Coyle wrote thirteen novels, among them *The Widow's House* (1924), *Youth in the Saddle* (1927), *It Is Better to Tell* (1928), *A Flock of Birds* (1930), *The French Husband* (1932), *Family Skeleton* (1934), *Undue Fulfillment* (1934), *Immortal Ease* (1941), *Morning Comes Early* (1934), and a memoir, *The Magical Realm* (1943) (culturenorthernireland.org 2008). Using stream of consciousness (a method perhaps emulating her friend James Joyce's approach in *Ulysses*), *A Flock of Birds* conveys a woman's jumbled thoughts while she worries about her imprisoned son's fate: she hates childbirth yet bears children, she longs to engage in sexual intimacy without losing oneself, and she enjoys the company of other women who despise their husbands. Also writing during this period was Kay Boyle, who published more than forty books, including fourteen novels that explored power differentials in male-female relationships. Yet another relatively obscure Irish American writer, the Scots-Irish Bernice Kelly Harris, developed the Irish penchant for satire in plays, short stories, and seven novels about family life. *Sweet Beulah Land* (1943) is perhaps her best-known work.

Labor activist and journalist Dorothy Day also began publishing during this period. Early in her career she worked for the Socialist newspaper *The*

Call and then moved on to *The Masses*, where she served as a reporter. When *The Masses* was closed down after dubious charges of espionage (based on their antiwar cartoons and editorials), she left journalism and entered nursing school. Seven years later, drawing on these experiences she published an autobiographical novel, *The Eleventh Virgin* (1924). A co-founder of *The Catholic Worker*, Day was a lifelong activist, ultimately publishing over one thousand articles as well as *Houses of Hospitality* (1939), which recounted the founding of the *Catholic Worker*; *The Long Loneliness* (1952), an autobiography; and *On Pilgrimage: The Sixties* (1972) (Simkin).

But all of these writers pale in comparison to Margaret Mitchell. Christopher Dowd maintains that *Gone With the Wind* "is one of the most significant and popular works by an Irish American woman. . . . Mitchell offered a unique female voice and created a female character that appealed to Irish American women in a way that a character like Studs Lonigan never could. . . . [A]ny study of Irish American literature that ignores the importance of *Gone With the Wind* is missing one of the biggest pieces of the puzzle. . . . In rewriting the story of Irish America, Mitchell established one of the most enduring myths of post-immigrant Irish identity" (2011, 174–75).

Scarlett's ethnic roots are reinforced throughout the novel. Her father tells her she cannot escape her "Irish blood," Rhett Butler characterizes her temper as getting her "Irish up," and neighbors refer to her as "highflying, bogtrotting Irish," while Atlanta's society mavens dismiss her as an "Irish peasant" (Mitchell 1937, 39, 195, 528, 89). Scarlett sees herself as more than this, and as a second-generation immigrant, she is. Her temperament represents an amalgamation of positive and negative Irish traits, accurately depicting the contradictory nature of Irish Americans (Dowd 2011, 175).

Scarlett's character also personifies aspects of Mitchell herself. Better known as a novelist than an Irish American, Margaret Mitchell was the daughter of the Irish Catholic suffragist Mary Fitzgerald Mitchell, who cofounded what eventually became the League of Women Voters. Margaret grew up in a staunch, first-wave feminist environment that emphasized the importance of fighting for one's rights (Pyron 1992, 41). Although mother and daughter did not always see eye-to-eye, this early influence was evident throughout Mitchell's life. After capturing everyone's attention at a debutante ball—à la Scarlett O'Hara in low-cut gown and provocative gaze—she later took to the stage to belittle marriage, stating that she and her friends were "coming down off the auction block . . . and going to work" (quoted in Pyron 1992, 161). At her mother's insistence, she entered that bastion of feminism, Smith, but lasted only two semesters (82). When she returned home, under the nom de plume Peggy Mitchell, she worked as a reporter for the *Atlanta Journal*, where she focused on women's rights. "She wrote as a woman, with women, and for women, and women dominated the content of her essays" (169).

Just as Mary McCarthy's *The Group* imposed a 1960s sensibility on a story set in the 1930s, *Gone With the Wind* reflects a 1930s worldview in an 1860s setting. One purpose of the novel was to invert Irish stereotypes still prevalent at the time: thus Scarlett credits her heritage for the courage to ignore the Southern insistence on good manners, to disregard Southern society's expectations of women, and to fight for Tara and her family even if it involves murder (Dowd 2011, 178). Totally overlooking her mother's influence, Dowd credits Mitchell's Irish American uncles for these traits and maintains that Mitchell used the novel "as a metaphor for contemporary ethnic confusion"; however, Pyron's biography suggests that through Scarlett, Mitchell (like Flannery O'Connor) was more likely rejecting Southern expectations regarding proper female behavior, as evidenced in Scarlett's refusal to be passive or submissive, and engagement in "unladylike" work and behavior (Dowd 2011, 187).

Unfortunately, Southern mores and society's expectations failed to recognize, let alone appreciate, Mitchell's message, so women continued to be bound by Southern social conventions. Consequently, such traits in a female character actually perpetuated negative perceptions of the Irish (Dowd 2011, 178). Nevertheless, these traits—which run throughout the works of Irish American women writers—enabled Scarlett O'Hara to endure.

Quest for the Self

The model set by Irish American women became more widespread during World War II, when prohibitions against women working changed rapidly: media propaganda encouraged women to support their country not only as wives and mothers but also "as workers, citizens, and even as soldiers." By 1945 the female labor force, three-quarters of whom were married, had doubled in size (Hartmann 1982, 20–21). By war's end, married women represented the majority of female workers (Chafe 1991, 13). Although their jobs were neither glamorous nor creative, women "enjoyed the companionship of fellow workers, the pleasure of mastering a new skill, the opportunity to contribute to a public good, and the gratification of proving their mettle in jobs once thought beyond the powers of women." As one housewife put it, "some just love their jobs. I think they for the first time in their life feel important" (Hartmann 1982, 20).

But as the war wound down, the same forces that encouraged women to work ensured that they returned to their "true calling" as wives and mothers:

• Businessmen, labor leaders, and government officials told women to relinquish their jobs.

• Returning veterans compared American women unfavorably to the "womanly" ones they had met abroad.

• Social welfare and child-care experts called upon women to pay more attention to their maternal duties.

• Psychologists and psychiatrists emphasized women's biological destiny and diagnosed feminists as "neurotic or worse." (Hartmann 1982, 21)

• Industry followed suit: across the country, 60 to 90 percent of all postwar job ads were once again "for men only." (Hartmann 1982, 21)

By the end of World War II, the Cold War mentality was urging conformity and obedience to authority in clothing, housing, and behavior, best exemplified in the move to suburbia, where a failure to conform might lead to "painful ostracism." During this period, with capitalism flourishing, the auto industry quadrupled output from 2 million to 8 million cars. Thanks to improved transportation, the suburbs exploded: between 1950 and 1960, 11 million of the 13 million homes built in America were in the suburbs. Suburban dwellers were expected to have the "right" number of cars, children, and spouses. Private backyards behind uniform tract homes were frowned upon; instead, neighbors shared a common area and socialized together in the neighborhood and at the local schools. Women were expected to marry young, bear children, and stay home to raise them (Woods 2005, 126–35). This message was reinforced by the media.

In the comics—the primary texts for 60 million readers in 1946, 80 percent of whom were young men and women between the ages of six and seventeen—wartime strips had featured women so courageous and resourceful that they could rescue male heroes like Buck Rogers and Flash Gordon. Among these powerhouses were Sheena, Queen of the Jungle; Mary Marvel, Captain Marvel's twin; Miss Fury, Batman's counterpart; and of course Wonder Woman. But after the war, these paragons gave way to simpering teens like Betty and Veronica of the "Archie" comics. Likewise, Wonder Woman and her feminist cohorts gradually devolved into the hero's love interests (Hartmann 1982, 190, 202).

Whereas the four major prewar magazines—*Ladies' Home Journal*, *McCall's*, *Good Housekeeping*, and *Woman's Home Companion*—had featured stories about young career women who not only worked but were also attractive and beloved by their husbands, these same magazines did an about-face as the war wound down and the men came home. *Ladies Home Journal* set the stage with "Occupation: Housewife," whose (female) author dismisses the housewife's ennui by pointing out her many skills and reminding her that even if she feels thwarted, "a world of feminine genius, but poor in children, would come rapidly to an end. . . . Great men have great mothers" (Thompson, quoted in Friedan 1963, 42). Beginning in 1949, subsequent articles such as "Femininity Begins at Home," "Have Babies While You're Young," "Are You Training Your Daughter to Be a Wife?," and perhaps the most insulting, "Why GIs Prefer Those German Girls," perpetuated these messages. By 1950, only a third of magazine heroines were pursuing a career outside the home—and they were usually getting ready to quit after realizing they really wanted to be housewives and mothers (Friedan 1963, 38–44).

By the late 1950s, a review of the above magazines (minus *Woman's Home Companion*, which had folded) yielded roughly one career woman per hundred articles, a focus echoed in other women's magazines like *Redbook* and *McCall's*. Worse, magazines such as *Life* presented supposedly fact-filled stories that attacked educated working women. *Life's* 1956 Christmas issue referred to them as the result of "that fatal error that feminism propagated," so masculinized that they emasculated their husbands. Even former career women were suspect, for their education had led them to be discontented with housewifery, disrupt the PTA, dominate their husbands, and destroy their children. In contrast, *Look* praised the contented housewife: "No longer a psychological immigrant to man's world, she works, rather casually, as a third of the U.S. labor force, less towards a 'big career' than as a way of filling a hope chest or buying a new home freezer. She gracefully concedes the top jobs to men. This wondrous creature also marries younger than ever, bears more babies and looks and acts far more feminine than the 'emancipated' girl of the 1920's or even '30's" (quoted in Friedan 1963, 59).

These messages were echoed at the movies. During the war years over 100 million Americans attended the movies every week; indeed, the demand for escapism was so great that in some cities theaters remained open all night. To encourage women's participation in the war efforts, producers cast Betty Hutton in *Here Come the Waves* (1945), Lana Turner joined the WACs in *Keep Your Powder Dry* (1945), and Lucille Ball portrayed an heiress working in a munitions plan in *Meet the People* (1944). To reinforce the notion that women could survive and succeed in the workforce while their men were gone, Hollywood produced films such as *Mrs. Miniver* (1942), *Since You Went Away* (1944), and *Tender Comrade* (1943) (Hartmann 1982, 191–92).

But as the war wound down, these messages changed. Suddenly career women were less admirable. In *Spellbound* (1945), the psychiatrist Ingrid Bergman is frigid; in *Together Again*, the mayor Irene Dunne abandons her career for marriage (1944); in *Mildred Pierce* (1945), obsessive business-woman Joan Crawford neglects and alienates her daughter. With the rise of postwar film noir, Barbara Stanwyck and Rita Hayworth seduce and manip-ulate their male paramours in *Double Indemnity* (1944) and *The Lady from Shanghai* (1947), respectively, while Olivia de Havilland tries to murder her twin sister in *Dark Mirror* (1946). If they weren't killing or manipulating, postwar female stars were often portrayed as victims. Ingrid Bergman is driven mad in both *Gaslight* (1944) and *Notorious* (1946); Barbara Stanwyck is terrorized in *Sorry, Wrong Number* (1948). Whereas women had appeared confident and competent when the war began, within a matter of years they had become helpless, insecure ninnies (Hartmann 1982, 202).

In this, the church was complicit. The Jesuit Daniel Lord wrote Hol-lywood's Production Code while the Irish Catholic Joseph Breen enforced it, thus brokering a deal between Jewish producers and Catholic bishops (Dezell 2001, 27). Films like *Going My Way* (1944) not only helped align American Catholics with the nation's commitment to war, but they also moved away from Depression mores of collaboration and mutual support toward a "moral economy of pragmatic leadership" (Smith 2010, 68). Henry Luce's *Life* magazine contributed to this reassessment. Whereas prewar articles had depicted Catholics as "ethnic Others," postwar photo essays represented them as good American citizens, in the process eliding any hint of ethnic difference. This message was underscored in a 1944 *Life* editorial, "The Kremlin and the Vatican," which attacked Russia for criticizing the pope, and in numerous articles featuring Cardinal Francis Spellman, praise for the pope, and photo essays about cherubic altar boys (Smith 2010, 104).

Luce's campaign was aided by Irish Americans Margaret Bourke-White and Bishop Fulton Sheen. Bourke-White was the first female photojournalist hired by *Life*. In fact, one of her photos graced the inaugural cover (Bois 1997). Bishop Sheen helped revise the public image of Catholics with his television show, *Life Is Worth Living*, which ran from 1952 to 1957. During this period Sheen was featured in a cover story in *Time* magazine, won an Emmy for "most outstanding personality," and became a permanent member of the top-ten list of most admired American men. What was his appeal? The promotion of "faith, home, and family as the foundation for collective American identity" (Smith 2010, 140).

Responses to this retrenchment varied. Like their foremothers, some Irish American women who were themselves professional writers supported the move. Betty Smith's novels of Irish America—*A Tree Grows in Brooklyn* (1943), *Tomorrow Will Be Better* (1948), and *Maggie-Now* (1958)—reiterate the belief that when women married, they quit working outside the home. Indeed, the preoccupations of Smith's heroines are "romance, marriage, childbirth, and death" (Scott 1979, 90–92).[3] Other Irish American novels of the time such as Mary Doyle Curran's *The Parish and the Hill*, Mary Deasy's *Hour of Spring*, and Ellin Berlin's *Lace Curtains* (all published in 1948) sound a comparable note. In a 1948 interview with *The Boston Post*, Curran describes her novel by saying: "mine isn't a love story. There isn't a drop of sex in it. . . . [I]t is my family of whom I am writing. . . . My mother was born in Ireland. She taught her children the true Irish value of life. . . . My mother

---

3. In contrast, Smith's *Joy in the Morning* (1963) is notable for its racy sex scenes.

believed in education for her children, moral and intellectual. . . . [W]e must return to those values" (quoted in Halley 2002).

But many prominent Irish American women writers refused to go that route. A descendant of John McCarthy, an Irish immigrant who settled in Newfoundland in 1837, Mary McCarthy married immediately after graduating from Vassar and then married three more times; nevertheless, she worked from 1937 through 1962 as a writer and editor for the *Partisan Review*, the most intellectually elite "old boys' club" in New York City (Brightman 1992; Showalter 2001). McCarthy's prominence in this imbalanced work environment is all the more striking given the low stature of its women contributors: in the *Partisan Review Reader*, a collection of the "best and most representative" essays published from 1939 to 1944, only fourteen of the ninety-two selections are by women. However, over a third were written by Irish Americans—McCarthy and the poets Louise Bogan and Marianne Moore—and they were soon joined by Flannery O'Connor.[4] O'Connor's short stories "The Heart of the Park" and "The Peeler" (which became part of her first novel, *Wise Blood*) were published by the *Partisan Review* in 1949 (Getz 1980, 19).

Irish American women maintained professional lives long before it became common or necessary. Louise Bogan, granddaughter of an immigrant from Derry (Frank 1995), began judging applications for Guggenheim Fellowships in 1944, a job she held into the 1960s. She later served as Fellow in American Letters of the Library of Congress, Consultant in Poetry to the Library of Congress, and consultant on belles lettres to Doubleday. Bogan also taught at the universities of Washington and Chicago, New York University, and Brandeis while continuing to publish prodigiously and win awards (Bogan and Limmer 1980, xxxi–xxxiii). Mary Cantwell worked as a copyeditor at *Mademoiselle* and *Vogue* in the late 1950s, rising to features

---

4. Despite her surname, O'Connor's works have not been previously viewed as Irish American, but she possesses the requisite bona fides. A descendant of the Treanor-Cline family on her mother's side and the O'Connors on her father's, Mary Flannery O'Connor was Irish Catholic (Getz 1980, 121).

editor and eventually managing editor (Barron 2000). Mary Doyle Curran, whose mother was from Kerry, wrote novels praising housewifery while teaching at the University of Massachusetts-Boston, Queens College, and Wellesley (Halley 2002). Elizabeth Cullinan worked for William Maxwell at *The New Yorker* from 1950 to 1959 before becoming an author in her own right. In the same years, the Irish-born Maeve Brennan wrote for *Harper's Bazaar* and later became a staff writer for *The New Yorker* (Bourke 1992).

Later authors have written memoirs in which they too attribute their careers to the role models provided by Irish American mothers who worked outside the home after marriage. The parents of the novelist-journalist-memoirist Caryl Rivers met in law school in the 1930s. Although her mother took what would now be considered maternity leave when Rivers was born in 1937, she soon resumed practicing law in Washington, DC (Rivers 1973, 10). The memoirist Maureen Waters's mother worked at Macy's (Waters 2001). The novelist Mary Gordon recalls watching enviously as her mother carefully dressed and applied makeup for her job as a legal secretary. "Early on," she writes, "the word 'work' took on for me a gravity, a luster, like the stone in a monarch's signet ring. 'Work' was a word I savored on my tongue like a cool stone'" (2007, 18).

Even though they refused to rejoin the ranks of housewives, literature by Irish American women of this era is unique for its inclusion of "Catholic themes, Catholic language" (McDermott 2000). In this regard, they refute historians who claim that "the absence of Irish Catholic intellectuals meant that perspectives born out of Catholic thought or Irish American experiences would have little effect on American thinking in this era" (Meagher 2005, 136). Depending on the authors' backgrounds and place of birth, these themes run the gamut.

Mary McCarthy rejected her faith at age eleven; nevertheless, her early Catholic training is evident throughout her oeuvre. Although McCarthy grew further and further from the mores of her Catholic girlhood, she could not escape herself. An infamously autobiographical writer, her heroines reflect her childhood beliefs, for "all of McCarthy's characters are unable to mediate between the traditional definitions of femininity embraced by the church, and the modern revisioning, an Irish Catholic fatalism and a belief in free will" (Donoghue 1996, 91). Her heroines believe in—and practice—sexual freedom, demonstrate intellectual independence, and work after marriage, yet all fall prey to Catholic guilt. Worse, without the church as a model, they lack a clear moral compass (Donoghue 1996, 93).

Catholicism is a strong undercurrent in the works of Flannery O'Connor. In her hometown of Milledgeville, Georgia, there were no Catholic churches; consequently, in 1847 the first Catholic mass was said in the apartment of O'Connor's great-grandfather. Three decades later, still lacking a church, her great-grandmother, Mrs. Hugh Treanor, donated land to construct one. Despite the scarcity of Catholics in the deep South at the time (the religion was not recognized in Georgia's charter), O'Connor, like her Irish American peers in other parts of the country, attended parochial schools—St. Vincent Grade School and Sacred Heart High School. Nevertheless, her preoccupation with Catholicism amazed even her teachers. In the third grade, for example, when assigned a sentence reading, "Throw the ball to ___," O'Connor substituted "St. Cecilia" for the expected "Rover" (Getz 1980, 6–10).

O'Connor was fascinated with life and death as viewed through her role as a Catholic woman living in the midst of Protestant fundamentalists (Getz 1980, 24). Juxtapose these worldviews and you get Hazel Motes, the main character in *Wise Blood* (1952), a young man who has lost his faith and sets out to create his own religion, "the Church without Christ." In the introduction to its tenth anniversary reissue, O'Connor described it as "a comic novel about a Christian *malgre lui*, and as such, very serious, for all comic novels that are any good must be about matters of life and death" (quoted in Daniel 1962, C2).

Similar themes are evident in the works of O'Connor's friend and patron, Caroline Gordon, an Irish American Southern Agrarian whose religious faith rivaled O'Connor's. Gordon was something of a holdover from the Irish American school of didacticism. As she wrote in one letter, she believed "there was only plot, the 'scheme of Redemption.'" Thus it should come as no surprise that her novels *The Strange Children* (1951) and *The Malefactors* (1956), both roman à clefs, are rife with Catholic themes. Loosely autobiographical, the characters of *The Malefactors* are based on Gordon's main religious influences: Claiborne is Gordon's husband Allen Tate, Horne Watts is Hart Crane, Catherine Pollard is Dorothy Day, and Joseph Tardieu is Peter Maurin in what Flannery O'Connor described as "a fictional study of religious conversion" (Labrie 1997, 16).

Despite the prevalence of Catholic themes, thanks to the enormous "pressure to conform" (Meagher 2005, 130) immigrants and second-generation Irish preferred to ignore their cultural heritage. McCarthy, O'Connor, Elizabeth Cullinan, and Maureen Howard distanced themselves from the Irish. McCarthy associated the Irish with the abusive relatives who took her and her brothers in after their parents' death, whereas Howard picked up on her mother's disdain. "Oh, the Irish," her mother would say. "We were taught to take the Irish lightly" (Howard 1975, 11). Elizabeth Cullinan's family was even more vehement: "Mother hated the Irish," she recalls. "We were supposed to be above all of that" (quoted in McInerney 2008, 99). The Scots-Irish were even further removed. O'Connor preferred to be known simply as a Southern writer, whereas Carson McCullers's association with the Irish was limited to a visit to Ireland when John Huston was filming *Reflections in a Golden Eye* (Savigneau 1995, 318).

Ambivalence runs throughout Maureen Howard's memoir of her 1950s childhood, *Facts of Life*. Her parents were devout Catholics, but they tended to mock "the world we came from . . . the *Catholic Messenger* with its simpering parables of sacrifice, its weekly photos of saintly missionaries and their flock of mocha children with souls like ours, rescued for eternity." Still, for her parents' generation, "Religion was a serious business" (Howard 1975, 12–13). Perhaps as a result, she found that her "religious periods have been genuine only as dramatic exercises" (35). Her first novel, *Not a Word about Nightingales* (1960), displays this pattern. Although the Irish Catholic culture is central, religion is used "more for mood and dramatic effect than anything else" (Durso 2008, 57).

Given her background it is not surprising that religion played only a minor role in the work of Carson McCullers. Irish Protestants differed significantly from their Irish Catholic counterparts. Because they were non-Catholics, they were able to assimilate into WASP society and to a certain extent become "indistinguishable" from any other American (Cochrane 2010, 2). So although Lulu Carson Smith McCullers was half Irish (on her mother's side) (Savigneau 1995, 11), she was also a Southern Baptist. Music was her religion until it was replaced to a certain extent with Marxism, and then again by feminism when she began developing the character of Mick Kelly. McCullers rejected Marxism because it considers men bourgeois and women the proletariat (Call 2009). She wanted more for her persona, and Mick Kelly goes far beyond the role of women proscribed by Marx and Engel: she wants to compose music and be a world-famous conductor who wears "either a real man's evening suit or else a red dress spangled with rhinestones" (McCullers 1983, 241).

Maeve Brennan's ambivalence is more reflective of her place of birth: her earliest stories take place in the Dublin suburbs where she grew up, while the later stories are set in New York, where she lived as an adult. Chapters 1 through 7 in *The Springs of Affection* (published in *The New Yorker* between 1953 and 1955) are first-person narratives featuring each member of her family, accurate in age, appearance, and name. At age twelve Brennan and her sister Derry began attending the Cross and Passion boarding school. Brennan's stories "The Devil in Us" and "The Barrel of Rumors" detail the meager food served at the school as well as familiar themes of guilt and apprehension. At the end of her second year, Maeve left school with the public denunciation by the nuns—"'damned, damned, damned'"—ringing in her ears, about which she said she "had never felt so holy" (Bourke 2004, 102).

Ethnic communities began to disappear by the end of the 1940s. By the 1950s, Irish Americans were moving into the middle class and out of the city, both of which threatened to weaken their religious and ethnic ties (Takaki 1993, 163). Nevertheless, parochial schools were instrumental in distinguishing between Catholics and Protestants. Drawing on her satiric heritage, Caryl Rivers writes: "The nuns made it clear that prolonged exposure to non-Catholics was not healthy. They gave off a subversive perfume; unseen, like radiation, but deadly. . . . We were urged to have Catholic friends, to attend none other than Catholic schools, to date Catholic boys, and if we married one, to live in Catholic neighborhoods. . . . Our minds were kept innocent of anything but praise for the Church" (1973, 129–54). Likewise, Maureen Waters writes of growing up at midcentury knowing "our souls were in mint condition, bright and glittering although vague in detail. . . . We kept them that way by a continual round of devotions: Mass on Sundays and holy days, rosaries, novenas, stations of the cross, little acts of self-denial . . . in a curious, paradoxical way [the nuns] encouraged independence." They demanded hard work and concentration, which in turn fostered autonomy (Waters 2001, 69).

Like other baby boomer Irish Americans, Alice McDermott, born in suburban Long Island (an Irish American enclave) in 1953, was raised in a family bent on assimilation. Nonetheless, McDermott attended parochial schools and religious icons dotted the house; she even slept with a rosary beneath her pillow until she was a teen (McDermott 2000, 13). Conversely, Madeleine Blais, born in 1947, identified strongly with her ethnic and religious background. When her widowed mother needed a job the Blais girls wondered "if we should say a novena. . . . We believed that good things happened not so much because you lifted yourself up by your bootstraps, the Protestant explanation, but when luck and prayer collided in heaven" (Blais 2001, 75).

Blais's contemporary, Mary Gordon, born in 1949, was raised by an exceedingly devout Irish Italian Catholic mother: from 1935 until her death more than sixty years later, Anna Gordon was a member of the Working Women's Retreat Movement. For these women, mostly widowed or unmarried, this group "provided a situation in which their spiritual life could be taken seriously," brought similarly minded women together, and provided, in essence, a room of their own where they could get away from their families. Several times a year, the women traveled around the country to meet, usually in a convent, attend Mass, listen to sermons and talks by the priests, and visit their friends (Gordon 2007, 105). These retreats led to enduring friendships not only among some of the women but also with some of the priests. Unlike the current climate in which priests are almost by default considered suspect, clergy in the mid-1950s "were treated like princes—no, like kings. . . . Nothing was too much to do for them. . . . You will say that I am naive, that many of these women served priests sexually," but the ethnic composition of the midcentury church provided a crucial distinction: "I am talking of the American Church in the triumphalist years of 1920–60, a church entirely under control of the Irish, who had no toleration for the wink-wink, nudge-nudge, 'we're all human after all,' 'a man's a man' comprehension found in other parts of the world" (Gordon 2007, 131–32).

Sex and the Irish American Woman Writer

Prior to World War II, Freudian theory had seemed like the key to women's emancipation. Acceptance of Freud's belief in the necessity of "freedom from a repressive morality to achieve sexual fulfillment" could be observed in the flappers' bobbed hair, short skirts, smoking, drinking, and independent lifestyles. But after the war, Freudian psychology was used to explain women's unhappiness. Drawing on the obsolescent notion of penis envy, everyone from sociologists, teachers, clergymen, and counselors, to advertisers, magazine editors, and pop psychologists attributed Freudian theory to everything "wrong" with American women. Indeed, such widespread beliefs were responsible for women's sudden stasis, if not regression. As Betty Friedan explains, "Without Freud's definition of the sexual nature of woman to give the conventional image of femininity new authority, I do not think several generations of educated, spirited American women would have been so easily diverted from the dawning realization of who they were and what they could be" (1963, 104–5).

This decade saw the introduction, acceptance, application, and misapplication of Freudian theory, which "led women, and those who studied them, to misinterpret their mothers' frustration, and their fathers' and brothers' and husbands' resentments and inadequacies, and their own emotions and possible choices in life" (Friedan 1963, 103). Eugene O'Neill's *A Long Day's Journey Into Night* (1956) certainly casts women in a sadly dependent and destructive light, as does Tennessee Williams's *A Streetcar Named Desire* (1951). An often-cited academic study of such misapplication is *Modern Woman: The Lost Sex*, which enjoyed wide popularity, and in many, a wide-eyed acceptance of claims such as, "The more educated the woman is, the greater chance there is of sexual disorder, more or less severe" (Farnham and Lundberg 1947, 142). Actually, the authors blamed all of society's ills on women, "from alcoholism to crime to war—to 'neurotic' career women who abandoned their children to the care of others, neglected their husbands, and competed with men in a man's world" (Woods 2005, 136). In postwar society, the stay-at-home mom was considered essential to American success, for her nurturing presence and welcoming hearth provided a safe place to escape the competitive world of the gray flannel suits.

Like the generations before them, Irish American women writers not only refused to accept this mindset, but they also displayed their resistance in their fiction. Carson McCullers appears to be the first Irish American woman to come cautiously out of the closet. All of McCullers's work contains a "significant homoerotic theme." This is not to say that her works feature specifically lesbian or gay characters. Rather, "same-sex love" is a given in McCullers's fiction. This should not be surprising, for McCullers's "crushes" on female partners permeated her marriage. Still, McCullers should not be considered lesbian per se. Since she also pursued affairs with male partners, married and remarried Reeves McCullers, and believed herself to be a man born in a woman's body, it is easier to call McCullers bisexual. Nevertheless, her literature and her friendships suggest a knowledge of gay and lesbian codes and lifestyles (Kenshaft 1996, 220–22).

One of the main characters in her first novel, *The Heart Is a Lonely Hunter*, is the tomboy Mick Kelly. Although Mick loses her virginity to Harry Minwitz, the description of her orgasm—"like her head was broke off from her body and thrown away" (McCullers 1940, 55)—is unprecedented in heterosexual novels of the time. But not within pseudo-Irish American pulp fiction. During the 1950s, a spate of supposedly Irish American lesbian novels emerged. Between 1957 and 1962, Ann Bannon published five lesbian novels featuring Beebo Brinker. Although these novels were acclaimed for their treatment of sexuality, Ann Bannon was not Irish; she was Ann Weldy. Claire Morgan's lesbian novel *The Price of Salt* sold over a million copies, but Morgan was actually Patricia Highsmith. Isabel Miller's *Patience and Prudence* features a loving lesbian couple; however, "Miller" is actually Alma Routsong (Bona 2004). In contrast, McCullers remained true to herself despite a somewhat schizophrenic sexuality.

McCullers's second novel, *Reflections in a Golden Eye* (1941), established her reputation as well as the genre of the Southern gothic. The plot includes a murderer, a madwoman, and a "homoerotic triangle," one of whom is a dwarf. McCullers's third novel, *The Member of the Wedding* (1946), is also a somewhat autobiographical bildungsroman recounting the coming-of-age of another tomboy, Frankie Addams. Frankie—who sports a crew cut—"wanted to be a boy and go to the war as a Marine. She thought about flying aeroplanes and winning gold medals for bravery" (23) and wished that "people could change back and forth from boys to girls whichever way they felt like and wanted" (97). McCullers's novella, *The Ballad of the Sad Café* (1951), was written during her stay at Yaddo, where she suffered from unrequited love for Katherine Anne Porter (Showalter 2009, 370). This is not typical Irish American fare.

Nor was Mary McCarthy's book of short stories, *The Company She Keeps* (1942), which offers sordid details of a divorcee's dalliances, most notably in "The Man in the Brooks Brothers Shirt." This story describes Meg Sergant's seduction by/of an unattractive traveling salesman, Mr. Breen,[5] during their cross-country train trip to the West Coast. Divorced and engaged to a new man, Meg coolly analyzes the seduction and her alternating feelings of pleasure and disgust for herself and Breen. Intermittently self-aware, at one point she realizes, "Dear Jesus . . . I'm really as hard as nails." Vowing to redeem herself, she goes to bed with Breen again, thinking, "This . . . is going to be the only real act of charity I have ever performed in my life; it will be the only time I have ever given anything when it honestly hurt me to do so" (114).

McCarthy's novels and memoirs from this era display a marked disregard for the sanctity of marriage. In scenes more graphic than 1950s readers of women's novels were accustomed to, McCarthy's works explicitly address sex, usually adulterous. *A Charmed Life* (1955)—a roman à clef satirizing McCarthy's relationship with Edmund Wilson (Brightman 1992, 243)—is perhaps most notable for the rape scene between Miles/Wilson and Martha/Mary after both have remarried.

> She wanted it, obviously, or she would not have asked him in. The angry squirming of her body, the twisting and turning of her head, filled him with amused tolerance and quickened his excitement as he crushed his member against her reluctant pelvis. . . ."Don't," she cried sharply. . . . She sat up in indignation, and his hand slipped in and held her breast cupped. . . ."Please don't," she begged, with tears in her eyes, while he squeezed her nipples between his fingertips; they were hard before he touched them; her breath was coming quickly. . . . Compunction smote him; he ought not to have

---

5. In yet another example of McCarthy's satire, the amoral Mr. Breen shares his name with the Catholic League film censor of the time, Charles Breen.

done this, he said to himself tenderly. Tenderness inflamed his member. Clasping her fragile body brusquely to him, he thrust himself into her with short, quick strokes. A gasp of pain came from her, and was over. (McCarthy 1955, 199–203)

In keeping with the tradition of Irish American women writers, McCarthy's frank departures from conventional fare anticipated societal changes emerging in the late 1940s. In 1948, Alfred C. Kinsey revolutionized the way Americans thought about sex with the publication of *Sexual Behavior in the Human Male*. Although this study was followed in 1953 by *Sexual Behavior in the Human Female*—which demythologized the belief that women were unable to enjoy sex—American consciousness seemed more attuned to male pleasure. The 1950s saw the entrée of Hugh Hefner's *Playboy* magazine, which essentially "legitimized sex outside the marriage bond." The popularity of Vladimir Nabokov's *Lolita* (1955), which glamorized statutory rape, underscores this mindset. But not everyone agreed. Margaret Mead, whose anthropological study *Male and Female* (1949) had cautioned against allowing women to take men's jobs and glorified women's essential femininity, condemned Kinsey for potentially undermining morals; consequently, in 1954, the Rockefeller Foundation, which had funded Kinsey's research, cut off his grants (Woods 2005, 139–40).

Paralleling these schizophrenic attitudes, the novels of this decade might be classified as reflecting the "three faces of Eve"—the housewife/mother, the intellectual, and the bad girl (Showalter 2009, 290). Mary McCarthy's characters in *The Oasis* (1949) and *The Groves of Academe* (1952) represent "the intellectual." In *The Oasis* she satirizes the "intellectual passivity" of liberals, most notably Philip and Nathalie Rahv (Hardwick 1972, xiv). In *The Groves of Academe*, she argues for academic freedom (within limits) through the predicament of Henry Mulcahy, fired by the president of his university for supposedly being a Communist sympathizer, while satirizing the resultant protests from his liberal colleagues. *A Charmed Life* (1955) and *Memories of a Catholic Girlhood* (1957) reprise her "bad girl" persona, Meg Sergant. *A Charmed Life* exacts revenge on ex-husband Edmund Wilson, while *Memories of a Catholic Girlhood* does the same to her abusive aunt and uncle. Both novels explore the female persona's sexuality. In so doing,

McCarthy "began to create a new image for American women" (Showalter 2009, 398).

This image extended well beyond the message of unhappy married life implicit in Irish American women's prewar writing. Forced to give up their jobs, their new-found independence, and the accompanying satisfaction and self esteem, many women developed feelings of anger, frustration, and guilt. But rather than suffer silently or wait for widowhood, Irish American women expressed these feelings through accounts of domestic pressures, thwarted ambitions, divorce, and depression.

Maeve Brennan focused on marriage and motherhood, neither of which was fulfilling. Her posthumous collection, *Springs of Affection*, features short stories originally published in the late 1950s and early 1960s, which recount the unhappy union of Rose and Hubert Derdon, whose portrayal is said to reveal "the emotional landscape of Ireland" (Bourke 2004, 173). But this landscape is not so different from Brennan's America: housewives are unhappy, husbands resentful. Rose and Hubert alternately long for and loathe the other, even going so far as to dream of each other's death. Hubert so dislikes his wife that he avoids her whenever possible. "Her pretensions, the pitiful air she wore of being a certain sort of person, irritated him so much that he could hardly bear to look at her on the rare occasions—rare these days, anyway—when they went out together" (Brennan 1966, 72). Yet he never confronts her, preferring instead the silence and avoidance Lawrence McCaffrey attributes to Irish men, for when Hubert finds himself about to address the issue, he "would have to stop himself, because he could begin to feel his anger against her getting out of hand. The anger was so dreadful because there seemed to be no way of working it off. It was an anger that called for pushing over high walls, or kicking over great towering, valuable things that would go down with a shocking crash" (Brennan 1966, 78).

Maureen Howard's memoir, *Facts of Life*, is less angry but more cynical. In her determination to be the ideal wife, Howard became "the compliant young matron." As a young faculty wife, she played the role even as she clung to the hope that someday she would move beyond "the hot competition in the hors d'oeuvres department" (1975, 76). In fact, she *was* moving along, for in 1960, she published her first novel, *Not a Word about Nightingales*, which describes a man's attempts to flee his wife and conventional job only to return in the end to resume the "dull garment of his past" (61). Despite favorable reviews, Howard apparently saw the work as a reflection of her life at the time. "I wrote a mannered academic novel, actually a parody of that genre and so at a further remove from life. If there is any strength there . . . it can only be in what I wanted that book to reflect: a sense of order as I knew it in the late fifties and early sixties with all the forms that I accepted and even enjoyed: that was the enormous joke about life—that our passion must be contained if we were not to be fools" (1975, 80). But Howard was not laughing. Viewing herself in the mirror, she laments, "I am as dull as the picture I ripped out of the frame, dull as the idea of a mirror over the couch. Impersonation of wife and mother. I have begun to wonder what I am like in real life" (1975, 86).

Irish American women writers did not accept the status quo. Despite their Catholic upbringings, they greatly exceeded the national probabilities for divorces in their time. Although the divorce rate had declined to a steady rate of 2.5 percent by the end of the 1950s, these authors out-performed their peers. They also embraced the fad of seeking psychoanalysis to understand themselves and self-medicated with drugs and alcohol to avoid the pain. Mary Doyle Curran divorced her first husband; over the course of her life she suffered from depression and alcoholism, for which she sought help through psychoanalysis (Halley 2002). Louise Bogan married and divorced twice; she also suffered from "nervous breakdowns" and depression and was hospitalized three times over a thirty-year period (Bogan and Limmer 1980, xxvii–xxxiv). Maeve Brennan married and divorced; suffering from alcoholism and mental illness during her last years, she had to be institutionalized (Bourke 2004). Carson McCullers married her husband Reeves, divorced him, and married him again (Showalter 2009, 370). Mary McCarthy married four times, divorced three. She began undergoing psychoanalysis while married to Edmund Wilson, ultimately seeing three different psychiatrists before declaring them unnecessary (Brightman 1992, 229). Maureen Howard, married twice and divorced once, also sought analysis at one point. Describing her early married life, she writes sardonically, "Look, I'm perfectly happy. . . . I've finally learned not to want things I cannot have" (Howard 1975, 174).

Unmarried and childless, Flannery O'Connor's stories nonetheless reflect the frustration engendered by a lack of independence. After graduating from the Georgia State College for Women in 1945, O'Connor moved north to enter the University of Iowa Writers' Workshop. There she worked with key Southern writers such as Robert Penn Warren. The short stories she published there—"The Geranium," "The Barber," "Wildcat," "The Crop," "The Turkey," and "The Train"—established her reputation. In 1948 she was invited to continue working on her writing at Yaddo, the Writers' Colony in Saratoga Springs, New York. There she found an agent, Elizabeth McKee, who placed "The Capture" with *Mademoiselle*, "The Woman on the Stairs" in *Tomorrow*, and "The Heart of the Park" and "The Peeler" in the *Partisan Review*. After leaving Yaddo, O'Connor tried living in New York but found she preferred a less populated area, so she moved to Connecticut to live with her friends Robert and Sally Fitzgerald, both Catholics and writers. During that period she fell ill and was diagnosed with lupus, causing her to return home to live with her mother in 1951. Initially they resided congenially: "You run the farm and I'll run the writing," O'Connor told her mother (quoted in Getz 1980, 28).

Following an interview, Richard Gilman wrote, "her mother, who enters into so many of her stories as the fulcrum of their violent moral action . . . was a small, intense, enormously efficient woman, who, as she fussed strenuously and even tyrannically over Flannery, gave off an air of martyrdom" (1969, 26). In so doing she reinforced another key Irish American archetype: the domineering matriarch. After 1955—when O'Connor's dependency on her mother increased and her mobility decreased owing to the need for crutches—this persona takes on a greater presence (Liukkonen 2008). In stories prior to that date the mother figure is interfering but not infuriating. She may be the grandmother in "A Good Man Is Hard to Find" (1953) whose bull-headed actions cause her family's death (Hendin 1970, 149). Mrs. Hopewell in "Good Country People" (1955) could be channeling Regina Cline O'Connor, for she "thought of her [daughter] as a child though she was thirty-two years old and highly educated. . . . She thought of her still as a child because it tore her heart to think instead of the poor stout girl in her thirties who had never danced a step or had any *normal* good times" (O'Connor 1955, 170, 173). This tone, as well as the adult child's gender, begins to shift in 1955, for O'Connor would not go so far as matro- or patricide (Hendin 1970, 99). Nevertheless, O'Connor "was among the American women writers of the fifties who confronted matrophobia, or the fear of becoming one's mother" (Showalter 2009, 401). Forced to live with her mother as an adult, O'Connor knew firsthand the tensions of this life.

Because she never married, O'Connor's works evoke fierce arguments among critics regarding her feminist side. Some claim that O'Connor avoided the reputation as a "lady writer" by focusing her satire on male char- acters (Showalter 2009, 402). Whereas early versions of *Wise Blood* feature strong, positive women characters, by the publication of *The Violent Bear It Away*, they had virtually disappeared. Thus the doctorate-holding Joy in "Good Country People" is not only hideous and deformed but also dis- plays poor fashion sense, while her genteel backwoods mother "could not help but feel that it would have been better if the child had not taken the Ph.D." (O'Connor 1955, 175)—an indirect slap at the postwar Freudians who advocated housewifery.

Apparently Carson McCullers did not fear that stigma, for feminist themes permeate her work. *The Ballad of the Sad Café* is emblematic of women writers' struggles against male domination, a necessity in the face of increasingly aggressive, bellicose attacks on "female autonomy" exempli- fied in the works of William Faulkner and Henry Miller.[6] Tall and tough, the character of Miss Amelia Evans suggests no need for men (Gilbert and Gubar 1989, 148). Descriptions of her wedding and brief (unconsummated) marriage to Marvin Macy support this reading. However, Miss Amelia's subsequent involvement with the hunchback dwarf Lymon Willis and even- tual fight with Macy years later—in which she is ultimately defeated because of Lymon's intervention—offer a strong allegory for woman's status at the time. After her defeat, Miss Amelia has been transformed from "a woman

6. This feeling is evident in male reviewers' delight in the eventual capitulation of the heroine, as well as the primary critical focus on male characters rather than the females. For further examples, see Huf, "Carson McCullers' Young Woman with a Great Future Behind Her," in *A Portrait of the Artist as a Young Woman*.

with bones and muscles like a man" to "thin as old maids are thin when they go crazy" (McCullers 1951, 70). Like McCarthy's characters, women may fight but they cannot win.

Although this situation was true across the country, it was particularly dire in the South, where women were expected to be ladies once they reached the age of consent (Heilbrun 1979). This losing fight against femininity is exemplified in McCullers's tomboy characters (Westling 1996). After Mick Kelly loses her virginity she essentially loses her freedom, for she is now afraid of the dark, and so unable to roam the streets; after Frankie Addams enters puberty and becomes first F. Jasmine and then Frances, she transforms into a silly teenager much less attractive than her tomboy persona.

The memoirs of Caryl Rivers and Maureen Waters, born before the war (1937 and 1939, respectively), adumbrate the feminist concerns of their baby-boomer successors. Rivers's childhood games alternated between arguing and fighting. "I was convinced that being a girl was an O.K. thing. Could I not do anything the boys could do, and do it better? Except, of course, pee on target" (1973, 20). Rivers grew increasingly disenchanted during high school. To her, the nuns' insistence on the rhythm method implied that it was "a woman's duty to be a brood mare, even it if destroyed her health, her marriage, her family life, and kept them all in bleakest poverty." The idea that it was "better to die in the state of grace than to commit [the] mortal sin" of using contraceptives was unacceptable (1973, 185).

Maureen Waters had similar experiences. "Nobody played with dolls," she writes. "What a strange group of girls we were, children of immigrants, fighting for a toehold in the promised land." As Waters grew older these attitudes intensified. A teenager in the 1950s, she writes, "the last thing in the world I wanted to be was a housewife. In high school my electives were math and science; I wouldn't be caught dead in home economics." The last straw occurred at her all-girls college. Because there were no males, the female students became responsible for responding to the chaplain during Mass, a role Waters assumed with pleasure. However, when she learned that she would not be allowed on the altar, that she would have to kneel "on a pretty little *prie-dieu* just outside the sanctuary," she rebelled. "Despite the thrust of my religious upbringing or, paradoxically, because of it," she writes, "I expected to be treated like everyone else, men included" (2001, 95).

Waters was not alone. America experienced a spike in divorces after World War II, jumping from approximately 16.7 percent in 1936 to 26.4 percent in 1946 (Day 1964, 511). Despite the Catholic prohibition against divorce, these figures varied little between Catholics and Protestants, averaging 21 and 25 percent, respectively (Robinson 2008). Divorce rates dropped in the 1950s, when approximately 80 percent of Americans were married. But it would be a mistake to infer that these statistics reflect overall marital satisfaction, for couples in those days separated much more often than they divorced (Gerson 205–7), and there is enormous anecdotal evidence to suggest countless unhappy marriages. Nor do these statistics suggest a general acceptance of divorce among Catholics. Mary Gordon notes that her mother, a legal secretary, explained that her boss did not "'handle divorce.' She said this as if divorce were a particularly nasty, possibly toxic species of effluvia, which they very well knew better than to touch" (2007, 23).

Despite their Catholic upbringing, this sampling of midcentury Irish American women writers greatly exceeded the national average of divorces long before they became commonplace. Perhaps as a result, they also conformed with the fad of seeking psychoanalysis to understand themselves. Caryl Rivers offers one explanation: "I would love to see the data on how many female alcoholics and frigid wives evolved out of that crazy indoctrination" (1973, 185).

Work + Religion + Education = Assimilation

Regardless of their marital or psychological problems, Irish American women writers at midcentury outperformed their unhyphenated peers. In 1959, while the average American woman was engaged at age seventeen, married by twenty, and mother of four by twenty-four, Irish Catholic families were encouraging their daughters to postpone marriage. Although the proportion of women attending college dropped from 47 percent in 1920, to 35 percent in 1958—increasing numbers of Irish American women went to college and worked throughout their lives (Woods 2005). "A century earlier, women had fought for higher education; now girls went to college to get a husband" (Friedan 1973, 150). Not so with the Irish Americans.

Just as "Teaching ultimately allowed daughters . . . of immigrants to leave the working class and enter the educated lower middle class" (Nolan

2004, 137), education in the postwar years ensured that Irish American women writers continued to move up. They went to college when other women were dropping out; they were among the 15 percent who married and kept working. They established careers that granted them membership in the top tier of Catholic professionals, the 9 percent of Catholics in the upper class (Schneider 1952). That they did so long before the advent of second-wave feminism no doubt accounts for their above-average rates of marriage, divorce, and psychoanalysis.

The works discussed here confirm these statistics; more important, they also relate aspects of Irish America that challenge its conventional portrayal as a conformist patriarchy in which women were at most housekeepers or nannies, their parents pious simpletons or atavistic ethnics. This picture of Irish America not only offers a convincing response to the traditional monolithic view; it also reveals how Irish American women laid the groundwork for future generations.

2

The 1960s

The Rise of Feminism

> I am as dull as the picture I ripped out of the frame, dull as
> the idea of a mirror over the couch. Impersonation of wife and
> mother. I have begun to wonder what I am like in real life.
> —Maureen Howard, *Facts of Life*

The Eisenhower era provided a seedbed for American feminism. Whereas the war years had encouraged married women to leave their homes to support the war effort, the postwar years pushed them back. As chapter 1 outlined, a cultural and public relations blitz resulted in a "consolidated attack on women's new-found freedom." Women were urged to stay home, take advantage of all the new labor saving devices, and view their roles as wife and mother as embodying "autonomy and responsibility" if not destiny (Whelehan 1995, 7). Many succumbed. Across America, the average marriage age fell to twenty, the lowest since the 1900s; overall 70 percent of young women were married by age twenty-four. Worse, single women over twenty-four were considered old maids (Davis 1991, 17). But although motherhood is important it is hardly glamorous, and while vacuum cleaners and washing machines made housework easier, they could not make it fun. Regardless of age or ethnicity, many American women felt alienated and dehumanized by housework (Whelehan 1995, 9). Thus it is not surprising that, apart from the civil rights movement, the most important and enduring social phenomenon of this decade was women's liberation (Woods 2005, 363).

This chapter traces the growth of the women's movement as portrayed in Irish American women's writing in the 1960s. Through their novels and short stories, these authors reminded readers that in love, marriage, work, and religion, women were second-class citizens and they were not happy about it—an attitude most often conveyed via satire to illustrate the "feminine mystique." The 1960s saw Irish American women's novels lamenting unhappy marriages, condescending husbands, and domestic abuse, themes characterizing their status at home, at work, and at church.

Why such a consistent message? Because Irish American writers had an advantage unavailable to their peers. Whereas many women found it difficult to organize because they lived in different neighborhoods or lacked a central organizing body and could not build the critical mass necessary to effect political change (Woods 2005, 364), through the mid-sixties Irish Americans were still bound by their religious beliefs and thus possessed a "collective consciousness" (Cochrane 2010, 2). Most important, as members of the largest, most enduring, and most literate of American ethnic groups, Irish American women not only had a long history of voicing displeasure through their writing but they also anticipated the need for change.

In this they consistently pre-dated their closest literary rivals, Jewish American women. Whereas Ruth Herschberger's *Adam's Rib* (1948), Alva Myrdal and Viola Klein's *Women's Two Roles* (1956), Rona Jaffe's *The Best of Everything* (1958), and Alix Kate Shulman's *Memoirs of an Ex-Prom Queen* (1971) have been cited as the earliest twentieth-century feminist novels (Brownmiller 1999, 40, 45), Irish American women were actually the first to raise these issues. Mary McCarthy published *The Company She Keeps* in 1942 and Maeve Brennan's "Talk of the Town" had been satirizing male vanity since 1949. During the 1960s, Helen Gurley Brown gained fame for *Sex and the Single Girl* (1962); Maureen Howard put a satirical, feminist spin on the message in *Bridgeport Bus* (1963); Elizabeth Cullinan criticized the influence of the Catholic Church in her 1960s *New Yorker* stories; and Mary Daly blew them all away by arguing for women's equality in *The Church and the Second Sex* (1968). Given their history, it is not surprising that Irish American women were ready for the women's movement, for they had been fighting this battle throughout their adult lives.

During the 1960s, Women's Liberation movements sprang up all over the country, among them the New York Radicals, the Chicago Women's Liberation Union, and Boston's Cell 16 of Female Liberation. After the

New York Radicals grew too unwieldy, the Redstockings formed as a splinter group. WITCH—known variously as Women's International Terrorist Conspiracy from Hell, Women Inspired to Tell Their Collective History, or Women Interested in Toppling Consumer Holidays—was formed to move from raising consciousness to raising hell, with factions in New York, Washington, DC, and elsewhere. Angered by Jewish feminists' assumptions that their Catholic counterparts were "intellectually inferior" because of their working-class backgrounds, the Irish American Redstocking Sheila Cronan formed a separate group—the Class Workshop—to discuss how their upbringing had affected Catholic women's confidence and political rhetoric (Brownmiller 1999, 65). A radical feminist, Cronan instigated the plan to hang a banner from the Statue of Liberty reading "Free Abortion on Demand," an idea unfortunately scuttled; she was also one of the first to argue that marriage enslaved women and that to achieve equality, it should be abolished (Echols 1989, 142).

Irish Jewish friction was clearly a by-product of World War II. Prior to the war, Irish American women dominated the female sphere of the publishing world, representing the major female ethnic group among the literati. But after the war, thanks to the influx of Jewish immigrants and Americans' response to the Holocaust, anti-Semitism faded in the face of postwar prosperity, necessitating an expanded workforce; consequently, Jews became a part of the mainstream, entering the white-collar echelons and moving to the suburbs. Whereas the best-known female Jewish writers (surrounded by uber males Alfred Kazin, Philip Roth, and Saul Bellow) had been Ayn Rand, Anzia Yezierska, and Gertrude Stein, the postwar era saw the emergence of Hannah Arendt, Jane Bowles, Martha Gellhorn, Diana Trilling, Fay Kanin, Maxine Kumin, Adrienne Rich, and Susan Sontag, to name just a few. And whereas prewar fiction by Jewish writers had centered around typical immigrant themes, postwar fiction became generically Jewish. Moreover, to maintain their identity, Jewish literature often featured the Jewish intellectual (Hoberek 2005, 71).

This attitude stood in sharp contrast to that of Irish American writers, who had been raised with the desire to assimilate. Unlike the Jewish populace, Irish Americans were often ashamed of overt intellectualism. As Daniel Patrick Moynihan explained, "Derision of the hifalutin all too easily shaded into contempt for intelligence and learning, particularly on the lace-curtain fringe" (quoted in Dezell 2001, 30). This view was not held by Irish American women writers, however: highly educated, they wrote to protest infringement on women's rights. They did not need to preserve their ethnicity, for Irish American traits were simply a part of their cultural inheritance.

Further evidence of Jewish-Catholic intellectual rivalry was evidenced in 1963, when the two most popular publications to explore feminist issues were Mary McCarthy's novel, *The Group*, and Betty Friedan's investigative study, *The Feminine Mystique*. *The Group* spent almost two years atop the *New York Times* best-seller fiction list and made McCarthy an international figure, selling over 370,000 copies during 1964 and over 5.2 million by 1991 (Brightman 1992, 480, 484, 486). At the same time, *The Feminine Mystique* spent six weeks at number 1 on the nonfiction list, selling over 3 million copies in just five years (Menand 2011). Both authors illustrate the push-pull of feminism for women of their generation who had "made it" without the benefit of second-wave feminism (Howard 1997).

Although McCarthy graduated from Vassar and Friedan from Smith, themselves seedbeds of feminism, both women conveyed mixed messages on the subject. McCarthy's motto was taken from Chaucer's Criseyde—"I am myn owene woman, wel at ease" ("Brooks Brothers," 104). Nevertheless, she was often quoted as saying that feminism "is bad for women. . . . [I]t induces a very bad emotional state," fomenting emotions such as "self-pity, covetousness, and greed" by indicting "self-dependency" and emphasizing "male privilege." Still, McCarthy admitted she was "sort of an Uncle Tom from this point of view," since she (like her Irish American foremothers) made her living in the male-dominated world of publishing (Brightman 1992, 343).

Prior to *The Feminine Mystique*, Betty Friedan had publicly disavowed an interest in feminism. But like McCarthy, her work belied her stance. Whereas Friedan claimed to have awakened to the "problem that has no name" after twenty years as a suburban housewife, she actually had her consciousness raised as an undergraduate at Smith, where she was an activist for labor issues and took what would now be considered women's studies courses. In 1943, just a year after graduating from Smith, Friedan was warning male readers that women's wartime factory jobs had made them aware of just how enervating housework was. Far from being a suburban housewife, through the 1950s Friedan keep repeating this message in her job as a labor journalist—while living in Sneden's Landing in upstate New York, the site of Maeve Brennan's 1950s satires about the nouveau riche. Friedan was unwilling to recognize feminism at this point, thanks in part to Joe McCarthy's Red scare. After observing Senator McCarthy's attacks on feminists and Communists, Friedan may have found it prudent to hide that element of her professional past (Horowitz 1998). Likewise, as McCarthyism grew more virulent, Mary McCarthy, who had initially viewed the Communist Party as the "pinnacle," disavowed and actually admitted embarrassment for her ardor in a 1953 piece, "My Confession"—published while working on the first chapter of *The Group*—which pokes fun in parts at her characters' political naïveté (Brightman 1992, 119, 352).

Even if McCarthy abjured feminism in her personal life, from 1942 to 1967 feminist themes dominated her fiction. These are best exemplified in *The Group*, the most infamous of her novels, in which she attempted to document the "idea of progress . . . in the female sphere" (1963, 62). In this novel McCarthy explores the aspirations of seven female graduates of the Vassar class of '31, juxtaposing early second-wave feminist desires for a meaningful career and a happy marriage with the realities of American society in the 1930s. In the process, McCarthy introduces the reader to formerly taboo subjects such as birth control, women's sexual pleasure, adultery, impotence, mental illness, homosexuality, spouse abuse, and the double standard. The main character, Kay (generally accepted as McCarthy's alter ego), lives openly with her fiancé, Harald, and shares details of their sex life with the other women in the group. In a time when birth control had only recently been legalized, McCarthy's characters discuss it openly. One of the males suggests it is used only by "adulteresses, mistresses, prostitutes, and the like," as opposed to respectable married women. Although Kay contradicts him, she is no better, declaring that "birth control . . . was for those who know how to use it and value it—the educated classes" (75). When McCarthy's antagonist, Norinne, visits a doctor to seek advice about her husband's impotence, she reports that the doctor asked "whether I wanted to have children. . . . When I said no, I didn't, he practically booted me out of the office. He told me I should consider myself lucky that my husband didn't want intercourse. Sex wasn't necessary for a woman, he said" (165).

Another character, Lakey, has a lesbian lover—a daring inclusion in the pre-Stonewall era. Although Marguerite Duffy, aka Megan Terry, was gaining notoriety for her gender bending plays, such as the off-Broadway production of *Ex-Miss Copper Queen on a Set of Pills* in 1963 (Bona 2004), most Irish American women writers had not fully exited the closet. More notable is Dottie's first sexual encounter—which she openly pursues. The graphic foreplay and seduction cover several pages, culminating in the following passage: "while she was praying for it to be over, surprise of surprises, she started to like it a little. She got the idea, and her body began to move too in answer, as he pressed *that* home in her slowly, over and over, and slowly drew it back. . . . Her breath came quicker. Each lingering stroke, like a violin bow, made her palpitate for the next. Then all of a sudden, she seemed to explode in a series of long, uncontrollable contractions that embarrassed her, like the hiccups, the moment they were over, for it was as if she had forgotten Dick as a person" (McCarthy 1963, 41).[1]

McCarthy uses *The Group* to remind readers of the unfortunate disparity between the group's liberal theories and the reality of their marriages, for once they marry independence disappears. At the beginning of the novel Kay is a strong-willed, independent woman, but as the story progresses she becomes increasingly helpless and miserable. Soon she is tiptoeing around husband Harald, eager to please and afraid to upset him. Priss, another group member, is introduced as a political activist; however, after she marries and gives birth she becomes so weak-willed that she lets her newborn cry for hours rather than disobey her husband and nurse the baby before he is "scheduled" to be fed.

Although reviewers such as Norman Mailer and Norman Podhoretz dismissed *The Group's* focus on women's lives and manners, McCarthy's Irish American contemporaries understood: Louise Bogan recognized the satire inherent in the "patois of privilege," and Robert Kiely's review for *The Nation* termed the novel a "virtuoso display of 'narrative mimicry,'" while

---

1. This description rather contradicts Thomas Flanagan's assertion that McCarthy's sexual descriptions were written in a "deliberately dry, clinical, wryly self-observant, and deflationary" manner (130–31).

Hayden Carruth called it a "whopper" (quoted in Brighman 1992, 481, 486). What non-Irish reviewers apparently overlooked was that McCarthy was "taking the mickey": like her pre-Famine ancestors, she used satire to mock people unlike her—in this case, the very rich. To illustrate their vapidity, she makes practically every pronouncement an indictment. When, after a one-night stand, Dottie's lover tells her to buy a pessary, or diaphragm, her reply underscores her naïveté: "'Yes, Dick,' Dottie whispered, her hand twisting the doorknob, while she let her eyes tell him softly what a deep reverent moment this was, a sort of pledge between them" (61). Priss Hartshorn makes them all look bad when she expounds on the difficulty of great wealth—"a frightful handicap; it insulated you from living" (31). Such "linguistic subversion" should come as no surprise from the orphan among the Vassar elite who tried to fit into their social circle even as she abhorred their snobbery.

McCarthy was in good company. Amidst a literary field dominated by male Jewish intellectuals, Irish American women were making their mark. Although Maeve Brennan's "Talk of the Town" columns appeared to be aimed at the *New Yorker's* advertisers, she was actually speaking directly to her women readers. Brennan wrote in a "feminine code, a parody of 'girl talk,' the breathless italics making a vivid piece of aural and visual description seem like a fuss about nothing, or a joke" (Bourke 2004, 189). In "Skunked," an article about the failure of a furrier to understand that he was to make a collar to match her skunk fur purse, she begins, "A rather long-winded lady has just given us an example of the death of the faculty of attention, which she believes is rampant," concluding, "today they called up in *agony* to say that the little man had turned up with the collar, but when they said, 'Where's the bag?' he said 'Well, I didn't think she'd want the frame, so I threw it away.' He *said* he only wanted the bag to match the skin, and then he *chopped* up this madly expensive bag and made a measly little collar out of it. Well, there you are, in case you've paid any attention'" (Brennan 1954, 27).

Beneath the surface, the Long-Winded Lady was skewering the male sex—and her readers knew it. Brennan's essays about working, shopping, drinking, and watching her fellow New Yorkers provided a subversive counterpoint to the postwar campaign to rid the workplace of women, to advertising's efforts to compensate paid employment with "fun" appliances, to

Joe McCarthy's attempts to curtail feminism, and to the fashion industry's emphasis on sexy, nonutilitarian women's clothing (Brightman 1992, 189).

This confluence of discrimination provided a strong impetus for feminism's second wave. While Mary McCarthy and Maeve Brennan had been raising these issues since the 1940s, Betty Friedan's research in *The Feminine Mystique* provided indisputable facts. Although she undertook the research to disprove the postwar canard that "higher education somehow masculinized women and prevented them from finding happiness as housewives and mothers," her findings revealed that this was partially true. College-educated women *did* regret not using their degrees; they just did not know why they felt so disenchanted with housewifery. They had bought into "the feminine mystique," the belief that woman's true happiness lay in marriage and motherhood (Friedan 1963). Brennan's short stories "The Carpet with the Big Pink Roses on It" (1964) and "The Sofa" (1968) illustrate this mindset: cleaning the carpet or getting a new sofa become major events, for they give housebound mothers something to fill their days and enliven their conversations.

Like her Irish American predecessors, Brennan focuses on marriage and motherhood; like her contemporaries, she inverts those themes. Hers are not happy stories. After thirty years of marriage, Hubert Derdon despises his wife and the feeling is mutual. In "An Attack of Hunger" (1962), Rose and Hubert's son John has left home to enter the seminary. Resentfully setting out cups and saucers for tea, she reflects, "Oh, if only Hubert had died, John would never have left me, never, never, never" (26). After the Derdons, Brennan began writing about Rose and Martin Bagot. These stories offer snapshots of unhappily married life in the 1960s. "The Shadow of Kindness" (1965–66) describes the condescending attitude of the working man toward his stay-at-home wife: "Martin had warned her often enough against thinking, because thinking led to self-pity and there was enough of that in this world. What he had really told her was that she must stop forcing herself, stop *trying* to think, because her intelligence was not high and she must not put too much of a strain on it or she would make herself unhappy" (30).

Brennan's personal life provided plenty of fodder. "Maeve fell in love recklessly and had her heart broken more than once," writes biographer Angela Bourke (2004, 133). Her first serious boyfriend, Solly Paul, was Jewish. When he decided they could not marry, Maeve was "distraught" but she soon recovered and fell in love with Walter Kerr. Described as "ambitious, good-looking, witty, and hugely energetic," he and Maeve seemed the perfect match. However, he broke off their engagement after meeting another clever Irish American woman, Bridget Jean Collins, who under the pseudonym Jean Kerr went on to recount their life together in *Please Don't Eat the Daisies*. Bourke asserts that the resulting heartbreak was the primary source of the "naked pain that is so strong in [Brennan's] fiction" (2004, 136).

This pain stands out in the second set of stories in *Springs of Affection* about Rose and Hubert Derdon. Although this couple might be confused with Brennan's parents, their portrayal may be more reflective of her marriage to St. Clair McKelway. When they wed, she was thirty-seven to his forty-nine. She had not married before, whereas he had already married and divorced three times and carried on countless affairs. Neither he nor Maeve could handle money or alcohol, and neither friends nor family believed the marriage could last (Bourke 2004, 179–80).

The final Derdon story takes place after Rose has died. Its title, "The Drowned Man" (1963), suggests a poignant picture of regret, yet Hubert believes he cannot mourn because he feels their marriage was a sham. But looking around Rose's room, he begins to cry: "The tears did not run down his face and away. They poured all over him and stayed on him and encased him, and when he tried to stop crying, because he was afraid he might smother in them, imprisoned in them, they poured out all the more and there seemed to be no end to them" (*Springs*, 210). Bourke posits that this anguish in the midst of ambivalence parallels Brennan's feelings at the death of her mother, Una, in 1958. But "The Drowned Man" was not published until 1963, and in the intervening years something else happened: in 1959, Brennan divorced. Even though no one thought the marriage would last, its waning days clearly impacted her. "Maeve was certainly heartsick at the time. With her mother dead, her marriage to St. Clair McKelway sinking ever deeper into debt, and her own writing in difficulty, she was clearly feeling diminished" (Bourke 2004, 209). This accumulation of negative events may well have contributed to those endless tears.

Similar relationships provided impetus for the women's movement. The National Organization for Women, founded in 1966, was "dedicated to the proposition that women, first and foremost, are human beings." NOW's liberal feminist stance also affirmed that "women's work," that is, mother-hood and housework, was indeed work. At the same time, NOW hoped both to "socialize domestic labor" and "remove the naturalized association of women with the home" (Whelehan 1995, 34–35)—a theme Elizabeth Cullinan explores in "The Time of Adam" (1960). During the summer, the mothers take the children to the beach while the fathers work in the city. When they arrive en masse on Friday night, they are treated like gods—the wives wait on them and the children, who adore them, are allowed to stay up late until their mothers whisk them off to bed (Cullinan 1960). As "The Reunion" (1961) and "The Nightingale" (1961) detail, these gender roles are no different at home. With "The Power of Prayer" (1961) this theme grows darker, for the father not only works in the city but also neglects his family, staying out all night to drink and gamble while his wife and daughter postpone dinner in the hope that he will eventually arrive.

In her memoir and novels Maureen Howard details these effects on the formation of one's personal identity. Describing her inbred attitudes about marriage in *Facts of Life*, she writes, "Girls were made to marry and marriage was my only serious pursuit. My education and career were sham intentions. . . . The endless dalliance of girls' waiting for a man, for the man, was my heritage. . . . My bridal picture tells too much: I am absolutely fierce, set in my purpose, impatient with the bouffant dress and illusion veil, the hate-ful lace mitts—all chosen by my parents" (1975, 73). Still, as a third-genera-tion Irish American woman, marriage did not occur until after Howard had graduated from Smith and worked for a few years. In this regard *Facts of Life* reflects the lives of women in *The Feminine Mystique*: after marriage, reality, not to mention boredom, sets in. Envying the relative freedom of another wife who teaches dance, Howard realizes she is not locked into domestic-ity; she can refuse to spend her days making elaborate dinners or passing her time shopping (Howard 1975, 76). This unsentimental exploration is a recurrent trope in Howard's body of work, as well as that of her Irish Ameri-can contemporaries as they delve into the impact of family history. In fact, her first novel, *Not a Word about Nightingales* (1960), suggests the results of a failure to do so. Not so with Howard and her cohorts.

Having grown up before Vatican II, Elizabeth Cullinan's protagonists mirror the mindset of many Irish American young women during that period, torn between their first-generation parents' expectations of marriage and the desire to gain an individual identity and independent lifestyle. Indeed, Cullinan's female personae reflect these conflicted desires (Murphy 1979, 14). The child of second-generation, lower-middle-class immigrants, Cullinan grew up under the close watch of her mother. This relationship, in conjunction with her mother's repudiation of their Irish roots, led to a struggle for identity evident in her young female characters (McInerney 2008, 98). In an attempt to break these bonds, Cullinan moved to Ireland in 1960.

The settings in *The Time of Adam* recall her three-year stay as well as her difficulty moving between "tradition and modernism" (Casey and Rhodes 2006, 656). In "A Sunday Like the Others" (1967), Cullinan's persona, Frances Hayes, is involved with the overbearing Michael Callan. After he blames her for their missing lunch with a prominent director, she finds herself apologizing. "Then, furious with herself, she tried to take back the apology." Yet she also tries to fulfill the woman's role, "a conviction of [Michael's]—that a woman should be able to come up with something decent to eat no matter what ingredients or what equipment she was given." Rather than complain or refuse, each time she visits she tries and fails: "She could feel his disapproval as he took the plates." Later, still pondering his missed luncheon and potential career opportunity, Michael muses, "We would have got nice and drunk . . . and then we would have come back here and been nice and close," to which she quickly responds, "I don't get drunk. . . . And we're never close" (26). Cullinan's heroines reveal the mindset of many young women during this period, torn between traditional expectations of marriage and family and the desire to establish their independence and carve out their own identities.

Shattering the Green Ceiling

Irish American women writers chose work and independence. By the 1960s, Flannery O'Connor had published short stories in *The Sewanee Review*, *Mademoiselle*, *The Partisan Review*, *Kenyon Review*, and *Harper's*; received four O. Henry Awards; and published two novels, *Wise Blood* and *The Violent Bear It Away*, plus her first collection of short stories, *A Good Man Is Hard to Find*. She had also begun lecturing and publishing book reviews. In recognition of her work, she received an honorary doctor of letters from Notre

Dame in 1962 (Getz 1980). In 1960, Maureen Howard emerged from the shadows of faculty wifedom to publish *Not a Word about Nightingales*, followed three years later by *Bridgeport Bus*. Elizabeth Cullinan, who worked for William Maxwell at *The New Yorker* from 1955 to 1959, so honed her craft that she was able to support herself as a freelance writer (McInerney 2008, 99). During this decade, Joyce Carol Oates published three novels, all of which were nominated for the National Book Award; she also became the second female professor hired at the University of Detroit (Showalter 2009, 430). Jean Kerr's *Please Don't Eat the Daisies* was a Broadway hit, while Mary Cantwell, Kathleen Ford, and Ramona Stewart were turning out memoirs and novels.[2] That so many Irish American women were publishing is not exceptional per se, since they enjoyed a long literary history; that they were highly visible and successful members of the New York literati during the sexist sixties is, however, notable—for women's rights were not yet protected under the law.

Despite the postwar propaganda sending women back to their homes, when the 1960s began, almost half of all American women ages sixteen and over were employed, although the majority were in poorly paid "women's jobs"—secretaries, sales clerks, nurses (Davis 1991, 59). In other words, while many women were working, their jobs were neither well paid nor intellectually challenging (Woods 2005, 376). Of course, it was hard for women to advance without higher education. At the undergraduate level, advisors discouraged female students from pursuing majors in traditionally male fields and pushed them into "women's" jobs such as nursing, teaching, or home economics (Woods 2005, 364). At the graduate level, sexist practices were evident in male-only admissions policies or miniscule quotas for females,

2. Those genres were rare in the 1960s. Ramona Stewart's historical novel, *Casey* (1968), tells the story of Irish Americans living in the Five Points section of New York, embellished on by Martin Scorsese in the movie, *Gangs of New York*. Kathleen Ford's *The Three-Cornered House* (1968) pre-dates the fantasy-romance genre with characters such as Lieu Lieu, Sir Lien, Erin de Rocca, Semi Iskatov Disser, and Khar. At the opposite end of the spectrum, having established her literary reputation, Mary McCarthy published two highly political works, *Vietnam* (1967) and *Hanoi* (1968). Neither was very popular (Brightman 1992, 555).

making it virtually impossible to be admitted into graduate schools of law, medicine, engineering, architecture, or veterinary medicine (Brownmiller 1999, 2). Even then, the few admitted were not treated equitably. Without exception, the contributors to *Changing Subjects*, a collection of personal reflections on the emergence of feminist literary criticism, describe the dismissive treatment by their male professors as well as the many ways in which these men impeded their progress in the academy (Greene 1993). While male graduate students were welcomed and mentored, females were discouraged or ignored. In the business world, married women who might have been promoted were passed over on the grounds that they might become pregnant or fired when they conceived (Davis 1991, 59). Even with a job, women were denied credit. Regardless of position, women were paid considerably less than their male counterparts (Hartmann 1982).

Granted, there were some notable exceptions: among Irish American women, Margaret Fogarty Rudkin sold her Pepperidge Farm Bakeries to Campbell's Soup for $28 million in 1960. Rachel Carson, who held a master's degree in zoology from Johns Hopkins and had worked at the U.S. Bureau of Fisheries since the 1940s, finished her research at the National Institute of Health and began writing *Silent Spring* (1962), which exposed the environmental damage wreaked by pesticides and led to the eventual foundation of the EPA (Lear 2008). Doris Kearns Goodwin, who earned a doctorate from Harvard University, went to work as an assistant to Lyndon Baines Johnson in 1967. After working for Douglas Aircraft as an engineering draftsman during World War II, Esther McCoy was refused admission to pursue graduate course work in architecture thanks to the aforementioned quotas; nevertheless, she went on to research and critique California's "neglected architecture" in *Five California Architects*, establishing the basis of modern California design and eventually publishing six books on the subject (Morgan 2011, 59–60). But not every woman was so accomplished.

An Irish American helped change the sexist status quo. John F. Kennedy's 1960 election was considered a victory for both Irish Americans and Irish Catholics, most of whom belonged to both groups (Dolan 2008, 272). Kennedy won in part because he directly addressed anti-Catholic prejudice, a political and rhetorical ploy that helped win enough Protestant votes to sway the election. Such cross-over votes were increasingly necessary. Across the country, Kennedy won 70 percent of the Irish Catholic votes, but in New York he received only 60 percent from his fellow Irishmen. Ironically, despite the Irish-Jewish rivalry, if not for the votes cast by Fordham University's mostly Jewish School of Social Work, its conservative Catholic undergraduates would have given the nod to Nixon—early signs that in reaction to the Vietnam protests, sexual revolution, and Civil Rights movement, the Irish were trending Republican (Meagher 2005, 164). Kennedy also won votes because he presented a more moderate image than his Irish American predecessors Joe McCarthy and Father Coughlin; rather, Kennedy "proved to be the Father O'Malley—portrayed by Bing Crosby in *Going My Way*—of Irish Catholic politicians for the postwar American consensus" (Smith 2010, 87).

It could also be argued that Kennedy achieved this status thanks in part to the women in his life. Doris Kearns Goodwin's *The Fitzgeralds and the Kennedys* describes his strong female role models and forebears. His great-grandmother, Rosanna Cox Fitzgerald, who raised eleven children before dying in childbirth, was "indispensable" to the family's success (1987, 59). His paternal great-grandmother, Bridget Murphy Kennedy, was a widow who single-handedly raised four children and saved enough money to send her son P.J. through private school. After entering politics, P.J. met Rose, the daughter of Mayor John "Honey Fitz" Fitzgerald, who defied her father to marry P.J.'s son, Joseph Kennedy. Before meeting her husband, Rose had aspirations of furthering her education at Wellesley. Denied this opportunity by her vote-counting father, she spent the rest of her life sublimating her desires for the good of the men in the family, an unfortunate family trait passed down to the Kennedy wives and daughters (Dezell 2001, 112–13).

Despite these family dynamics, the Kennedy presidency effectively brought an end to anti-Irish bigotry. One sign was the 1960 establishment of what later became ACIS, the American Conference for Irish Studies. Another sign was the appointment of the "Irish Mafia"—top advisors David Powers, Ken O'Donnell, and Larry O'Brien—"Irishmen skilled in the art of politics" (Meagher 2005, 276). Following Kennedy's election, Mike Mansfield was named majority leader of the Senate; the following year, John McCormack became Speaker of the House (Meagher 2005, 331–32). They were joined by national security advisor McGeorge Bundy and secretary of defense Robert McNamara (Woods 2005, 165), but Kennedy was the key.

Although his family's wealth set him apart, his Irish American traits—education, wit, political expertise, and oratorical skills—changed Americans' views of the Irish and ushered in feelings of acceptance and respect, thus opening the door for Irish American ascendancy into the middle class and breaking through the "green ceiling" (Hamill 2006, 529). Consequently, "By 1960, the Irish had become one of the most prosperous and best-educated ethnic groups in the nation" (Dolan 2008, 278). Indeed, the proportion of Irish Americans holding white-collar jobs was well above the national average, surpassing every other ethnic group except the Jews (Meagher 2005, 132). The Irish moved out of the cities into the suburbs, where their endogamy—and defensiveness due to their immigrant identity—gradually diffused. Thanks to their education, Irish American males were gaining access to highly paid, prestigious positions previously denied them; thanks to John Fitzgerald Kennedy, women of all ethnic backgrounds were able to progress in the workplace.

Within a year of his election, Kennedy created the PCSW, the President's Commission on the Status of Women. Its first job was to tackle the question of the Equal Rights Amendment, first introduced in 1920 and still unresolved. As the PCSW wrangled over the amendment, Kennedy ordered all federal agencies to "hire, train, and promote employees regardless of sex." The following year, Congress passed the Equal Pay Act a mere eighteen years after it was first proposed. In 1963, Kennedy created the Citizens' Advisory Council on the Status of Women as well as an Interdepartmental Committee on the Status of Women, both of which survived until Ronald Reagan took office. In the year following Kennedy's assassination, Congress passed the Civil Rights Act, which included Title VII, banning "sex discrimination in the workplace, along with racial discrimination [in] jobs at all levels and to most American businesses" (Davis 1991, 37–39). By 1967, this legislation also included affirmative action and Title IX, which extended equal rights to women and minorities.

The changing roles of women were supported, to a certain extent, by the media. In television shows such as "The Bionic Woman" and "Charlie's Angels," women were depicted as tough (but attractive) crime fighters. The "Mary Tyler Moore Show" actually featured an independent working woman. Irish American Moore was self-sufficient, sexually active, and assertive, leaving her boyfriend when he balked at marriage, openly taking the pill, and willing to demand equal pay. Granted, she was an exception. For the most part, Irish American females in television land relied on the wisdom and advice of their male bosses, colleagues, and husbands, as evidenced in *The Real McCoys, June Allyson, Donna Reed, The Brady Bunch, My Sister Eileen,* and *Leave it to Beaver.* Irish American males were even more popular, with hosts such as Pat Boone, Tennessee Ernie Ford, Dick Clark, Garry Moore, Glen Campbell, Andy Griffith, Ed Sullivan, Arthur Murray, Jimmy Dean, Johnny Cash, Bing Crosby, Phil Donahue, Dick Powell, Jackie Gleason and Art Carney, and shows such as *Ben Casey, The Brothers Brannagan, Burke's Law, Ensign O'Toole, Harrigan and Son, Hogan's Heroes, McHale's Navy, The Travels of Jaimie McPheeters,* and *The Trials of O'Brien.* And these were just some of the better known.

Among the 1960s movies, *Bonnie and Clyde, Breakfast at Tiffany's, The Sound of Music, The Graduate,* and *The Unsinkable Molly Brown* have been cited as the best feminist films of the decade. Yet of the first three, Bonnie Parker is a thief, Holly Golightly is a loose woman, and Maria is a nun who leaves the novitiate to marry. Fictional Irish American women fare better. Katherine Ross's character in *The Graduate,* Elaine Robinson, positively represents a strong, educated woman who refuses (at least for a while) to associate with the man who supposedly raped her mother, finds the courage to disobey her parents, and leaves her marriage right after the ceremony. *The Unsinkable Molly Brown* celebrates the bravery of Margaret Tobin, also known as the eponymous Brown, who helped a lifeboat of people survive the sinking *Titanic.* Fluent in several languages, Brown was able to organize the lifeboat's international crew: before the lifeboat was picked up, she had raised ten thousand dollars from her fellow passengers for the families of those who had not survived (Dezell 2001, 46).

More powerful were the Irish American women providing momentum and media exposure for the Women's Liberation movement. In 1965, Helen Gurley Brown founded *Cosmopolitan* magazine, an early crusader for women's rights amidst the sexual revolution. In 1968, Robin Morgan—the "best known 'politico'" in New York City (Brownmiller 1999, 69)—led the New York Radicals in a protest at the Miss America pageant. As journalist Charlotte Curtis described it, "Women armed with a giant bathing beauty puppet and a 'freedom trash can' in which they threw girdles, bras, hair curlers, false eyelashes, and anything else that smacked of 'enslavement'" (quoted in Woods 2005, 364). That same year, more than ten thousand women protested the Vietnam War by participating in the Jeannette Rankin Brigade.

Rankin, an early suffragist and the first woman elected to Congress, was a co-founder of the ACLU and the Women's International League for Peace and Freedom (Smith 2002). The Rankin Brigade captured the media's attention when they buried an effigy of the "traditional woman" during their demonstration. Other Irish American activists included Marilyn Webb, Ellen Willis, Jane McManus, and Nancy Hawley, who went on to found the Boston Women's Health Book collective. The following year, Sheila Cronan, a caseworker for the Bureau of Child Welfare, joined the movement after observing NOW's week-long demonstration against Colgate-Palmolive because they refused to promote women to management. To capture the public's attention, Kate Murray Millet designed a "giant toilet bowl with feet, to make the point that Colgate flushed women's aspirations down the toilet." They were soon joined by Pam Kearon, who became known for her satirical essay, "Man-Hating" (Brownmiller 1999, 45–46).

Although they tended to credit their own courage and independence rather than the women's movement, Irish American journalists contributed to the new image of women and transformed the role of women as war correspondents from an aberration to a norm (Hoffman 2008, 8). Years before her colleagues acknowledged the war's futility, the Radcliffe alumna Frances FitzGerald was analyzing the multilayered Vietnamese society. *Fire in the Lake: The Vietnamese and the Americans in Vietnam*, published in 1972 when she was thirty-two, won a Pulitzer Prize for contemporary affairs writing, a National Book Award, and the Bancroft Prize for historical writing (traditionally a scholarly award). Unlike FitzGerald, the *New York Herald Tribune* correspondent Marguerite Higgins—who had won a Pulitzer for her reporting on the Korean War—"was a hawkish, anti-Communist" with regard to Vietnam (Hoffman 2008, 7). Nevertheless, her subsequent book, *Our Vietnam Nightmare* (1965) revealed her concerns about the role of the American military. Back home, Mary McGrory, who had established her reputation reporting on the McCarthy hearings in the 1950s and won a Pulitzer for her commentary about Watergate, enhanced her national standing with her reporting on John F. Kennedy's assassination (Dezell 2001).

Lyndon Johnson supported Kennedy's efforts to cut taxes and further civil rights, not only because he believed in them but also because he felt these successes would improve his chances in the next election. Thanks to his commitment, the Civil Rights Act of 1964 put an end to discrimination in housing, federal funding, educational access, and "on the basis of race, color, religion, sex, or national origin" (Woods 2005, 182–83). Although the category of "sex" was added by conservatives as a means of blocking passage, the bill passed and thus opened the door for women. After winning the 1964 election in a landslide, Johnson continued to promote and protect civil rights, passing the Voting Rights Act in 1965. The following year he reinforced this initiative by issuing an executive order mandating that employers practice affirmative action to ensure equal representation in the workforce. Having apparently overlooked the need for affirmative action on the basis of sex, that category was added in 1967 (Woods 2005, 195). Unfortunately, the 1968 election of Richard M. Nixon put a halt to such forward progress. Nixon opposed Title IX, the ERA, abortion rights, even day-care centers (Woods 2005, 334).

Joyce Carol Oates's 1960s novels brought a feminist awareness to these disparities. Oates is not generally known to be Irish American, for like Flannery O'Connor she rarely addresses her Irish roots, but the paternal Oateses emigrated to upstate New York during the Famine. Her great-great-grandmother (a Mullaney) brought her six children to America after the death of her husband, Dominic Oates.[3] Oates shares other traits with her Irish American contemporaries. Like Maureen Howard, she experiments with narrative style, for example interrupting the chronology in *Expensive People* (1968) with commentaries on memoirs, faux reviews, a short story ("The Molesters"), and an analysis of same. Again like Howard, as well as Brennan

---

3. Letter to Susanna Araujo, 2008. Cited in Susanna Araujo, "I'm Your Man: Irish American Masculinity in the Fiction of Joyce Carol Oates," in Ebest and McInerney, *Too Smart to Be Sentimental*, 157–70.

and McCarthy, Oates satirizes the aspirations and affectations of the upper middle class, poking fun at the huge houses and requisite maids, the mothers' ennui and affairs, the fathers' uneasy distance from their own children, and the children's subsequent alcoholism, drug use, and homicidal impulses. She also shared their resentment of (and revenge on) the white male literati at the *Partisan Review*, who did their best to exclude women writers, through her characterization of Moe Malinsky, a "'professional intellectual' and radical editor of *The Transamerican Quarterly*" (Showalter 2009, 393).

During this decade, Oates published *A Garden of Earthly Delights* (1966), *Expensive People* (1968), and *them* (1969). She intended these novels to be "critiques of America—American culture, American values, American dreams—as well as narratives in which romantic ambitions are confronted by what must be called 'reality'" (Oates 1966, 221)—a theme characteristic of Irish American women's novels in the 1960s. The sardonically titled *Garden of Earthly Delights* features migrant workers, while *Expensive People*, in the tradition of Kathleen Norris, satirizes the suburban nouveau riche. Unremittingly grim, *them* looks at the post-Depression era, reads like the muckraking exposes of Norris's brother-in-law, Frank Norris, and features doomed heroines as hapless as Mary McCarthy's. Women get pregnant or beaten, they are worn down by childbearing, take to drink, lose their husbands. As Clara says in *Garden*, "There had been nothing else in the world for them, nothing, except to give themselves to men, some man, and to hope afterwards that it had not been a mistake. But could it be a mistake? There was no other choice" (Oates 1966, 147).

Critics such as Richard Ohmann have claimed that Americans' postwar middle-class status led to dissatisfactions that translated into narratives of illness; however, Irish American fiction was more likely to parallel the message implied in the works of Mickey Spillane, who correlated the author's agency with that of his characters (Hoberek 2005, 17). As befitting a writer who suffered from chronic illness and lack of agency, Flannery O'Connor conflated the two. Drawing on interviews with O'Connor's mother, Josephine Hendin argues that the theme of entrapment running throughout the later stories reflects O'Connor's dependence on her mother. Worse, the "code of Southern genteel womanhood" (against which Margaret Mitchell and Carson McCullers similarly rebelled) dictated that young women be pleasant and keep their personal business to themselves. Hendin points out the problem with this mindset: "But what if one's 'business,' one's most essential feelings are not the stuff pretty gestures are made of? What if, from girlhood, you have known you loathe the Southern belle you are supposed to become? What if you have felt 'other' and 'different' in a milieu that is horribly embarrassed by anything unconventional? And what if your business later on is dying slowly, being filled with impotent rage at your own weakness? And what if, through it all, no one will even tolerate your 'fussing' about it?" (1970, 12).

O'Connor displaced her anger and frustration by fictionalizing it (Hendin 1970, 13). This strategy certainly describes the stories in *Everything That Rises Must Converge*. Written after O'Connor had lived as a semi-invalid with her mother for ten years, they feature obnoxious yet loving mothers and equally obnoxious but well-educated sons who believe themselves superior to everyone. In the opening story as well as in "Greenleaf"—originally published in 1956, the year after O'Connor could no longer walk (Liukkonen 2008)—and "The Comforts of Home," the mother dies. In "A View of the Woods" and "The Lame Shall Enter First," children die because of an adult's self-righteous beliefs. O'Connor sublimated her frustration in characters whose unexpected rage often takes readers aback. These fictional sons and daughters resent the need to depend on mothers whose overbearing ways keep them in a state of perpetual adolescence (Hendin 1970, 14–15). Indeed, *Everything That Rises Must Converge* might also be called *Everyone Who Grows Up Must Confront His Parents*, for practically every story concludes with a confrontation leading to a parent's death. If the adult child is unable to cause the death, he collapses. Like O'Connor, these angry adult children are wholly reliant on their mothers even as they long to rebel, feel guilt-ridden, and fear punishment (99).

To deal with these feelings, O'Connor often created doubles—mothers' doubles so that the violence is shifted to a look-alike, children's doubles who enact vengeance on the offending parent, or animals who do the job guilt-free for the angry child. In the title story of *Everything That Rises*, Julian Chestney's mother has a heart attack caused by her double—a black woman wearing a hat just like hers—who conveys Julian's rage through her anger at Mrs. Chestney's racism. "Revelation" (1964) is set in a doctor's waiting room where Mrs. Turpin converses with a woman she considers her equal about the failings of their inferiors, including the woman's unattractive daughter, Mary Grace, who cannot help but overhear. In the story's denouement, Mary Grace attacks Mrs. Turpin, her mother's doppelganger, in retaliation for their mirth at her expense. In "The Comforts of Home" (1960), Thomas is furious because his mother has allowed Star, a convicted "nimpermaniac," to stay with them. Although Thomas intends to shoot Star, he accidentally kills his mother, who is Star's mirror image (Hendin 1970, 116–17). To punish Sheppard, the self-righteous father in "The Lame Shall Enter First" (1962) who ignores his son Norton while trying to rehabilitate the misfit Rufus, Rufus befriends Norton and convinces him to hang himself. Surely it is no accident that in almost every case, the angry "child" is a weak, needy intellectual. Like her predecessor Kathleen Conway, O'Connor exposes the psychic damage inflicted by a domineering Irish American matriarch.

Fouling the Catholic Nest

By focusing on female experiences and value systems, Irish American women in the 1960s produced novels with which millions of women could identify. Mary McCarthy and her contemporaries were the inspiration for generations of women because they wrote about "a woman's domestic strategies, her finances, her female friendships, her minute biological concerns" (Donohue 1996, 95–96). Anyone who has read these novels and biographies recognizes the constant interweaving of fiction and reality—a reality that includes Irish American women's relationship with the Catholic Church. Herein lies an interesting contradiction. Despite their assimilation in the 1960s, the feminist novels of Irish American women often suggest the influence of their Catholic background, for throughout most of the twentieth century, Irish Americans still defined themselves as American Catholics (Meagher 2005, 146).

When Kay Peterson declared that "Birth control . . . was for those who know how to use it and value it—the educated classes" (McCarthy 1963, 75), Mary McCarthy took on not only the church but also the birth control movement itself, which was aimed at "controlling" the growth of the working class. Since the majority of the working class was Catholic and thus prohibited from practicing birth control, this propaganda was viewed as a deliberate slight. The church did not dispel this perception. During the period in which *The Group* occurs, contraception had just been accepted by most Christian, non-Catholic denominations. Only the Catholic Church refused to budge, instead issuing *Casti Connubii: On Christian Marriage*, which stated that "any use whatever of marriage, in the exercise of which the act by human effort is deprived of its natural power of procreating life, violates the law of God and nature, and those who do such a thing are stained by a grave and mortal flaw" (quoted in Tobin 2008, 211). In addressing this and other taboos, McCarthy effectively spat in the face of the Mother Church.

Although McCarthy rejected the Catholic Church, she was unable to shake its tenets—a tendency characteristic of most Irish American women writers of this period. McCarthy's conflicted attitudes, characters, and behavior stem from her heritage, for despite her ostensible anti-feminism she struggled with "the Church's restrictive definition of women, and a historically and culturally Irish fatalism" (Donoghue 1996, 87–88). And even though McCarthy grew further and further from the mores of her Catholic girlhood, she could not escape herself. Despite her anti-feminist statements, her characters represent conflicting tensions as they are pulled between the desire for sexual and intellectual freedom and their internalized Catholic sense of guilt (Donoghue 1996, 93).

Catholic women are not generally associated with feminism. This group was not involved in feminism's first wave (1898–1920), which was closely tied to women's suffrage, because it was "implicitly anti-Catholic . . . vilifying the growing Catholic working-class political leadership of cities, such as Boston and Chicago, as the epitome of 'rum, Romananism, and rebellion'" (Ruether 2003, 3). However, between 1920 and 1950 many of the Catholic lay movements became involved with leftwing political issues, among them feminism. Founded in 1956, the Conference of Major Superiors of Women (CMSW) quickly grew disenchanted with Rome. Although twenty thousand women religious had willingly responded to the Vatican's request for American sisters to serve in Latin America, the Pope refused to reply to the sisters' unanimous petition to have representation on panels dealing with their own lives. Consequently, under the direction of Sister Marie August Neal, the CMSW distributed the National Sisters' Survey to ascertain the degree of support for structural change within the church (Weaver 1985, 83–84).

During the 1960s and 1970s, groups such as the Grail—Catholic lay-women who believed women had the potential to change the world—and the Catholic Family Movement (CFM) promoted a feminist agenda linked with social action. Both groups ran afoul of church authorities (Kalven 2003, 6–7). Following Vatican II, Grail members began to question Rome's authority over their lives; consequently, their leadership decentralized into three task forces: "the bonding of women, the search for God in traditional and nontraditional ways, and liberation." In 1968, the National Assembly of Religious Women (NARW) declared itself an explicitly feminist movement committed to giving all Catholic women a voice and engaging in feminist social justice initiatives such as the ERA, financial rights, and protection from domestic abuse (Weaver 1985, 126–28). Perhaps even less popular with the Catholic hierarchy was the so-called Army of Three—Patricia Macgin-nis, Lana Clarke Phelan, and Rowena Gurner—who started the movement to put abortion rights in the hands of women rather than male doctors, lawyers, or politicians. Begun in the late 1960s, this work continued into the next decade as they and other women worked to overturn antiabortion laws (Baehr 1990). Thanks to their efforts, NARAL—the National Abortion and Reproductive Rights Action League—was founded in 1969.

An Irish-born Catholic, Maeve Brennan did not much concern herself with religion, for thanks to Eamonn de Valera, the church had become inter-twined with the Irish government and was more or less taken for granted. However, in her short story "An Attack of Hunger," she makes a strong point. Throughout, Rose and Hubert bicker, reflecting spousal tensions gen-erally unaired at the time in women's fiction. Rose glares at Hubert. He watches her "with dislike and alarm," shouting, "You shut up! . . . Do you hear me? Shut up before I say something you won't want to hear." As the fighting escalates, Hubert accuses Rose of driving their son John from home. "He was sick of you and I'm sick of you, sick of your long face and your moans and sighs—I wish you'd get out of the room, I wish you'd go, go on, go away. . . . All I want is not to have to look at you anymore this evening" (Brennan 1962, 26). Forcing herself out the door, Rose resists the urge to beg his forgiveness. She considers borrowing money from her parish priest to go to John, but realizes "he would disapprove. He would tell her to go back to her husband," the plight of many a married Catholic woman in the 1960s (Dezell 2001, 105). And so she fulfills her only option: she returns home.

Irish American women's critiques of the church can be attributed, in part, to the aftermath of the Second Vatican Council. The core of the ensuing document dealt with internal conflicts: structural issues regarding the church's hierarchical authority and more pragmatic issues dealing with the duties, responsibilities, and lifestyles of men and women religious (Seidler and Meyer 1989). Reflecting the spirit of the 1960s, younger members disputed the church's authority to govern their behavior. In addition to changing from Latin to English masses, the Vatican Council dropped many of its parochial demands and adopted a more ecumenical stance toward other religions. As a result of these changes, and despite the shift to the suburbs, 70 to 85 percent of Irish Catholics regularly attended Mass (Dolan 2008, 284–85). More pertinent to the present study were women's issues involving "abortion, women's rights, the role of women in the Church, and the ordination of women," which could be further subdivided into issues related to marriage, birth control, divorce, remarriage, and sexuality, and the rights of women religious (Almeida 2006, 79–81).

With the advent of the birth-control pill in 1960, contraception became a topic of discussion outside the bedroom. In fact, one positive outcome of Vatican II had been Pope John XXIII's decision to reconsider the ban on contraception and Paul VI's convening the Papal Commission on Birth Control in 1964. After hearing the findings of the Catholic Family Movement, which reported widespread dissatisfaction with the abstinence method, accounts of its ineffectiveness, and serious demoralization among married partners, a majority of the commission voted to overturn traditional church teaching and allow the use of "medically approved method[s] of birth control within marriage" (Ruether 2003, 6–7). Unfortunately, minority members were able to dissuade the Pope, who went on to issue *Humana Vitae*, which reaffirmed the ban in 1968.[4]

4. Valerie Sayers's first novel, *Who Do You Love?* (1969), touches on this theme. Following two days in the lives of the Irish Catholic Rooney family, the overriding

These events coincided with the 1968 publication of Mary Daly's groundbreaking work, *The Church and the Second Sex*. Written in the years between Vatican II and *Humana Vitae*, Daly had viewed Vatican II as the first step toward a revitalized, more modern church, but with the emergence of *Humana Vitae*, change was no longer in the air. After her work was published, Daly was denied tenure at Boston College; however, in a striking example of irony, Daly's superiors reversed their decision after twenty-five hundred *male* students signed a petition in protest (Boston College did not admit females until 1970). Known as one of the best feminist minds of the twentieth century, Daly was neither an upstart nor an apostate. The daughter of Francis Xavier and Anna Catherine Daly, she was a cradle Catholic, attending parochial schools as a child, earning her B.A. at St. Rose and an M.A. at Catholic University (Lewis 2011). When Catholic University would not allow her to study theology because she was a woman, she earned her first doctorate from St. Mary's College/Notre Dame University in 1954 and subsequent degrees in theology and philosophy from the University of Fribourg in 1963 and 1965. The following year she was hired in the theology department at Boston College (*Encyclopedia* 2011).

The Church and the Second Sex traces the history of misogyny in the Catholic Church, taking care to point out that this could not occur or continue without secular approbation (Daly 1968, 8). To analyze the types of discrimination, she adopts the paradigm established by de Beauvoir:

• Patterns of oppression and deception such as hostility to women's emancipation, promise of heavenly rewards, enforced passivity, the illusion of equality, emphasis on service over intellectual efforts.

• Perpetuation of anti-female dogma such as the belief that women are "naturally inferior" and encouragement to identify with the Virgin Mother to assure purity and servility.

• Negative moral indoctrination through adherence to Greek and Jewish beliefs that women were morally inferior, essentially sinful, played a minor role in procreation, caused the expulsion from Eden, and essentially unclean—all

---

trauma concerns Mrs. Rooney's fifth pregnancy, an unforeseen consequence that promises to upset the family's already shaky finances.

of which supported bans on contraception and abortion—which in turn maintained woman's status as a slave to, if not a parasite on, man.

• Exclusion from the male hierarchy, which creates an inherent feeling of inferiority.

• The myth of transcendence through salvation—assuming one can emulate the actions of St. Theresa of Avila. (Daly 1968, 15–25)

To demonstrate these forms of prejudice, Daly traces the history of the church. To establish a record of contradiction if not hypocrisy, she compares pro- and anti-woman passages from the Old and New Testaments, noting that the church promoted the latter while illustrating that certain doctrinal aspects, such as obedience, fidelity, and mutual respect have always been applicable to males and females alike (Daly 1968, 33). Likewise, despite historical views of Eve as inferior because of her sex, Daly points to passages in Genesis confirming that originally Adam and Eve were equals. Despite the use of historical facts and direct quotations from the Bible, as well as recognition of signs of change and offers of "modest proposals" toward a peaceful coexistence, this work outraged the male hierarchy within and beyond the church. But their anger was nothing compared to that of the laity—whose ire was directed at Rome.

Following *Humana Vitae*, church attendance dropped from 65–70 to 50–55 percent by the 1970s (Dolan 2008, 285). Catholics began to question the idea of papal infallibility and to follow only those doctrines they could support. Whereas only 29 percent had supported the idea of female priests before *Humana Vitae*, within a month of its decision that number rose to 31 percent, and to 66 percent by the 1980s (Dezell 2001, 175–76). But the encyclical also had severe consequences: the number of priests and sisters declined by a third, while the ranks of teaching sisters and seminarians fell by 90 percent—a drop that in turn had serious consequences for parochial schools (Shelley 2006, 601). With the loss of women religious, the Catholic identity of these institutions faded away. After a record enrollment in 1964, over 40 percent of the elementary and 27 percent of the high schools closed. With these losses, the Irish American identity with and dominance of the Catholic hierarchy also began to fade (Meagher 2005, 332).

Vatican II shook the foundations of observant Catholics. These feelings are evident in Irish American women's novels of the 1960s, which reflect a loss of innocence, certainty, and security, as well as feelings of dislocation, emptiness, and rootlessness. Included beneath this rubric are the *Bildung-sromane* of the 1960s. In Catholic fiction, the death of a parent and the child's reaction generally parallel or stand as a metaphor for the "dissolution of American Catholic culture." Interestingly, "within the Catholic culture . . . innocence survived longer than in most other groups of its size in the United States"—at least through the 1950s—because the church answered all questions and mapped out the way to heaven. This is evident in the sentimental novels written during that era such as Ramona Stewart's *Casey*. Up to this point, American Catholicism had been a "clearly identifiable paradigm" (Gandolfo 1992, 1–3). But a new paradigm developed following Vatican II and *Humane Vitae*. World War II certainly upset many people's worldview; however, the upward mobility experienced by Catholics, along with the rest of the country, helped alleviate any sense of crisis. Yet this period also marked the beginning of a shift from the unquestioning piety of the "immigrant church" toward a period of growing intellectualism as children of first- and second-generation immigrants comprised the majority of Catholic college students (Meagher 2005, 143).

A parallel development was the move of Catholic novels from sentimental to realistic. The former basically adhered to the Catholic belief that such works should be didactic. Since the Civil War, American Catholic fiction had been characterized as "fiction with a parochial purpose" in the tradition of Mary Ann Sadlier (although the aforementioned women clearly had moved beyond that). However, the crisis instantiated by Vatican II resulted in a different type of Catholic novel based on personal experience—even if the church did not appreciate the shift. Traditional Catholics disapproved of any novel that criticized the church; indeed, conservative clerics such as Bishop Norbert Gaughan characterized such novelists as having "'fouled the Catholic nest.'" Conversely, if not hypocritically, male Catholic writers who took issue with the church were rarely castigated (Gandolfo 1992, 18–20).

Caught in the middle, Irish American women writers began sharing their stories. These 1960s novels were highly autobiographical as well as thematically related, featuring guilt-ridden, sometimes brow-beaten women trying to break out of suffocating social, cultural, religious, and political paradigms. Although literary critics have traditionally criticized women's autobiography, dismissing it as "merely autobiographical—'merely' in the sense of 'uncreatively' or even 'unintelligently'" (Hite 1989, 121), for women such fiction was empowering. Indeed, "the autobiographical novel continues to remain a major literary form for oppressed groups, as a medium for confronting problems of self and of cultural identity which fulfills important needs" (Felski 1989, 78).

This definition was particularly appropriate for Irish American women at midcentury. Trapped between their personal desires and the dictums of the church, many felt isolated. Although some married women worked outside the home, this was not yet an American staple (or necessity). In Catholic parishes, working women were still anomalies. If they did work outside the home, they had to contend with "overt prejudice, sexist remarks, sexual suggestiveness, . . . —the whole gamut of sexual and gender discrimination and second-class citizenship" (Du Plessis 1985, 101). Perhaps moreso among Irish American women than almost any other minority, this combination yielded "oppressed groups" greatly in need of "confronting problems of self and cultural identity" (Felski 1989, 78). Irish American novelist, memoirist, and satirist Caryl Rivers explains the dilemma. Catholic girls "were expected to be, in a word, docile. Like well-broken riding mares, we were to do what we were told, quietly and with the least amount of trouble for our handlers" (1973, 164). To escape, Irish American women began producing highly critical, highly autobiographical novels.

Not surprisingly, these novels were not only autobiographical but also feminist. Their works include some if not all of the following traits: The purpose is to "change the world"; in other words, gender and politics are intertwined (Schweikert 1986, 38). Connection and community and the "struggle against patriarchy" are often prominent themes leading to feelings of optimism about the prospect of future change. In these novels, male characters are no longer the most interesting, and powerful women are no longer monstrous or unfeminine. Instead, female experiences and value systems are examined and more likely to be valued, leading women readers to identify more easily with the characters and plots. The text/story is viewed as a manifestation of the author because these novels rely on a personal voice conveying a sense of "interiority"—that is, the authors provide an inside look at the character's heart and mind, which in turn often triggers a desire to connect with the text (Schweikert 1986, 46–48). Feminist novels by Irish American women reflect most if not all of these traits. As Maureen Howard notes, "it is in the telling of our stories that we reveal how bound we are to the rituals of family life, yet how we strain against them" (1997, xi–xiii).

Some Irish American women writers were able to balance this strain through the use of humor, for using comedy lessened the severity of questioning the church (Del Rosso 2005, 149). Maureen Howard learned from the master—or mistress, in this case. "For a woman coming of age in the 1950s," she wrote, "to read Mary McCarthy was a jolt in the right direction. That direction is the arrow (a bright, pulsing neon) pointing upstairs. Upstairs is the head bone, gray matter" (1975, 195). McCarthy's satire, political critiques, and feminist messages laid the contextual groundwork for Howard's scathing *Bridgeport Bus* (1965).

Set in Howard's hometown of Bridgeport, Connecticut, the novel explores "the thematic roots of her own Irish Catholic upbringing" (Fanning 2001, 344). When compared with Howard's memoir, *Facts of Life*, it becomes clear that she based the novel on her family members; however, to protect the innocent, the real life characters' roles are reversed and enlarged on—the sarcastic comments of Howard's father are placed into the mouth of the fictional Mrs. Keely; her lonely, put-upon brother's personality is grafted onto the character of Mary Agnes—while the need to escape one's roots becomes a journey from present to future as well as from past to present. In short, Howard takes the traditional Irish trope of a daughter who has devoted her life to caring for a widowed parent and turns it on its head.

Howard's protagonist, Mary Agnes Keeley, is thirty-five years old. Rather than endure a life of self-immolation in service to her widowed parent, "Ag" decides to leave home to experience life and discover herself, a quest characteristic of the feminist novel. In terms of maturity, Ag is a teenager; consequently, the novel revolves around her loss of sexual innocence. The plot is framed by Ag's rejection of the church because she associates it with her hypocritical Irish Catholic mother whom she has supported since high school (while her brother went off to Fordham). Because her mother has nothing better to do, most battles entail church-related guilt. When Ag cannot attend a Novena because she has a French class, Mrs. Keeley begins a familiar refrain: "'God knows'—she started the harangue right away—'you were brought up a good Catholic girl, that you should choose a lot of dirty French books over your religion. And thank the good Lord' (with a tremolo) 'your father is not here to see you an ingrate to your mother'" (Howard 1961, 10).

Tired of feeling belittled and ultimately betrayed by her mother, Ag moves to New York, finds an apartment and a job, and begins a relationship with her coworker, Stanley. Perhaps because he is the first man she has slept with, she believes she has fallen in love. However, she panics when it is time to meet Stanley's mother and impulsively sleeps with a young artist. Throughout this period, the novel breaks from chronological narrative to pursue Ag's streams of consciousness, thus illustrating Howard's "impatience with narrative conventions [as] part and parcel of healthy contempt for strictures on behavior that stifle the soul groping toward change for the better" (Fanning 2001, 342–43). After subsequent encounters with the artist, Ag finds herself pregnant, so she moves home, grows increasingly out of touch with reality, and kills her mother.

As the novel ends, thirty-seven-year-old Ag has been confined to a Catholic home for wayward girls to await the birth of her illegitimate child. When she asks why she was put there, a nun tells her to "pray to God." Periodically, the girls are "herded to Mass," where altar boys cover the rail with doilies "as if the swollen penitent girls who straggled up the aisle were not quite clean" (Howard 1961, 303–4). Taken piece by piece, these scenes are more funny than damning; taken as a whole, however, they offer a satirical view of Howard's perception of the church's hypocrisy.

At the same time, Ag's gradual mental disintegration exemplifies a theme common among novels of the era, whose authors reflect their Cold War anxieties and middle-class angst through their characters' demise: "a man (occasionally a woman) is doing pretty well by external measures; yet somehow the tension between his [or her] aspirations and his [or her] quotidian social existence grows unbearable. He [or she] stops doing what people expect . . . and enters a period of disorientation and disreputable experiment" (Ohmann 1984, 393). This theme can be found in Salinger's *Franny and Zooey*, Roth's *Portnoy's Complaint*, Bellow's *Herzog*, Updike's *Rabbit* trilogy—as well as Mary McCarthy's *The Group*, with heroine Kay's committal and apparent suicide. But anyone familiar with Howard's work recognizes the same theme, not to mention its stylistic brilliance. The same is true of Maeve Brennan's swan song, the novella *Springs of Affection*, and runs throughout the works of Flannery O'Connor.

Fiction by O'Connor and Cullinan are permeated with themes associated with traditional Irish American Catholicism: overbearing mothers, guilty daughters, and unnecessary veneration, if not fanaticism, for the religious life. O'Connor published her second novel, *The Violent Bear It Away*, in 1960. In an interview, she summarized it as dealing with "vocation." The main character, Tarwater, could become a religious fanatic like his great-uncle Old Tarwater—whom she describes variously as a "crypto-Catholic" (Wells 1962, 71) and as echoing her own Catholic beliefs (Daniel 1962, C2)—or choose the more secular path exemplified by his school teacher uncle, Rayber. This plot (and these characters) reflect the conflict between secular and religious life, a favorite O'Connor theme. Like *Wise Blood*, this novel explores the lives of "youths cursed by self-loathing" because of their own weakness and inability to break with their "parents," another theme running throughout her oeuvre (Hendin 1970, 58–61).

O'Connor passed away in 1964; shortly thereafter her second collection of short stories, *Everything That Rises Must Converge*, which later won the National Catholic Book Award, was published. O'Connor always maintained that she did not write for Catholics alone (*Motley* 1958, 29). Nevertheless, as a Catholic, she said, "death has always been brother to my imagination. I can't imagine a story that doesn't properly end in it or in its foreshadowings" (quoted in Mullins 1963, 35). That certainly describes the stories in this collection of angry children, overbearing mothers, and sudden death.

Elizabeth Cullinan's short stories featuring priests reflect Irish American women writers' ambivalence about the church. In "Estelle" (1976) and "Voices of the Dead" (1960) this feeling is symbolized by setting the matriarchs' home in the "shadow of the church" (Almeida 2001, 89). "The Reunion" (1961) contrasts the veneration of priests with the guilt of a failed priest. "The Ablutions" (1960) features Father Fox, a precursor to Father Phil in *House of Gold*. Like Father Phil, Father Fox is extremely close to his mother but secretly despises his sister and her family, who live with his mother in the family home—which he also hates: "the remembrance of the old house devastated him, driving away, as it always did, the peace and self-respect that twenty years of separateness from them had built in him" (Cullinan 1960, 103). With the publication of *House of Gold* (1969), all of these traits came together, exemplifying "contemporary Irish American domestic fiction at its best . . . a definitive portrait of crippling psychic damage that can occur within Irish-American families" (Fanning 2001, 335).

In this novel, the protagonist and eldest daughter, Elizabeth Carroll, and her siblings gather for an event familiar to Irish and Irish American fiction: the dying of the matriarch. Through the lens of the dutiful daughter, Cullinan reveals the power of the Irish American mother over her children's and grandchildren's lives and the pervasive effort of the matriarch to silence and control. In so doing, Cullinan debunks a number of sentimental Irish American stereotypes: the saintly Irish Catholic mother (Mrs. Devlin), the willing self-immolation of a daughter (Elizabeth) to care for her widowed parent, and the self sacrifice of children (Father Phil, Mothers Mary James and Helen Marie), who give their lives to the church.

As the novel opens, Mrs. Devlin is dying and her children, now grown, return to the family home. Each of them evidences the damage of an overbearing, overly religious mother, but her daughters suffer the most. Elizabeth and her family have recently moved out of Mrs. Devlin's home. Elizabeth feels guilty for having moved, even though she served as her mother's housekeeper and her family lived in her mother's attic. The nuns, Mother Mary James and Mother Helen Marie, who entered the convent in their early teens at their mother's bidding, are far from saintly: they cannot get along with each other but say nothing, for they have been taught to restrain their words and thoughts. To deal with such problems, Mother Mary James turns to Librium, Mother Helen Marie to sleep. Through these characters, Cullinan seems to conflate, if not equate, Mrs. Devlin's control with the power of the church, as evidenced in the book's title and the inappropriate, gold-plated touches throughout the house (remnants of the Devlin's fiftieth wedding anniversary celebration).

With characteristically Irish and Irish American gallows humor, Cullinan illuminates the psychic debts accrued by Irish Catholic women whose families seek respectability in the United States. Her characters struggle to resist the oppressive obedience fortified by an immigrant culture of anxiety and give voice to the psychological experience of creating an identity within, and despite, the constrictions of the Irish American culture of church and family. This sense is best illustrated in the novel's conclusion. After Winnie learns that her grandmother has died because of misdiagnosis and neglect by their so-called family friend, Dr. Hyland, she does not hesitate to say so. When the doctor's wife gushes that Mrs. Devlin's life was "'Not long enough . . . for those she's left behind,'" Winnie sees her opening:

"'I agree,' Winnie said. 'That's why it's too bad she wasn't operated on when she first got sick. Then, maybe her life actually would have been longer. . . . Our doctor, Doctor Sheridan, said that if there'd been an operation, my grandmother would very likely have lived a few years longer, and most certainly she'd have suffered less at the end.'" When Mrs. Hyland tries to stop her, asking, "'What on earth are you saying?'" Winnie does not hesitate.

"'Just that nine out of ten cases like hers are operable, regardless of age. . . . Nan had no heart . . . condition and . . . no responsible doctor would have said she did.'" With that, she walks away. When her sister finds Winnie in the restroom, she congratulates her. "'For a minute there I thought you were going to hit her.'"

"'I wish I had,'" Winnie replies (Cullinan 1969, 313–14).

This generation of Irish American mothers and daughters were not cowed by their so-called betters, nor did they keep their opinions to themselves: instead, they struggled to "escape this architecture of containment that is their inheritance" (McInerney 2008, 98). Through her fictional characters, Cullinan describes the effects of the church on a great number of Catholic women in the latter half of the twentieth century.

In 1969, William Maxwell revealed Maeve Brennan's identity as "The Long-Winded Lady." This was quite a coup: "Maeve achieved what only a handful of writers on *The New Yorker* in her generation did, in establishing an identifiable persona within the 'Talk' column, but the manner of her achievement was more daring than it looked, for she was unique in making a woman's voice heard regularly in that forum" (Bourke 2004, 190).

Brennan was not alone. In the 1960s, this cohort of Irish American writers presented a united front in exposing and rejecting the sexism inherent in church and society. Mary McCarthy's Kay Petersen, Maureen Howard's Mary Agnes "Ag" Keeley, Elizabeth Cullinan's Bernadette/Frances/

Cecilia/Winnie, Maeve Brennan's Rose Derdon and Delia Bagot—even Flannery O'Connor's Mary Grace Turpin and Joyce Carol Oates's Clara Walpole—represent women's struggles in the 1960s to gain personal identity, independence, and respect, not just from their husbands or lovers, but also from the non-Irish American community.

Manifestly autobiographical, these characters' struggles catch our attention because of their realistic insider's view. They are not just Irish American, for they also open the doors on American marriage and motherhood. They put a human face on the miserable women Betty Friedan represents in *The Feminine Mystique*, yet these writers are at the same time uniquely Irish American, for their stories are inextricably interwoven with the Catholic Church. Hence the themes of guilt and repression, anger and rejection, depression and disappointment. As Alice McDermott explains: "the language of the church, my church, was not only a means to an end in my fiction but an essential part of my own understanding of the world." Catholicism, she continues, "was the native language of my spirit" (2000, 12). As the coming chapters reveal, these traits endure.

3

The 1970s

A State of Upheaval

By the time I had reached adolescence, I was aware that society had carved out a niche for me, now that I was about to become a woman. I was offered one ticket, good for a lifetime, to the bleachers.

—Caryl Rivers, *Aphrodite at Mid-Century: Growing Up Female and Catholic in Postwar America*

The 1970s were a decade of turmoil. Every year brought another calamity—from Kent State, Watergate, Vietnam, and Nixon's resignation to Nixon's pardon, the Iran hostage debacle, and Boston race riots—violence and disaster dominated the headlines, leading historian Randall Bennett Woods to describe this era as "the most tumultuous and troubling through which the United States had yet passed" (2005, 351). In the midst of this tumult *Time* magazine declared feminists "Women of the Year" and announced that feminism had "penetrated every layer of society, matured beyond ideology to a new status of general—and sometimes unconscious—acceptance" ("Women" 1976, 1).

The truth of this statement could be observed in developed countries around the world. In France, women comprised 22 percent of lawyers, 18 percent of doctors, 40 percent of medical students, and 90 percent of pharmacists. Under Margaret Thatcher, British women were guaranteed equal pay for equal work. In Italy, more than twenty thousand women rallied to demand abortion rights; in Iceland, women went on strike and closed down the nation's phones, schools, and theaters. Japanese women were employed in every field and ruled the roost at home. Taking this trend to extremes, in India Indira Gandhi became the first female dictator ("Women" 1976). Meanwhile in Ireland, amidst the terrorism aroused by Bloody Sunday and retaliation by the IRA, the Women's Liberation Movement (WLM) issued a manifesto demanding equal rights and equal pay; removal of the marriage bar; equal treatment for widows, single mothers, and deserted wives; equal educational opportunities for women; and the right to legal contraception and equal housing. When the WLM collapsed, Irish Women United was formed; two years later, the Contraception Action Programme—an activist organization that deliberately protested where they were most likely to be arrested—was formed (Horgan 2001).

Back in the United States, a Harris poll revealed that 63 percent of Americans supported "most of the efforts to strengthen and change women's status in society." Despite major national and international disputes, women's issues came to the fore while women-centered legislation proliferated—as did the work of Irish American women. Among those recognized by *Time* as "Women of the Year," almost half were of Irish descent: Susie Sharp, the first female chief justice of the North Carolina Supreme Court; Jill Ker Conway, the first female president of Smith; Addie Wyatt, the women's affairs director for the Amalgamated Meat Cutters and Butcher Workmen; Kathleen Byerly, the top aide to the Navy's Pacific fleet command; Charlotte Curtis, the editor of the *New York Times* Op-Ed page; Joan Ganz Clooney, who started *Sesame Street* and ran the Children's Television Workshop; and Catherine Cleary, the president of First Wisconsin Corp Bank and board member for AT&T, Kraftco, and General Motors ("Women" 1976). During this period, the FBI hired its first female agents, Susan Lynn Roley and the former nun Joanne E. Pierce, and Jane Burke Byrne was elected the first female mayor of Chicago (Woods 2005, 365).

In universities, women's studies programs proliferated; by the end of the decade, more than twenty thousand women's studies courses existed (Ferguson, Katrak, Miner 1996, 45). Feminist research by Irish Americans was world renowned. This decade saw the U.S. publications of Kate Murray Millet's *Sexual Politics*, Robin Morgan's *Sisterhood Is Powerful*, Mary Daly's *Beyond God the Father* and *Gyn/Ecology*, Gail Sheehy's *Passages*, and the beginning of Carol Gilligan's research on female moral development.

Such studies raised awareness that previous research had focused almost exclusively on male subjects, which led to "an avid feminist reexamination of old studies" (Davis 1991, 222). By the end of the decade, publications by women across the academic disciplines had tripled (DuBois 1987, 16). Bonnie Zimmerman describes the era's zeitgeist: "we broke ground in virtually every area of society. We took risks and created dazzlingly new ideas and interpretations. Because we were pioneers—because we fervently believed (rightly or wrongly) that we had been born anew—we were also ideologues and fanatics, passionate about our new religion" (1990, 115). The spirit of the times was exemplified by a number of national events:

- 1970—the fiftieth anniversary of women's suffrage.
- 1971—Women's Equality Day.
- 1972—the Equal Rights Amendment was passed by Congress and sent to the states; National Women's Political Caucus established; Title IX passed.
- 1973—Roe v. Wade upheld.
- 1974—Equal Credit Opportunity Act passed; Coalition of Labor Union Women established.
- 1977—first National Women's Conference.

The women's movement was also reflected in pop culture. The biggest movie of the decade was *Star Wars*, in which Princess Leia played an equal role among male her co-stars. Other films made less subtle points. Molly Haskell's 1974 documentary, *From Reverence to Rape*, was one of the first to analyze how females were depicted in "women's films." Similarly, Jean Kilbourne's documentary, *Killing Us Softly*, revealed the many ways advertising oppresses women. *Looking for Mr. Goodbar*, starring Irish American Diane Keaton as Paula Dunn, was a cautionary film for independent women, while *Norma Rae* promoted courageous women. The heroine of *The Goodbye Girl*, Paula McFadden, is a single mom supporting herself and her daughter; likewise Alice Wyatt, the widowed mother in *Alice Doesn't Live Here Anymore*, takes her son on the road in an attempt to earn a living as a singer. Similar messages about independence, female friendships, and the sexual revolution came across in *An Unmarried Woman*. Yet in every Hollywood retelling, women's problems were resolved by remarrying or entering into a committed relationship. Hollywood was not quite ready for feminism.

The media were also reluctantly undergoing change. Groups such as Media Women (which consisted of female writers from the *New York Post*, Sunday Morning News at CBS, the Associated Press, *Women's Wear Daily*, *Newsweek*, Newsreel, and the Screenwriters Guild) organized to protest inequitable pay, sexist treatment in the newsroom, and the perpetuation of essentialist stereotypes by the postwar cadre of male editors. Media Women was joined by OWL, the Older Women's Liberation group. Despite their solidarity, radical feminists such as Shulamith Firestone (leader of the New York Radical Feminists) almost ruined efforts to negotiate with *Lady's Home Journal* editor John Mack Brown when she tried to tackle him. Thwarted by one of her own, she stomped out. The following month, Robin Morgan led a sit-in at Grove Press, demanding it cease publishing pornography (Brownmiller 1999, 91–92).

On television, two of the most popular programs were *Laverne and Shirley*—two young, independent, blue-collar women who worked in a beer factory—and *Mary Hartman, Mary Hartman*, a supposedly average housewife surrounded by hypocrites (Woods 2005, 387). *All in the Family's* bigoted Archie Bunker (played by Irish American Carroll O'Connor) raised eyebrows by calling attention to issues of race, class, and gender issues, but he was regularly called on his prejudice by his liberal daughter (Sally Struthers) and occasionally by his brow-beaten wife. Unfortunately, Archie Bunker's mindset was sometimes reflected among women just like him.

Most outrageous was Phyllis Schlafly, whose 1972 "Stop ERA" movement warned that ratification would force all women to work and to share restrooms with men. To foil pro-choice proponents, Henry Hyde (R-Illinois) introduced legislation prohibiting the use of Medicare and Medicaid funds for abortion, a decision not only upheld by the Supreme Court but also extended to members of the military and Peace Corps in 1978 (Woods 2005, 370). Turncoat Marabel Morgan, author of *The Total Woman* (1973), promoted the sexist behaviors railed against by Caryl Rivers in her memoir, *Aphrodite at Mid-Century: Growing Up Female and Catholic in Postwar America* (1973). Reviewing advice (repeated by Morgan) on how to catch a man, Rivers concluded: "And there she is, folks, Aphrodite at Mid-Century: Adaptable as Play Doh, possessed of no ego at all, fetching and carrying for hubby with her hair freshly done and the beef bourguignon simmering on the range, a pal who likes hockey, football, lacrosse, craps (you name it) because HE does, who never nags, who keeps hubby thin, puts the big chair by the fire for him and slinks about in a black negligee if HE is in the mood. And she always, *always* spends an hour a day cross-examining herself to make sure she is Making Marriage Work. She makes me want to throw up" (1973, 246).

Many women agreed. By 1970, women comprised 44 percent of the workforce while the birthrate dropped from a high of 25.3 births per thousand in 1957 to 14.8 by 1975 (Woods 2005, 367). Feminists took to the streets to protest, met privately in consciousness-raising groups, and argued for the inclusion of women's literature, history, and accomplishments in the academic curriculum. To do so, American women had to unlearn what they had been taught and decondition the ingrained tendency to sublimate their personal desires to serve their bosses, parents, boyfriend, spouse, or children (Rich 1979).

Sexually Transgressive Writing

In addition to protesting for equal rights, feminists raised awareness of stifling marriages, rape and domestic violence, and the desire for sexual freedom. On these issues, Irish American women were at the forefront. Whereas Mary McCarthy and Betty Friedan represented the needs of Irish Catholic and Jewish women writers in the 1960s, Mary Gordon encompassed both categories. Her mother, Anna Gagliano Gordon, was Italian Irish while her father, David Gordon, was a Jewish convert to Catholicism. This genetic confluence yielded a first novel set in Queens, a middle-class Irish American borough, featuring female friendships, teen-age and adulterous sex, rape and a lesbian relationship, domestic violence and self-loathing, priests and politicians, repentance and forgiveness. In other words, Gordon took Mary McCarthy's themes away from the upper-class Episcopalians, set them in a working-class Irish urban enclave, and added Catholics, priests, and guilt. Like *The Group*, *Final Payments* was a hit. It spent five weeks on *The New York Times* "Best Sellers" list, was named a *New York Times* outstanding book of 1978, and was nominated for a National Book Critics Circle Award. In 1979 alone *Final Payments* sold 1.25 million copies (Bennett 2002, 11).

After eleven years spent caring for her widowed, stroke-ridden father, a retired rightwing conservative Catholic professor of medieval literature,

Gordon's Isabel Moore finds herself unable to mourn his death because she is thrilled to be free: "I felt light, as from the removal of a burden, light as a spaceman in a gravity less universe" (1978, 9). Taking a feminist stance often misinterpreted as anti-Irish, Isabel rejects suggestions from the family lawyer that she, a college graduate, become a housekeeper. She has no desire to join "that network of Irish daughters, orphaned in their forties by the death of an invalid parent, [working] always for less than minimum wages at jobs found by some priest, some doctor, among their own kind" (26). Conflating feminism and Catholicism, Gordon explains, "I was brought up to take issues of justice very seriously. . . . And what is feminism except a desire for universal justice not bounded by gender roles?" (quoted in Wachtel 2002, 272).

Paralleling the feminist movement, Isabel's progress is slow and somewhat recursive. Her distaste for servile jobs stems largely from her association with Margaret Casey, the family housekeeper who hoped to marry Isabel's father and stop him from spoiling his daughter. A recurring figure based on Gordon's hated aunt,[1] Margaret is a horrid old woman constantly whining about her lot. Isabel wisely has no desire to join her company: "I always knew who I was; I was not Margaret. It gave me a great freedom. I could do whatever I wanted." This belief is fostered by Isabel's father, who "always said he was raising a Theresa of Avila, not a Therese of Lisieux: someone who would found orders and insult recalcitrant bishops, not someone who would submit to having dirty water thrown on her by her sisters in Christ" (27–28).

Although *Final Payments* garnered praise from critics, like *The Group*, it caused an uproar among the people it skewered: in this case, Irish Americans. A *New York Times* Book Review begins positively— "Along with her unmistakable talent Mary Gordon shows great respect for her craft: she cares about her diction, the rhythms of a sentence, the pacing of her paragraphs"—but then continues, "Mary Gordon's cleverness, like her heroine's, can be forced and somewhat parochial" (Howard 1978, 32). Charles Fanning's reaction is better-known and less tempered. Accusing *Final Payments* of being "fueled by personal rage and bitterness at the perceived excesses, distortions, and injustices of Irish-American family life," he describes the

---

1. See Gordon's autobiography, *Circling My Mother*.

plot as movement "from a caricatured constriction to an exaggerated escape into the open air." The father is depicted as "an intolerant Catholic conservative who makes William F. Buckley, Jr. look like Dorothy Day"; the family priest as "a mawkish, alcoholic priest who retards Isabel's growth"; and the working-class Irish neighbors as fractious and irrational (2001, 329). Later analyses accuse Gordon of blaming the bleak Irish American lifestyle on "tragic defects in Irish culture" (Meagher 2005, 166) and criticize such works as depicting "a parade of grotesques" (Ebest 2005, 182).

But Irish American sociological history suggests Gordon's depiction might be somewhat accurate—even though critics should take care not to conflate literature with sociology (Dezell 2001, 31). Regardless, such criticisms reflect Kerby Miller's depiction of Irish Americans as overly concerned with assimilation and respectability (Dezell 2001, 72). Clearly Gordon had moved beyond this. In fact, the New Irish immigrant Eamonn Wall defends the novel as representative of the genre. Noting that "Irish American writers usually present their ethnic group in an unflattering light," he explains that "this modus operandi, which has long been a feature of Irish and Irish American writing, is part of the writer's historical inheritance," a trait that can be traced from James Joyce through Edna O'Brien and Dermot Bulger (1999, 16). In this instance, Wall suggests that Gordon's characterization of Isabel Moore displays an understanding of how cloistered her life had been and how poorly her upbringing had prepared her for adulthood. At the same time, the plotline serves as an allegory for "the secondary role women have been forced to play in Irish American families" (Wall 1999, 32–33) while reminding us that most academics are more comfortable with Irish Americans portrayed by male writers who focus on pubs, cops, and "boyos" (Dezell 2001, 31).

A close reading of the novel, as well as Gordon's 1989 memoir, *The Shadow Man*, further refutes such criticism. As Maureen Howard did in *Bridgeport Bus*, Gordon draws on real-life personality traits to develop her main characters and then changes their identities. She reverses her own father's virulent anti-Semitism, turning it into ultraconservative Catholicism as a means of exposing the church's treatment of women. *Final Payment's* opening scene "reflects the views of most Catholic feminists . . . that the church's attempt to accommodate feminist ideals in recent years amounts to 'tokenism'" (Labrie 1997, 248–49). The priests are less than respectful: constant visitors to Isabel's home, they spend their time "determin[ing] the precise nature of the Transubstantiation, fumbling for my name as I freshened their drinks" (Gordon 1978, 1). Such commentary suggests consciousness, if not resentment, of the patriarchal relationships still present in the 1970s. But the burden of caring for her father and the apparent futility of change—for him and for her—further contribute to Isabel's rejection of the church. Afraid of upsetting her father, she takes long walks while supposedly attending Mass. Here too a bit of feminist anger creeps in: "when the Church ceased to be inevitable, it became for me irrelevant. And then there was the [Vatican II] Council, with its sixties relevance and relativity that interested me not a whit" (Gordon 1978, 17).

Guilt also plays a role. Isabel illogically believes that her father's stroke was a reaction to his discovery of her in flagrante with his star pupil, an attitude reflecting the church's view of extramarital or adulterous sex as illness or disease (Del Rosso 2005, 38). "My sex was infecting me; my sex was a disease," Isabel laments (Gordon 1978, 265). But although Gordon initially personifies the church through the character of Isabel's tyrannical father, through her reflections she ultimately matures and gains self-knowledge, in the process exploring her attitudes toward and rejection of the church. Indeed, by the novel's end, Isabel comes full circle. Her indifference fades as she begins to mourn her father and find solace in their shared faith. In this, the family priest is the key to her return to the church and eventual escape from self-immolation.

Although both Jeanna del Rosso and Charles Fanning maintain that Gordon is explicitly anti-Catholic, her depiction of Father Mulcahy is actually positive and comforting. In fact, his phone call prompts her awakening. Although he has never left the city, he offers to drive to upstate New York for a visit. After they speak, he advises Isabel to take care of herself: "'I think you should leave here,'" he tells her. When Isabel protests that she has promised to care for Margaret, he counters, "'Even God breaks promises. . . . Here,' he said, squeezing a crumpled bill into my hand, 'Get your hair done on me.'" Again countering her refusal, he tells her, "'Well, then, watch your weight, honey. God gave you beauty. If you waste it, that's a sin against the fifth commandment.'"

"'Thou shalt not kill?'" she asks. "'What does that have to do with it?'"
"'It means slow deaths, too,'" he replies, and takes his leave (297).

A review of Gordon's work notes that "neither in her fiction nor in her essays and interviews has Gordon ever revealed the personal vendetta against the Irish that Fanning suspects" (Hoeness-Krupsaw 2008, 204). Rather, she consistently hails her parents as "immigrant survivors" and credits the Catholic Church as a "formative influence." Another influence was Mary McCarthy, who praised the novel even before it was published. Likewise, Gordon gives a nod to McCarthy in her second novel, writing: "She had been warned about Mary McCarthy for years. Ever since *The Group* nuns had shaken their heads and breathed her name as a warning to the better students. 'What good do all those brains do her? Four husbands and writing filth,' they said. It was a comfort to have that book with her. She felt accompanied by a daring older sister whom defiance had made glamorous" (Gordon 1980, 90). Just as *The Group* raised eyebrows in the 1960s through its exploration of feminist issues, *Final Payments* epitomized Irish American women's writing in the seventies—as liberating—"for she employs traditional fictional elements to new effects that eventually broaden the parameters of the traditional Irish American novel" (Hoeness-Krupsaw 2008, 208).

In addition to *Bildungsromane* like Gordon's, the 1970s saw the rise of "feminist meta-fiction—novels in which the author 'revises' traditional phallocentric messages by inserting a feminist plot which quite often abandons the traditional path from parents' to husband's home" (Showalter 2009, 443). Like most Irish Americans, Joyce Carol Oates's novels reflect their author. Although Oates is not so explicitly autobiographical as other Irish American women, her works represent not only elements of her personal life but also, perhaps more important, a record of her creative life (Daly 1996, 223–24).

Oates's 1970s novels mark the end of her themes of violence and trauma per se and the beginning of a focus on discrimination and violence against women. Her fiction features a number of specifically "woman-centered novels"—*Do with Me What You Will* (1973), *The Assassins* (1975), *Childwold* (1976), and *Unholy Loves* (1979)—as well as a number of similarly themed short stories in *Marriages and Infidelities* (1972). In addition to feminist themes, Oates practices figurative "infidelities" against male-dominated institutions in the majority of her work during this decade—against science in *Wonderland* (1971); against law in *Do with Me What You Will*; against politics, philosophy, the visual arts, and religion in *The Assassins*; against literature in *Childwold*; against fundamentalist Christians in *Son of the Morning* (1978); against literary criticism in *Unholy Loves*; and against business in *Cybele* (1979)—each personified in a male character. Oates also criticizes patriarchal institutions. *The Triumph of the Spider Monkey* (1976) and *A Sentimental Education* (1979) critique social welfare and military institutions, respectively (Daly 1996, 69–75).

In this, her work was reflective of feminist efforts to publicize and eradicate sexual violence and male domination (Brownmiller 1999, 194). Prior to the 1970s, Americans seemed unaware that rape, incest, and domestic abuse were social problems (Davis 1991, 308). The women's movement— which included a significant number of Irish American women—helped raise the consciousness of the American public. Continuing Irish American women writers' tradition of protecting women's rights through their journalistic efforts, Marilyn Webb, a member of DC Women's Liberation, helped develop a counterculture journal, *Off Our Backs*. Its first issue discussed abortion, the Pill, and how to use a diaphragm. Collaborating with Martha Shelley and members of WITCH, Robin Morgan took over *Rat* magazine from its male editors. Her essay in the inaugural issue, "Goodbye to All That," which repudiated the male members of the New Left, is still considered "one of the most powerful documents of the emerging feminist era." In Pittsburgh, Jo-Ann Evans Gardner founded *KNOW, Inc.*, a fact-filled compendium of women's issues; in New York, Mary Cantwell, managing editor at *Mademoiselle*, contributed to the movement by running a series of profeminist essays. In Los Angeles, Varda Murrell, under the pseudonym Varda One, started *Everywoman* magazine, which eventually led to the founding of the Everywoman Bookstore. In Berkeley, Bay Area Women's Liberation members Trina Robbins, Lynn O'Connor, and Susan Griffin contributed to *It Ain't Me, Babe*, a twenty-four-page feminist newspaper (Brownmiller 1999, 74–77). Although Kate Millet's *Sexual Politics* was the first to identify rape as a "weapon of the patriarchy," *It Ain't Me, Babe* was one of the earliest feminist journals to draw attention to the issue. After running an article entitled "Anatomy of a Rape," the editors included essays on how to

"Disarm Rapists" and "Fight!" Diane Crothers brought this to the attention of New York's West Village-One, a feminist consciousness-raising group, after seeing an article describing how California feminists had exposed the men (including the groom) who raped a woman at a bachelor party. Consequently, the New York Radical Feminists held a speak-out on rape at which victims described their ordeals. Carolyn Flaherty, of the Brooklyn Brigade #5, ensured the event would receive adequate publicity by convincing Gail Sheehy, then writing for *New York Magazine*, to cover it. Sheehy's coverage led to the New York Radical Feminist Conference on Rape, whose publicists were Rosemary Gaffney and Sheila Michaels (Brownmiller 1999, 195–201).

The following year, Susan Griffin, poet and cofounder of Bay Area Women Against Rape, published "Rape: The All-American Crime"—considered a "trailblazing article, the first in a national publication to put rape in a historical context." Later that year, WAR (Women Against Rape) groups were founded around the country. In response, Kathy Barry, along with Joanne Parrent, Cate Stadelman, and eight other women published a handbook, *Stop Rape*. This work was the impetus for Liz O'Sullivan and others to form East Coast support groups for victims of rape, which led in turn to the DC Crisis Rape Center, a hotline women could call twenty-four hours a day. In 1974, Noreen Connell and Cassandra Wilson co-edited *Rape: The First Sourcebook for Women*, the first book on the topic to be published by a mainstream press. It was followed by *Against Rape*, coauthored by Kathleen Thompson, and *The Politics of Rape: The Victim's Perspective*, by Diana Russell (Brownmiller 1999, 205–23).

Irish American women were also active in the abortion rights movement. In 1966, Patricia Maginnis, Lana Clarke Phelan, and Rowena Gurner had begun publishing a handbook—emblazoned with Margaret Higgins Sanger's famous declaration, "A woman has the right to control her own body"—offering advice for women seeking illegal abortions. In 1969, the Austin Women's Liberation Group, led by Judy Smith, Bea Durden, and Victoria Foe, convinced the recent law school graduate Sarah Weddington—who went on to be co-counsel in *Roe v. Wade*—to join them in the fight to legalize abortion. In the 1972 inaugural issue of *Ms.* magazine, Jane O'Reilly contributed the lead article, "The Housewife's Moment of Truth," detailing her travails in attempting to secure an abortion. Such increased awareness led to passage of the marital rape law in 1976 and the establishment of the National Coalition Against Domestic Violence in 1977. In 1976, the feminist author Del Martin wrote *Battered Wives*, the first book exposing domestic violence. This work, as well as the establishment of shelters for battered women in England, inspired Lenore Walker to research and write *The Battered Woman*. Published by Harper and Row in 1979, this book introduced the "battered woman's syndrome" as a defense argument for women accused of killing their abusers (Brownmiller 1999). By 1979 forty of the fifty states had developed or revised their rape statutes (Ferguson, Katrak, Miner 1996, 47).

Irish American women exposed these problems in their literature. In the lesbian novel *Give Me Your Good Ear* (1979), the heroine Francie is involved with Ben, a man who verbally abuses her. For much of the novel she contemplates leaving him but stays for fear he will go berserk (Brady 1979, 16). In *Final Payments*, Gordon's Isabel Moore is raped by the politician John Ryan and later physically and verbally abused by her "ideal" man, Hugh Slade. Joyce Carol Oates further explores these themes in *The Assassins*. This message becomes more uplifting in *The Childwold*, which takes the themes and characters running throughout Nabokov's *Lolita* and turns them on their head. Rather than featuring a ruined and defeated nymphet, Oates's Laney Bartlett moves beyond the influence of her seducer, Kasch, for his tutelage has enabled her to expand her mind and her world. "Where are you, why have you gone so far?" he asks. "The books you read are not my books, the language you use is not my language. You are no longer recognizable! You are no longer mine!" (Oates 1975b, 290).

Unlike Nabokov's socially and intellectually stunted Lolita, Laney not only transcends Kasch but also actually returns to help him, for "she feels her own power to restore Kasch to life through her own imagination." Laney represents Oates's "youthful alter-ego," for like Oates her intellectual emancipation enables her to regain her voice and tell her own story as the novel concludes (Bender 1979, 121). As such this novel "rewrites *Lolita*, transforming Humbert Humbert, a monologic narrator, into a man named Kasch who fantasizes but does not act upon his 'paedomorphic' lust" (Daly 1996,

93). In this novel as well as Oates's *Unholy Loves* (1979), women free themselves from negative relationships with men (76).[2]

As the decade progressed, the Women's Liberation movement continued to raise the nation's consciousness by making social and political progress. In Supreme Court rulings, *Eisenstadt v. Baird* ended the ban on unmarried women using contraceptives, *Corning v. Brennan* put an end to job discrimination, and *Taylor v. Louisiana* allowed women to be part of jury pools—bans that seem unimaginable now. In 1975, Elaine Noble became the first openly gay candidate to be elected to the Massachusetts State Legislature; two years later, the U.S. Air Force academy graduated its first female cadet. A woman (Bella Abzug) was the first congressperson to call for Richard Nixon's impeachment, women-owned businesses were growing, and *Ms.* magazine's circulation grew to over four hundred thousand (Brownmiller 1999, 225).

Traditional attitudes were also challenged in the gay and lesbian community. Although the 1950s and 1960s saw some evidence of gay and lesbian writing—in pulp fiction and more notably in Jeannette Howard Foster's *Sex Variant Women in Literature* (1958) and *The Ladder*, which reviewed lesbian literature—the 1969 Stonewall Riot marked the official beginning of the Gay Rights movement. After two nights of rioting to protest police raids on gay bars in Greenwich Village, the Gay Liberation movement ushered in a spate of gay and lesbian-themed plays and novels exploring coming out, sexual experimentation in urban and rural environments, and sometimes "sexually transgressive" writing like pornography and sadomasochistic works (Bona 2004, 211). Among lesbian novels, the best known was Rita Mae Brown, *Ruby Fruit Jungle* (1973), published by Daughters Inc., a press cofounded by Parke Bowman, June Arnold, and Bertha Harris (a major influence on Dorothy Allison).

Given the attitudes toward homosexuality expressed by the Catholic Church, Irish American Catholic writers were not among this initial group;

2. Somewhat obtusely, in *Capitalism, the Family, and Personal Life*, Eli Zaretsky suggests that *Lolita* is actually a feminist novel because it stands as an implicit critique of the postwar reification of family life.

however, Blanche McCrary Boyd did not suffer from this pressure. Born and raised in South Carolina, Boyd belongs to the school of Scots-Irish Protestants of the American South—stubborn, prickly, independent "radical individualists" who refused to be cowed, or to bow, to anyone—particularly the Catholic Church (Webb 2004, 81). Indeed, her main themes—the exploration of sex and sexual preference—echo those of another Irish American Southerner, her predecessor Carson McCullers. Boyd's first novel, *Nerves* (1973), traces the feelings and frustrations of a woman who cannot be sexually satisfied by a man but does not know why. This theme, as well as the novel's locale, set Boyd apart, for Irish American lesbian novels have been almost completely overlooked.

Nerves intersperses chapters exploring friendship, betrayal, love and loss from the point of view of husbands, wives, and daughters. First Lena's friend Martha leaves her husband for a younger man, exclaiming, "You wouldn't believe how much freer I feel. Out of a cage." Martha's confession leads Lena to realize, "*something is wrong. Something is badly wrong and I don't know what it is*" (Boyd 1973, 21–23), a feeling she is embarrassed to confess to another woman. After Martha attempts suicide, Lena visits her in the hospital. Haltingly, Lena tries to explain her own unhappiness. "I'm sleeping on my back because I feel like a corpse," she admits (70). Feeling guilty because she does not enjoy sex, Lena stumbles through her emotions, ignoring her needs and forcing herself to just try, try again. On her anniversary getaway, after multiple couplings "each time [her husband] touched her, she would think *I can't, I just can't*," but then she "would find that she wanted him with a new and odd intensity." This is not lost on her worn-out husband. "He wished she would come back so that he could make love to her, and maybe this time the hunger would be gone. Over with. . . . [He] knew that whatever was wrong with her wasn't physical. For him, it was as if cracks had opened in her personality, and she was trying to break into pieces" (80–85).

A heterosexual reader might not consider *Nerves* a lesbian novel, for only after reading Boyd's subsequent works (or Bonnie Zimmerman's analysis of lesbian novels, *The Safe Sea of Women*) do the clues emerge. The first step—"At first isolated and inchoate, the lesbian discovers herself and shapes a definition of what it means to be a lesbian" (Zimmerman 1990,

32)—is only partially fulfilled. Lena is certainly "isolated and inchoate," but she does not know why. Yet her feelings of struggle and pain, her sense of difference, and her feelings of "speechlessness, invisibility, inauthenticity" (74) hint at the source of her problem. The fact that nothing specifically sexual occurs typifies the 1970s, for the "sexualization" characterizing heterosexual men and women during the decade "passed most lesbians by" (Faderman 1991, 247).

Boyd's second novel, *Mourning the Death of Magic* (1976), moves beyond that characterization. Like *Nerves*, *Mourning* is set in the South, alternates points of view, and uses doubles—sisters Galley and Mallory—who represent two halves of Boyd's persona. Galley is a closet lesbian; her sister Mallory is a feminist. Like Lena in *Nerves*, Galley is suicidal and depressed yet sexually insatiable. Just as Lena could not be satisfied by her husband, Galley has gone through numerous lovers: "she was fifteen and lost her virginity twenty or so more times before she reached seventeen," not only in the usual way, but also with "coke bottles, the hairbrush handles . . . the fingers inside her in bathrooms at school, in bed at home, the penises she sucked, wanting something, she didn't know what. Certainly not what she got." In college, Galley takes a lover—her female philosophy professor—"whose elegant, nervous hands brought Galley orgasms unmatched by her own frantic fingers, by the clumsy hands of boys." But rather than calm her searching mind, this relationship pushes Galley over the edge (Boyd 1976, 76).

What saves Galley appears to be a Southern gothic twist: Mallory realizes that Galley is uncomfortable and unhappy because she (Galley) loves her (Mallory)—not as a sister, but as a woman. Standing on the dock looking out at the water, an outdoors setting often used to symbolize that loving a woman is natural (Zimmerman 1990, 44), Mallory kisses Galley on the lips. Immediately, "There was a faraway sound, then Mallory felt light, a revelation"—also significant lesbian metaphors (Zimmerman 1990, 55). "Lust began to open inside her like a door, like a fist unclenching. Her nerves seemed to hang outside her like a web, like lace. It was right, and it was inevitable. She felt a relief, a sadness, a pleasure she had not even known about" (Boyd 1976, 208). This act and the lovemaking that follow make them whole and give them purpose. Given the novel's agenda, this act cannot be taken literally. Rather, Mallory represents Galley's mirror image—a lesbian trope first recognized in the late 1800s[3]—the half she has ignored. Once she acknowledges this element in herself, she becomes whole and the story can be read as "a novel of awakening" (Zimmerman 1990, 37).

Like Dorothy Allison, Boyd left the South. This literal detachment enabled both writers to observe how southerners differ from Yankees. "The contrast defines us: mildly barbaric, a little too earthy, profoundly sexual, living in the moment as easily as the past, and alienated from family and region, not only by political convictions but by a rude sense of embarrassment, a self-consciousness about the less admirable intransigencies of our heritage—that rockbound prejudice that seriously undermines sanity and intellect" (Allison 1995, xiv–xv). Indeed, one of the elements distinguishing the Scots-Irish novels is an ever-present consciousness of race and class. Despite the Catholic Church's strong stance against racism, this awareness is more evident in the Irish American novels of the South—generally Protestant—than in those by the Irish American Catholics in the rest of the country. Such an attitude is inbred, for in addition to a general prickliness, the Scots-Irish are particularly cognizant of racial inequity, in large part because the majority were neither slaveholders nor part of the aristocratic slave owners (Webb 2004). Boyd makes her stance clear: "Like every white American I've ever encountered, I am a racist." Of course, racism is not the only reason she left. For Southerners, homosexuality carried the same stigma as incest; worse, for Protestant Irish American woman writers, religion offered neither guidance nor solace, since "none of them . . . took religion seriously" (Boyd 1995, 189).

Captivity in the Sacrament and Ritual of Marriage

By the 1970s, Irish Americans were acquiring college educations and succeeding in business, outpacing every other "white ethnic group except the Jews" (Meagher 2005, 132). Such successes led the Irish to move away from the safe ethnic enclaves of the city. Some returned to Ireland (Almeida 2006, 554); in fact, more immigrants went home to Ireland during the 1970s than during any other period (Almeida 2001, 52). Others preferred the relative

3. See Dijkstra 1986, or Gilbert and Gubar 1989.

anonymity of the suburbs. Comprised of third- and fourth-generation children of immigrants, this group nonetheless remained staunchly Catholic and, consequently, outsiders (Meagher 2005, 139). At the same time, they did not necessarily feel like they belonged to the new parish either. *Humane Vitae* had resulted in fewer Irish religious, fewer students attending parochial schools, less reliance on the parish priest, and only a 50 percent attendance rate at Mass (Almeida 2006, 556; Dolan 2008, 285). While Vatican II had loosened church restrictions, these changes also contributed to "a loss of mystery and identity" (Almeida 2001, 99).

This sense of cultural isolation is exemplified in two very different works—Ann Beattie's debut novel, *Chilly Scenes of Winter* (1976), and Maureen Howard's third novel, *Before My Time* (1974). Beattie's characters, Charles, Sam, and Susan, exemplify the aftermath of the sixties youth culture: boredom, disillusion, and longing for the past as well as a preference for fulfillment over "rampant careerism" (Woods 2005, 357). Women have "put their brassieres back on and want you to take them to Paul Newman movies," the men complain. Charles yearns for his former lover, Laura, who has married someone else; Sam avoids the present through alcohol and sex; while the naïve Susan is simply lost. Although Charles and Susan worry about their alcoholic, suicidal mother (a recurring figure in Beattie's fiction), their concern is tinged with cynicism. When they learn she has been hospitalized yet again, Charles explodes, "She's not in pain. [Her husband's] out with some barfly and she's acting up" (Beattie 1976, 4).

To Beattie's chagrin, such characters led her to be categorized as a "chronicler of the disillusioned 1960s counterculture," although some reviewers consider this more a backdrop than a statement (L. Gordon 2011, n.p.). Certainly her setting rang true. This generation felt alienated from their country, from their parents, from traditional American beliefs in marriage, materialism, and monogamy (Woods 2005, 358). In sum, despite the use of Irish surnames and reliance on alcohol, Beattie's exploration of the characters' ennui is more representative of a lost generation than of Irish Americans specifically.

Conversely, the third-generation Maureen Howard dwells specifically on denizens of the Irish American diaspora. In *Before My Time*, Howard explores the marriages of two Irish American cousins, Laura Quinn and

Mill Cogan, whose unions represent "uneventful, deeply felt, nonprogress, of captivity in the sacrament and ritual of marriage, of life as a series of inconsequential events, poignant and terrible, signifying little" (Grumbach 1975)—a theme that might be said to capture the mindset of many women during this decade of feminist unrest.

Laura is the unhappy wife of a Boston lawyer; her cousin Mill is the unhappy wife of a Brooklyn gambler. Whether Laura's unhappiness stems from losing her ethnicity and Mill's from being mired in it, the fact remains that both women find their lives unsatisfactory. To survive, they escape into the past. Taken together, the two women become an amalgamation of Howard as she describes herself in her memoir, *Facts of Life*. Winner of the National Book Critics Circle Award for nonfiction and the PEN Kaufman Award, this work stands as "a significant document in Irish-American cultural self-definition" (Fanning 2001, 345). *Before My Time* likewise stands as a significant feminist document, for it recounts the cultural sexism and personal angst Howard encountered as a young wife.

Just as Laura passes her time as a housewife writing, Howard divided her days between writing her first novel and cooking gourmet meals for other young graduate student couples. "I have glazed patés and salmon late into the night. In a sense I have dined out in my own house, hoping to enter a world I can't belong to and that I now hold in contempt" (1975, 72). Just as Howard and her husband lived in married student housing while he finished Harvard graduate school, Laura recalls their "love nest, a roach infested sublet in Cambridge" (1971, 46). And just as Mill finds solace in gin, Howard sprinkles her memoir with wine, whiskey, daiquiris, and martinis. Similarly, Mill's admission that "for years now she had lost the knack of wanting these small domestic treasures" (Howard 1971, 30) echoes Howard's lament, "I've finally learned not to want things I cannot have" (1975, 174).

Whereas *Bridgeport Bus* introduced Howard's persona in the guise of thirty-three-year-old Mary Agnes Keely, *Before My Time* shows her at forty, somewhat successful as a writer but saddled with children (Howard was forty-three when the novel was published). She has escaped Bridgeport's suffocation only to find it a state of mind. Moreover, *Before My Time* includes Howard's ongoing lament about not doing her best work, as well as experimental strategies for elucidating her tales, such as individual vignettes for each character and journal excerpts to shed light on their actions and beliefs. What distinguishes this novel from Howard's subsequent work is the absence of tragedy, which tends to shake up the characters and convince them to change their ways. Instead, Mill and Laura engage in feminist consciousness-raising, revisiting their pasts and confronting reality. There is agency in self-awareness. Howard's characters make conscious decisions to put the past behind them and make the future better—an Irish American feminist conclusion enabling them to clarify their identities and move "toward change for the better" (Fanning 2001, 343).

Irish Americans who stayed in the city did not always fare so well. Although the early part of the decade saw Irish festivals and musicians, many of them organized by Gertrude Byrne, by 1976 she and her husband had relocated to the Catskills and taken their festivals with them (Moloney 2006, 435). As a result of similar moves, by 1970, the Irish population in New York City had fallen from 4 percent overall in 1960 to only 2.8 percent (Almeida 2001, 45). These numbers remained flat thanks to the 1965 Immigration and Nationality Act, which reduced Irish immigration to approximately fifteen hundred per year through the 1970s (Almeida 2006, 555). As racial demographics changed, some boroughs emptied out, while the Irish population in others dropped precipitously—Manhattan by 46 percent, Brooklyn by 39 percent, and the Bronx by a quarter. Some parishes went from all-Irish to Afro-Hispanic within a matter of months (Almeida 2001, 47). The ensuing tensions and court-ordered public school integration contributed to race riots in Chicago and Boston, some of which were led by Irish American politicians Louise Day Hicks and John Kerrigan (Meagher 2006, 638). Nevertheless, in the 1970s, Irish Catholics were more tolerant of integration than Protestants or Catholics of other ethnicities (Greeley 1985, 167). All the same, Richard Nixon, who had never championed civil rights, saw this mindset as key in his efforts to win over blue-collar workers, conservatives, and Catholic "ethnic groups"—whom he cast as the silent majority—to throw out the policies of the New Deal (Woods 2005, 321).

On the positive side, racial tensions raised ethnic awareness. Although urban areas were no longer the hubs of Irish activity, Irish Americans maintained an interest in their heritage. The 1970s saw the rise of genealogical organizations such as the Irish Ancestral Research Association, the Buffalo

Irish Genealogical Society, and the Ballykilcline Society. Suddenly traditional Irish music was popular, as evidenced in the rise of the Clancy Brothers and the Chieftans. In 1975, the first Irish American music festival was sponsored by the Philadelphia Ceili Group. Its popularity gave rise to similar events such as the Snug Harbor Irish Traditional Music and Dance Festival on Staten Island, the Providence Irish Festival in Rhode Island, and the Glen Echo Irish Festival in Glen Echo Park, Maryland (Moloney 2006, 430–31). In academia, Irish Studies programs, which emerged in 1966, began to proliferate around the country (Meagher 2005, 167–68).

Some of Elizabeth Cullinan's short stories in *Yellow Roses* (1971) celebrate this ethnicity (Fanning 2001, 372). In "Life After Death," for example, the female narrator reflects, "There's no such thing as the whole truth with respect to the living, which is why history appeals to me. I like the finality. . . . The reasons I love Mass are somewhat the same. During those twenty or so minutes, I feel my own past to be not quite coherent but capable of eventually proving to be that. And if my life, like every other, contains elements of the outrageous, that ceremony of death and transfiguration is a means of reckoning with time" (178). Likewise, "Commuting" celebrates the liberation of ethnic doubleness. As the narrator travels from her job in Manhattan back to her home base in the Bronx, she reflects on the disparate sights, comparing present and past, success and failure, to conclude: "Riding that last half-mile, my head swam with relief, my heart sang—they do every week, as this realization comes over me: I've reenacted, in spirit, the journey that has given my life its substance and shape, color and brightness. I've escaped!" (35). Such comparisons allow the narrator to examine her life and its arc of success as she "escapes" from the poverty of the Bronx to success in Manhattan. But rather than repudiate her ethnic roots, she celebrates the dynamic role they have played in shaping the richness of her life (Fanning 2001, 375).

Joan Bagnel's historical novel *Gone the Rainbow, Gone the Dove* (1973) reflects Irish Americans' nationalistic interests with a tale of doomed Irish lovers torn apart by the Troubles. Jamie Daley longs to fight for Irish sovereignty, only to fall in love and find he must choose between love of country and love for young Margaret Culhane. Recounted in flashbacks by his cousin Jerry, the tale traces the boys' fascination with Fianna Faille and their desire to drive out the British. This novel puts a human face on the Troubles following Bloody Sunday and the growth of the IRA. Initially, Irish Americans rallied around the cause, often sending money through NORAID. Indeed, in 1972, the theme of New York's St. Patrick's Day Parade was "Get England Out of Ireland"; and in 1978, Governor Hugh Carey was booed because of his conciliatory speeches regarding Northern Ireland (Almeida 2006, 559). Always attuned to popular trends, Hollywood churned out a number of movies prominently featuring people of Irish descent: Joe Curran, the anti-hero in *Joe*, represents the Irish American hawk thanks to his brutal attack on antiwar hippies. *Serpico*, *Ragtime*, *True Confessions*, *The Godfather*, and *LA Confidential* include violent or corrupt Irish cops, not necessarily because the Irish were perceived as such but because they represented the anti-establishment counterculture of the era (Dezell 2001, 165).

Of the Irish Americans remaining in the city, over a third were at least seventy years of age (Almeida 2006, 555). Among the remaining two-thirds there was sometimes a sense of defeat, for the 1970s was a time of economic deterioration thanks to Lyndon Johnson's attempts to pay for the Vietnam War without raising taxes, thus creating a $10 billion trade deficit, 10 percent inflation, the 1973 oil crisis, a lowered industrial production rate of 1 percent a year, and massive unemployment. The sense of Irish unity was failing as well. Among Catholic conservatives, the attempt by Reverend Phillip Berrigan to kidnap Henry Kissinger was not looked on favorably (Woods 2005, 356–59). Within the city centers, Irish societies were dwindling away, networking declined, even attendance at Gaelic Park eroded as its former population moved away. While there was still a strong sense of identity among the remaining Irish, it was based on family traditions rather than social associations (Almeida 2001, 56–57).

The Personalist Revolution

American Catholic fiction of the 1970s reflects the uncertainty of the church (Labrie 1997, 13). Attendance at Mass fell by 20 percent while the use of birth control rose from 45 to 83 percent, interrelated factors stemming from the *Humana Vitae* anti-birth control stance—a move many women viewed as a means of keeping them "in their place" as nurturers and second-class citizens (Weaver 1985, vii). This decade saw an increase in priests' resignations from the clergy, 50 percent fewer seminarians entering the clergy, and apostasy doubling from 7 to 14 percent (Weaver 1985, 2). More troubling were women's feelings of alienation. While the church's patriarchal structure had been acceptable in medieval times, its exclusive model of male leadership and view of a masculine God was considered regressive, if not repressive, among many women congregants (Seidler and Meyer 1989, 10).

In response, Catholic women began to initiate change and Irish American women began to speak out. Throughout the 1970s, the Leadership Conference of Women Religious encouraged its members to work toward women's equality. Mary Lynch, a Catholic laywoman, convened a group of like-minded women to discuss promoting women's ordination during 1975, International Women's Year; this movement in turn resulted in the Women's Ordination Conference. At that conference Elizabeth Carroll accused participating bishops of failing to enter into serious dialogue, while Margaret Farley encouraged women to challenge the traditional hierarchy and "claim a 'moral imperative' for ordination" (Weaver 1985, 112–13). While such statements claimed the headlines, they did not alter the church's stance. In 1972 and 1973 the Grail reached out to women by sponsoring consciousness-raising workshops and co-hosting Women Exploring Theology conferences that addressed the need for theological inclusivity. Between 1974 and 1979, the Grail's Seminary Quarter went even further, promoting an "emerging feminist theology that begins, not with God, but with a theological reflection of women's experience." Likewise, in 1974 the Institute of Women Today was founded to address women's religious oppression; that same year, Catholics for a Free Choice was formed to protect women's reproductive rights (Weaver 1985, 127–30).

The feminist theologian Mary Daly experienced this sense of alienation more strongly than most. In *Beyond God the Father* (1973) she deconstructs Christianity and urges women to leave the church. Begun in the giddy days following Vatican II, Daly had already moved from "reformist" feminism to characterizing herself as a "postchristian radical feminist." *Beyond* not only reevaluates her 1968 study, *The Church and the Second Sex*, but also outlines the many ways she disagrees with her earlier stance as a result of anger and disillusion. Like other 1970s feminists, she points out the prevalence of rape and physical violence against women and children. Addressing the myth of transcendence, which promises women heavenly rewards for their earthly travails, she dismisses it as "dead circles of repetition going nowhere." On the subject of conflict and vindication, she concludes that the latter is impossible as a result of "perpetual oppression." As for the mythic paradigm of integrity and transformation, Daly argues that these planes can be attained not through the church but through other myths with a "biophilic context," described in chapters subtitled "Sisterhood as Antichurch" and "Sisterhood as Cosmic Covenant." Such arguments underscored the need to move feminism out of the "ruts, already violently embedded into women's psyches," which had frozen them at the most basic stages of feminism and discouraged them from realizing the "full implications of patriarchal power" (Daly 1973, xiii–xv).

Although traditional church leaders dismissed the study, feminist theologians such as Mary Jo Weaver and Rosemary Radford Ruether supported it. A relative moderate compared to Daly, Ruether argued that "unless one is willing to take the journey into that deeper anger, even to risk going a bit mad, one really will never understand the depths of the evil of sexism" inherent in the Catholic Church (1993, 187). With *Gyn/Ecology* (1978) Daly moved beyond a critique of Catholicism to deconstruct the rationales, or rationalizations, underlying long-accepted worldwide methods of torturing women, ranging from Chinese foot binding, African genital mutilation, and European witch burnings, to American gynecology. With this, she firmly established her reputation as the angriest and most outrageous Irish American lapsed Catholic feminist of the era.

The literary works of the Irish American Ramona Stewart in some ways exemplify this sense of alienation. During the 1970s, Stewart published five novels: *The Possession of Joel Delaney* (1970), *Apparition* (1973), *Age of Consent* (1975), *Seasons of the Heart* (1978), and *The Sixth Sense* (1979). Cinephiles no doubt recognize the first and last of these, for both were made into movies. *The Possession of Joel Delaney* centers around Santeria, a religion in which only males can be priests, influenced in part by Roman Catholicism and the "deviant worship of saints" (Pichardo 1998, n.p.). In this novel, the possessed Delaney commits various murders until he is stopped by the police. Its closing scene, in which a young naked boy (presumably his nephew) dances maniacally, suggests the possibility of reincarnation. *The*

Sixth Sense, the story of a young boy who sees—and is ultimately helped by—dead people, continues this theme. One could not move much farther from the church, although Maura Stanton's *Molly Companion* (1977)— whose eponymous heroine shares some parallels with the journalist Nellie Bly, is set in 1864 and tells a love story during the wars between Paraguay and Argentina, Brazil, and Uruguay—is a good try.

Other reactions were less extreme. With easy access and increased acceptance of artificial birth control, women gained control of their bodies; with the profusion of labor saving devices, women were no longer tied to their homes. According to the theologian Andrew Greeley, "These changing structures challenged the assumption of traditional Church teaching about family life, birth control, family planning and size, and women's place in the home." Coinciding with the feminist movement was the rise of what Greeley termed the "personalist revolution": "the call for individuals to become more fully themselves" (1985, 21). For women, this revolution centered around hotly contested canonical issues—abortion, women's roles in the church, women's ordination—in sum, women's rights. Between 1973 and 1975, the National Coalition of American Nuns publicly denounced a study by the U.S. Bishops' Committee on Pastoral Research and Practices because it refused to support the ordination of women; a young American girl took her plea to become an altar girl all the way to Rome; a woman who had run an abortion clinic was denied a requiem mass; and priests were ordered to deny Communion to members of NOW (Seidler and Meyer 1989, 79).

This anger was reflected in Irish American women's autobiographical novels, wherein individuals subordinate the church to the needs of the individual. Writers following this path strive to overcome their past—represented by Catholicism—which they view simultaneously as "repressive" and "an ethical ideal and a source of security." Within the Catholic autobiographical novel, the death of a parent and the child's reaction generally parallel or stand as a metaphor for the "dissolution of American Catholic culture"—a theme evident in Gordon's *Final Payments*. Whereas men grieve their loss of faith, women write about the promise of a life without the restrictions of religion. Meaning is located in relationships rather than institutions (Gandolfo 1992, 162).

Given the patriarchal authority of the church, these opposing viewpoints should come as no surprise. Mary Gordon herself suggests that this distinction led women toward collaboration and the view that other women were important, key themes in her work. This tendency also becomes evident in a novel's characterization: whereas male writers feature the lone wolf, females put their characters into a pack. These women tend to be seeking some sort of "awakening"—not religious or spiritual, but psychological. "Characteristic of the female vision of American Catholicism is a refusal to either glory in or condemn the past but to note its strengths as well as its weaknesses. There is no reductive identification of the Church with oppression, but a realization that the situation is far more complex" (Gandolfo 1992, 163–71).

Such feelings are illustrated in Irish American fiction of the 1970s, for it reflects the attitudes and, at times, the animosity generated by the feminist movement amidst the church's inflexibility. Such work "offers Catholicism two different visions of American individualism. The first . . . is ostentatiously 'Catholic,' clinging to the name in an assertion of autonomy that does not simply reject heteronomy [read patriarchy] but appropriates its codes." Especially in the years following *Humana Vitae*, women writers' views of reconciliation differed considerably from those of the opposite sex. Although women in the 1970s were realizing that the church was out of touch and its doctrines difficult to preserve in the modern world, they also understood that because of their experiences they were better able to understand life's temptations as well as the church's role in helping them to persevere. For these writers, Catholicism took on a Proustian shape, its importance "limited to a 'remembrance of things past'" (Gandolfo 1992, 109–13). Reconciliation occurs when these writers reveal how their early religious training framed their contemporary behavior. Elizabeth Savage's *A Good Confession* (1975) is a good example.

Like Maeve Brennan's Delia Bagot, Maureen Howard's Laura Quinn and Mill Cogan, and Blanche Boyd's Lena and Martha, Elizabeth Savage's Meg O'Shaughnessey Atherton evinces what Betty Friedan termed "the problem that has no name," the ennui of the American housewife. Although Meg holds a bachelor's degree, she does not work and she has no children; she had a dog, but he ran away and she has no desire to replace him. She and her husband, Spencer, do not quarrel; they just don't talk. As the novel opens

Meg is confronted by her husband's mistress. Although Meg's first response is, "'You realize I'm a Catholic?'" she nevertheless decides to leave him.

Meg is plunged back into childhood memories when she is summoned to the deathbed of her grandfather, Big Jim. He and his wife, Kate, raised Meg, so naturally she will go home. With the move to this setting, Savage reincarnates the Irish American trope of children returning to honor their dying parent, or in this case parent-substitute. At the same time, Savage uses the figure of the grandmother (Kate)—a recurrent trope among Irish American female poets—as a reserve of wisdom (Monaghan 2004, 344). Clearly such a figure will lend commonsense advice and stability to her granddaughter's life. This change of scene also allows Savage to alternate between past and present to illustrate the influence of Meg's grandparents as well as her relationship with Val, a teenage crush who spurned her for the priesthood.

The combination of a cheating husband and a rejecting boyfriend elicit acerbic comments about the male sex typical of 1970s feminist novels. Spencer "defeated me with a cold, sustained courtesy such as I had never seen on Mahoney Street" (34). In response to a misstatement from Val, Meg remarks, "But then, men are dense" (35). Recalling Spenser's annoyance at her illness, she echoes Maeve Brennan: "But then, I understand many men are annoyed when their wives are ill. They at first—say for the first three hours—seem sympathetic; after that it becomes a nuisance, and then an affront. Malingering is suspected" (193). Such feelings are regularly contrasted to the relationship she recalls between her grandfather and grandmother. Watching Big Jim put his arm around Kate's shoulder or pat her hand, Meg reflects, "I thought that was what marriages were like" (65). Such recollections gradually soften Meg's feelings toward her adulterous husband, leading her to realize: "I don't hate Spencer. Perhaps it is not much fun to live with someone bored and disappointed. *Let not the sun go down upon they wrath*," she recalls, a lesson she learned from Kate (83–84). "By and large, and barring the odd case, Kate never wasted much sympathy on women who lose their husbands. She said they probably hadn't been generous," to which Meg counters, "I don't know how you're to be generous to a man who prefers another woman's generosity." Yet after reflecting on her role in this marriage, she recalls Spenser's comment, "'You don't share anything, do you, Margaret?'" (107).

The problems between Meg and Spencer occur, in part, because theirs is a mixed marriage. Meg's attitude toward the church reflects the 1970 mindset—insular yet critical, just like Irish siblings. Although she notes that "many of us escaped our faiths," she has not "escaped all the way." So when Big Jim dies, Meg immediately calls Spencer: "At the end you must go back, if only because you have promises to keep. Perhaps from now on it would be better for Spenser and for me, and perhaps not. But it was my promise for which I was responsible, and not his" (215). In a decade when women were leaving and divorces soaring, Catholicism made all the difference.

When comparing degrees of conflict in the church between the 1960s and the 1970s, women's issues stand out as "statistically significant" (Seidler and Meyer 1985, 86). Organizations within the church, such as the Leadership Conference of Women Religious (LCWR), a group of feminist nuns, began to speak out against injustice toward women (Ruether 2003, 5). Their study packet, *Focus on Women*, issued in 1975, decried the historical oppression of women, argued that the church had been a major force in these efforts, and called for women to unite and refuse "to accept such 'institutional injustice.'" Similarly, the Grail, a "noncanonical Catholic women's religious 'order'" established in 1921, developed an increasingly feminist outlook in the 1970s that attracted women religious leaders across sects. Although most Grail members viewed themselves as "100 percent loyal Catholics," many had begun to dissent following *Humane Vitae*. "With each succeeding statement on sexuality issues—contraception, divorce, abortion, homosexuality, use of condoms for prevention of HIV/AIDS, ordination of women—both dissent and Church efforts to control it have increased" (Kalven 2003, 35).

In the 1970s, the second model of the Catholic novel was developmental, often leading to abandonment of the church. This fiction, "which focuses on the search for a true religious self, is, not surprisingly, most evident in women's fiction" (Gandolfo 1992, 157). Prior to Elizabeth Cullinan no authors offered an alternative vision of the church.[4] In *House of Gold*, Cullinan presented an extended allegory revealing the authoritarian repres-

---

4. These views are echoed in the Irish American Susan Cahill's memoir, *Earth Angels: Portraits from Childhood and Youth* (New York: Harper & Row, 1976).

sion of the past and the possibility of a new vision of American Catholicism. These themes resurface in her short story collections In *The Time of Adam* (1971) and *Yellow Roses* (1977). As her persona, Louise Gallagher, says, "Fish will always mean Catholic to me, and . . . Catholic meant Irish and Irish meant lower class" (1977, 83). Even though Cullinan was second generation Irish American, she still felt the sting of her "immigrant" status. Thus it is perhaps not surprising that both collections "may be seen as Irish American escape stories" (McInerney 2008, 103).

Cullinan manifests this desire in recurrent themes and characters. One of the most prominent is the figure of the arrogant priest, an omnipresent character in her 1960 short stories. This figure becomes more menacing in "Only Human." Juxtaposed with the nuns' and her family's fond remembrances of Father Jim, his niece Marjorie recalls how he was "always taking you aside and telling you, in that beautiful, cultivated voice, some dirty joke; always, when he kissed you, touching you some place he shouldn't have touched you; always those wet kisses" (Cullinan 1971, 150). Although Cullinan seems to blame the church for its priests' arrogance, she finds the strictures imposed on women even more repressive. This theme is illustrated in her female personae.

In three interrelated stories—"Yellow Roses," "An Accident," and "A Forgone Conclusion"—Louise Gallagher contemplates ending her affair with Charlie, her married lover. Needless to say, any mention of his wife makes her "begin to dislike him" but also "to dislike herself." More damning is her recollection of their early flirtation before he married. When Louise asks, "Why can't you marry me?" his response, "It's out of the question"—because he is Protestant and she, Catholic—prompts her to throw his yellow roses into the trash.

The following story, "An Accident," reveals that the affair has continued. Although it is set in the liberal 1970s, the church remains a bulwark against divorce and remarriage. Louise realizes that while the affair could go on, it will lead to nothing because of her religious beliefs. In "A Foregone Conclusion," these feelings gradually build. After Charlie gives her his grandmother's ring, Louise dismisses it as inappropriate: "Rings belonged to explicit loves, loves with a context and a direction, but theirs, for all its durability, was an inconclusive affair. That they should go on indefinitely the way they were seemed unlikely, but that they should part seemed unnecessary, and anything else was out of the question since Louise was Catholic" (Cullinan 1977, 90). Looking at the ring, she thinks, "there was no way of reconciling this ring with what rings were meant to stand for," and surreptitiously slips it into Charlie's pocket as they prepare to leave. As the story concludes, "Though it seemed an irrational act, a senseless thing to have to say," her last words are "Goodbye, Charlie" (98). Cullinan's stories "bring the fresh air of considered moral perspective to Irish American life" (Fanning 2001, 334).

Although neither feminists nor Catholics have been associated with humor, comedy allowed them to raise questions without fear of punishment (Del Rosso 2005, 149). Always ahead of her time, Mary McCarthy's apostasy came well before the 1960s period marking the large-scale shift from the unquestioning piety of the "immigrant church" toward a period of growing intellectualism (Gandolfo 1992). McCarthy also moved away from feminist themes long before the post-feminist era. But regardless of topic (and sometimes despite her best efforts) McCarthy maintained her satiric voice. During and after the Vietnam War, she continued her satirical political analyses in *Birds of America* (1971) and *Cannibals and Missionaries* (1979), even though these works have been relegated "to a limbo in American letters" (Brightman 1992, 555).

Caryl Rivers's memoir, *Aphrodite at Mid-Century: Growing Up Female and Catholic in Postwar America* (1973), has been similarly consigned to limbo; nevertheless it represents a good example of how to "use humor to subvert the sexism" of the church. Rivers's humor is all the more potent because it is combined with feminism, "which is activist in nature . . . a call for change, for resistance, for revolution" (Del Rosso 2005, 154–55). In this she reflects the strategies introduced by McCarthy in *Memories of a Catholic Girlhood*: defiance, criticism, and commentary regarding the effects of the church on her personality (Evasdaughter 1996). This message is evident throughout: whether Rivers is discussing movies, sports, saints, or marriage, she laments sexism and the lack of female role models. At the same time, she gives the church its due, recalling the "changeless truth [and] simple moral choices."

Rivers's critical strategies come to the fore when she moves out of childhood. In her teens she realizes the church's insularity as she and her friends are warned against mixing with those outside the faith: "The nuns made it clear that prolonged exposure to non-Catholics was not healthy" (Rivers 1973, 129). She also suggests that Catholic teachings attack girls' self esteem, for they were inculcated with the belief that physical beauty—personified in the Virgin Mary—is the ideal and thus unattainable. This attitude is reinforced by the nuns, who held limited ideas about sex. They "made the whole thing seem dirty. It was clear that babies and bosoms and sex and reproduction were all low and disgusting, the sort of things hogs did in the trough. . . . The Marriage Act was for the purpose of creating children. Period. One was not supposed to enjoy it" (179). Furthermore, marriage per se was not enough. "If you didn't get married by a priest, you were living in sin, and if you died, off you went to hell." If you were married and poor, you prayed to avoid getting pregnant, for using contraceptives was a mortal sin. "Better to die in the state of grace than to commit a mortal sin," the nuns told her (183–84).

Rivers would have none of it. By adolescence she "was aware that society had carved out a niche for me, now that I was about to become a woman. I was offered one ticket, good for a lifetime, to the bleachers" (224). Used in this way, humor provides subversive liberation: "Perhaps the potential for change that feminists envision for the Catholic church can only come from a kind of religious syncretism, an opening up of the church's teachings to new (or old?) thought and fresh visions. And perhaps humor can play a large part in that change" (Del Rosso 2005, 167). If that were true, Mary Daly would have been a best-seller.

The 1970s were truly tumultuous. Just as Americans demonstrated for and against the war in Vietnam, the feminist movement warred within itself while Irish American women revolted against the strictures of the church. Assimilation played a major role in these decisions. First-generation writers such as Elizabeth Cullinan and Maureen Howard conflated the terms "Irish" and "Catholic" and thus attacked both, whereas writers like Maeve Brennan, who viewed herself as more Irish than American and thus took the church for granted, left it alone. Writers in the second generation such as Mary Gordon and Elizabeth Savage, more comfortable with their status, took a less jaundiced, more ambivalent stance. Women's roles and treatment by the religious hierarchy certainly influenced this decade's authors and their novels; conversely, despite the lack of a strong religious commitment among Protestant Irish Americans, the racism and sexism they observed helped shape their feminism.

Perhaps the most striking issue of the decade was sexuality. With Blanche McCrary Boyd's *Mourning the Death of Magic*, the 1970s marks the emergence of the first Irish American lesbian novel. Although Carson McCullers touched on this theme, her androgynous girls eventually succumbed to society's pressures—they put on a dress, grew out their hair, and lost their virginity—to a male. While Mary McCarthy's *The Group* (1963) included a lesbian character, she remained in the background, carefully closeted overseas until the novel's end. Even when she did emerge, the other characters expressed mainly curiosity and disbelief, and Lakey's character was not explored. The discovery of Boyd's novels is all the more striking because of their location in the 1970s, coincidental with the publication of the first "official" American lesbian novel, Rita Mae Brown's *Rubyfruit Jungle*. Boyd not only predates the topic in contemporary Irish women's novels (most notably Emma Donoghue's *Stir-Fry* in 2000), but also displaces Eileen Myles, who heretofore held the title as the first Irish American woman writer to exit the closet—in the late 1990s. Fellow Irish American southerner Dorothy Allison warns that in addition to being lesbian writers, she and Boyd are "expatriate writers, prickly and rebellious at being labeled any one thing too firmly" (Allison 1995, xii). This distinction merits attention, for its advent epitomizes the spirit of the decade.

4

The 1980s

The War on Women

She is not like other mothers, who make grocery lists and wear undergarments. Other mothers do not forget that you go back to school in September. . . . Although she preferred her mother, sometimes she was frightened.

—Susanna Moore, *My Old Sweetheart*

Anyone who has read the Irish Canadian Margaret Atwood's dystopian novel, *The Handmaid's Tale*, will recognize its genesis in Ronald Reagan's war on women. In Atwood's satire, set in a near-futuristic theocracy, women's rights have been stripped. They can no longer work, hold bank accounts, or walk the streets alone. With birth rates in decline, fertile and pregnant women are reified. But all women are assigned to castes: childless Wives, working Marthas, and the Handmaids—who are impregnated by the Commanders, give birth—and then must hand over their newborns to the Wives who, because of their chastity and social standing, are considered morally superior.

Published in 1985, *The Handmaid's Tale* articulated the fears of many American women following the 1980 election of Ronald Reagan. This vote marked a political turning point for Irish Americans. Although they had been trending Republican since the post-Kennedy years, more Irish Americans and American Catholics voted for the "Great Communicator" and his party than ever before (Almeida 2006, 557). Reagan's popularity coincided with the rise of nationalist support for Ireland. A year after his election, support for NORAID in the midst of Bobby Sands's hunger strike grew from

$5,000 a year to $55,000, much of it collected in pubs (Meagher 2005, 334; Dolan 2008, 297). Where did all of this money come from? By the 1980s, Irish Americans numbered 40 million. Moreover, they had attained the highest echelons of capitalist society and turned into "icons of conservatism" (Meagher 2005, 565–66). They had achieved this pinnacle largely because of their education, surpassing all other immigrant populations except the Jews and Japanese Americans and rivaling the financial success of Episcopalians on the East Coast and across America (Meagher 2005, 156)—an achievement that most likely contributed to the movement of many from the Democratic to the Republican Party (Almeida 2006, 557).

This achievement was not simply a matter of assimilation. While World War II had spurred upward mobility and the election of John F. Kennedy brought power and recognition, Irish Americans also benefitted from the changing definitions of the term "race." Whereas the early years of the century had spawned prejudice among Caucasians of various ethnicities, the Civil Rights movement of the 1960s erased those distinctions, making differences redound to black and white. Equally important, the civil rights, antiwar, gay rights, and women's movements had ignited a "healthy skepticism of authority and celebrated individual liberation and personal authenticity" (Meagher 2005, 159–60).

As the decade progressed, increasing numbers of Irish Americans supported Ronald Reagan's conservative agenda. They applauded his promotion of prayer in school and opposition to abortion (Dolan 2008, 293), and they were not overly concerned with his avoidance of homosexual issues. Such views no doubt helped swing the vote toward the Republicans and away from the Democratic candidate, Walter Mondale, and his running mate, Geraldine Ferraro, who was not only a feminist but also pro-choice. Indeed, Ferraro's stance, which she reiterated in a letter stating that Catholics were split on the abortion issue, so infuriated New York archbishop John O'Connor that he publicly castigated her—and likely cost Democrats the Catholic vote (Martin 2011, 153). Among the hawks, conservatives supported Reagan's strong stance against Russia. And just before the 1984 election, when rumors of his disengagement and poor memory were raising questions about his competence (Woods 2005, 456), Reagan cemented his chances by reminding supporters of his Irish roots with a televised visit to his great-grandfather's hometown of Ballyporeen in County Tipperary (Dolan 2008, 293).

Following his landslide re-election, Reagan further strengthened his Irish base by supporting constitutional change in Ireland and appointing a number of Irish Americans to his cabinet: Attorney General Edwin Meese, Secretary of Labor Raymond J. Donovan, Secretaries of the Treasury Donald Regan and Nicholas Brady, CIA Director James Casey, and U.N. Representative Jeanne Kirkpatrick. In the Senate, George Mitchell was majority leader; in the House, Thomas Foley was the Speaker. After Reagan's re-election, the House of Representatives, led by Democratic opponent Tip O'Neill, supported a resolution in favor of the Anglo-Irish agreement, which helped broker peace between the two countries. Thanks to Reagan's friendship with Margaret Thatcher and promise to help sustain the International Fund for Ireland, England supported the agreement (Almeida 2006, 560–61). Finally, as one of Reagan's last acts, he appointed Anthony Kennedy to the Supreme Court in 1988.

"Only in retrospect would it become apparent that Ronald Reagan was a shell, a stereotypical actor who went from one role to the next, who served as a façade for an inner core of advisers who in most respects actually ran the United States," writes Randall Bennett Woods (2005, 454–56). Ronald Reagan, famous for his recollections of an ideal childhood, had a father who was an often-unemployed, peripatetic, debt-ridden alcoholic. Beloved of rightwing conservatives, Reagan voted Democratic in the 1930s and 1940s. Fond of recounting tales of World War II heroism observed at the front, he never left Hollywood. President of the Screen Actors Guild, he betrayed writers, directors, and even fellow actors during the Red Scare. Remembered for his speech supporting Barry Goldwater, he plagiarized much of it from Roosevelt, Lincoln, and Churchill (Woods 2005, 445–56).

The man who ostentatiously prayed in public, supported prayer in schools, claimed to be "born again," and was beloved by Irish Catholics was a Protestant who rarely attended church. Although he was twice divorced and estranged from his children, he promoted family values—even as he and his cronies tried to cut funding for child care, refused to support the Equal Rights Amendment, blocked the rights of women to sue employers for sexual discrimination, and outlawed Medicare and Medicaid-funded abortions for poor women, promoting as an alternative "chastity clinics" (Woods 2005, 478–79). In his autobiography, Tip O'Neill attempts to explain Reagan's mindset: "Maybe it all boils down to the fact that one of us lost track of his roots while the other guy didn't. . . . As a man of wealth, [Reagan] really didn't understand the past thirty years. God gave him a handsome face and a beautiful voice, but he wasn't that generous to everyone. With Ronald Reagan in the White House, somebody had to look out for those who were not so fortunate" (1987, 330–31).

From the beginning Reagan's goal, articulated by the Heritage Foundation, was "to turn the clock back to 1954 in this country." Indeed, the New Right's argument—"that women's equality is responsible for women's unhappiness" (Faludi 1991, 230)—echoed the postwar propaganda blitz to get women out of the workplace and back into the home, where they supposedly belonged. The gains of the 1970s had threatened the traditional white male power structure: anti-Communists, economic conservatives, anti-abortion activists, and evangelicals (Davis 1991, 434). Believing they were losing power, members of the New Right felt the need to resurrect their status. They did so by attacking the women's movement. Feminists were conflated with the proposed Equal Rights Amendment, which was demonized as potentially destroying the traditional family and depriving the paterfamilias of his rightful role. More outrageously, feminists were castigated as "moral perverts" and "enemies of every decent society," who would "turn the country over to women." Still, such attacks underscored the growth and influence of the women's movement in the past decade (Faludi 1991, 231–32).

To counter these gains, within a year of Reagan's election the Heritage Foundation issued its *Mandate for Leadership*. This document essentially warned that feminists were taking over and proposed countermeasures to lessen their gains. The first of these was the oxymoronic Family Protection Act. Its title was intentionally misleading, for its goal was to overturn everything the women's movement had attained in the previous decade: "eliminate federal laws supporting equal education; forbid coed sports; require marriage and motherhood to be taught as the proper career for girls; deny federal funding to any school using textbooks portraying women in nontraditional roles; repeal all federal laws protecting battered wives from their husbands; and ban federally funded legal aid for any woman seeking abortion, counseling or a divorce" (Faludi 1991, 234–36).

Although these actions were appalling, they were not new; rather, they typified the fin de siècle mindset, which generally emerges approximately twenty years before the century's end. In Britain and France, for example, the 1880s had been notable for fears regarding "sexual anarchy" that gave rise to sexism, homophobia, and sexual scandals. These social upheavals led to moral outrage manifested in social purity campaigns and demands for anti-woman legislation coupled with pro-family initiatives (Showalter 1990, 3). Such historical precedent suggests that the 1980s were ripe for exploitation. More important, just as the 1880s saw reaction to such heavy-handed tactics through art and literature that questioned and ridiculed these fears, so did the 1980s. The majority of novels by Irish American women exposed the hypocrisy, if not the naïveté, of every fear, every prejudice, and every mandate regarding the sanctity of marriage and purity of maternity.[1]

Whereas the sainted mother had been a stock character in early Irish American sentimental novels, throughout the 1980s she became an object of scorn as she repeatedly failed or abandoned her daughter. Irish American women's novels of this decade feature crazy, addicted, abusive, distant, teenage, and working mothers—all of them bad. Such characterizations did not denigrate women per se; rather, they questioned the government's sexist attitudes by pointing out its fallacies. The only exception was the lesbian mother, for her goodness helped remind the Reagan administration that homosexuals were people too. In every regard, Irish American women were again ahead of their time. Whereas "most women novelists were, during the 1980s, engaged in the 'privatization and depoliticization of their concerns, the sentimentalization of the family, the resignation to things as they are'" (Greene 1993, 200), Irish American women took a stand: they rejected those myths.

---

1. One exception is the trade paperback novelist Nora Roberts, née Robertson. Her first novel, *Irish Thoroughbred*, was published in 1981; by 1984, she had published twenty-three more. Although she claimed her works were feminist because her female characters have to work at winning "this incredible guy," such a statement actually underscores her misunderstanding of feminism (quoted in Krug 2012, n.p.).

She Is Not Like Other Mothers

Susanna Moore's autobiographical novel, *My Old Sweetheart* (1982), is one of many to address the reification of mothers and motherhood.[2] In this plot, the eldest daughter is figuratively abandoned because of her mother's madness. She and her siblings are then literally abandoned when their philandering father "controls" the madness by sending his wife away. This theme has many predecessors—Charlotte Brontë's *Jane Eyre*, Charlotte Perkins Gilman's "The Yellow Wallpaper," Daphne du Maurier's *Rebecca*, and Jean Rhys's *Wide Sargasso Sea*, to name just a few. In retelling her mother's story, Moore reminds us that this tradition continued into the late twentieth century.

Early on, Lily knows her mother is different: "She is not the kind who bandages cuts, Lily thought. She is not like other mothers, who make grocery lists and wear undergarments. Other mothers do not forget that you go back to school in September. . . . Although she preferred her mother, sometimes she was frightened" (5). These fears lead Lily to guard her mother and tend to her younger siblings. Yet after learning that her mother has "left them" (has been committed to a mental institution), Lily's response is typical: she wonders "what she might have done to drive her mother away" (73).

Moore's subsequent novel, *The Whiteness of Bones* (1989), also questions the reification of mothers. Another version of *My Old Sweetheart*, Moore's main characters, Mamie and Claire, have a remote mother and a dead father and thus are left to fend for themselves, with tragic consequences. This theme recurs in Bobbie Ann Mason's *In Country* (1985), when the protagonist Sam (Samantha) is abandoned by her mother after she remarries and moves to the city. Always one to upset conventional wisdom, Erin McGraw's first book of short stories, *Bodies at Sea* (1989), turns this theme upside down. "Accepted Wisdom" and "Finding Sally" reverse the traditional Irish theme of a child's self-immolation in the service of her abandoned or widowed parent: in these stories, it is the lonely, needy parents who live their lives around their children, to no avail.

2. See Wadler's interview, "Dark Work, Written in a Sunny Spot," in *The New York Times*, June 21, 2007, D6, for the many parallels between Moore's life and that of her personae's.

Alice McDermott's first novel, *A Bigamist's Daughter* (1982), tells yet another story of an abandoned daughter. Growing up, Elizabeth's father was seldom at home, always coming and going without warning, supposedly for a government job. When Elizabeth meets Tupper Daniels, who is writing a novel about a bigamist, she begins to suspect her father. Elizabeth is an editor at Vista, a vanity press, and Tupper is one of her authors. Because Elizabeth is young and attractive and has confided her suspicions, they begin dating. Although the attraction is mutual, Elizabeth wants to fall in love, whereas Tupper hopes to discover the truth about her father and use it as his conclusion.

A Bigamist's Daughter differs from McDermott's subsequent works. First, it is funny. Although the plot centers around Elizabeth and Tupper's relationship, it is interwoven with humorous stories about the hapless, hopeful, naïve authors. Second, love, sex, and even feminist concerns pervade. Pondering her first date with Tupper, Elizabeth realizes it has been almost "a year since she's had anyone in her bed . . . because waking up with the feeling, 'Oh shit, who's this?' makes for wonderful jokes but lousy mornings and lousy days" (15). Yet Elizabeth makes the first move, inviting Tupper to her apartment, where they make love. As Tupper begins, "She closes her eyes and begins the slow, downward movement, the saddest, the loneliest"—she compares him to Bill, her former lover (67). As the current relationship develops, she compares it to other couples, especially her friend Joanne's. Married only a month, Joanne already feels the magic is gone. She also makes comparisons with her parents, for Tupper wants material for his novel. But Elizabeth retains control. Every time his questioning becomes too intrusive, she stands up, moves away, tells him to leave.

Both actions and words suggest something of a feminist characterization. In fact, when Elizabeth interviews for her position at Vista, she tells her boss "she wanted a career, not a job. Thinking of Bill, she said she thought it was important for every woman to have a career, something hers alone, something that would remain hers, that she could remain dedicated to, despite the ups and downs, gains and losses, of her personal life" (90). But what Elizabeth truly desires is "real love, she wanted true attention" (96). In other words, she is not so much a feminist as an idealist; like her friend Joanne, her views of love and marriage are based on Barbie and

Ken—the sentimental, unrealistic message promoted by government and the media.

Bill's story does not emerge until the novel's end. After falling in love, he and Elizabeth had lived together; however, her lack of maturity doomed their relationship. Recalling this, Elizabeth realizes the myth on which her beliefs were based: "Love will come to you, love beyond everything. It will change your life forever" (274). Almost simultaneously, she realizes that she does not love Tupper. Knowing he will smile at this and tell her she's simply afraid of falling in love, she says nothing. Instead, as the novel closes, she boards a train at Penn Station for an extended business trip and "looks around the car. In a little while, she'll get up to get a small bottle of wine. Maybe even meet someone on the way, invite him back to her seat. He'll see her manuscript bag and ask, What are you, a musician? A doctor? A traveling saleswoman? . . . If she likes him, she knows she'll lie" (290).

Although *A Bigamist's Daughter* was published in 1982, its conclusion (and its heroine) echo Mary McCarthy's "The Man in the Brooks Brothers Shirt," published four decades earlier. Despite the desire to be strong and independent, both sets of female characters are doomed by society's messages. Just as McCarthy's pre-feminist women are gradually transformed into compliant wives and mothers because neither their husbands nor postwar America would tolerate their independence, McDermott's conflicted feminist characters reflect the Heritage Foundation's efforts "to turn the clock back to 1954 in this country" (Faludi 1991, 230), a time when notions of true love prevailed.

While the Heritage Foundation promoted motherhood, it simultaneously targeted the Women's Educational Equity Act (WEEA) in the belief that it represented a "money machine for a network of openly radical feminist groups" (quoted in Davis 1981, 442). Reagan obliged by gutting its budget (Faludi 1991, 260). When GOP Congresswoman Margaret Heckler succeeded in restoring 40 percent of these cuts, members of Phyllis Schlafly's Eagle Forum were appointed to the WEEA board to ensure that its "feminist agenda" was curbed. They did so largely by rejecting grant proposals aimed to counter sex discrimination, justifying their decisions by denying that discrimination existed (Faludi 1991, 262). After the WEEA was demolished and its female staff dismissed, the Reagan administration installed men in many of the formerly pro-woman agencies. Gary Bauer was appointed to head the "family policy" arm of the Education Department. He is perhaps best known for "The Family: Preserving America's Future," in which he attacked women who worked, used day care, divorced, bore illegitimate children, or lived in poverty as a "result from personal choices." His proposed solutions: "bar young single mothers from public housing; revive old divorce laws to make it harder for women to break the wedding bonds; deny contraceptives to young women"; and give tax breaks to women who stay home and have babies. Married women, of course (Faludi 1991, 264).

Mary Gordon takes on this mindset in *Men and Angels* (1985). The protagonist, Anne Foster, is a mother of two who holds a doctorate in art history. Her husband, also a PhD, is a professor at tiny Selby College. Anne is a stay-at-home mom, but not by choice: "if the college didn't quite know what to do with women students and faculty, it knew even less what to do with faculty wives" (14). When she is commissioned to write the catalogue for an upcoming exhibition of a female artist's works, Anne hires Laura to care for her children. Some critics maintain that the plot explores "conflicts between materialism and spirituality," calls for ecumenism, and sympathetically portrays Laura to indirectly underscore this need (Watanabe 2010, 200–201). But given the overbearing influence of the Heritage Foundation during this decade, it could also be argued that rather than representing the evangelistic arm of the Apostolic Church, Laura personifies the rightwing, for she is an ignorant, self-centered, hypocritical, born-again Christian who believes she is "the chosen of the Lord" (8).

As the story opens, Laura is flying home from London after being dismissed from an au pair position because her religious fervor disturbed her employers' children. When Helene, a fellow passenger, begins sharing stories of her own faith, "Laura stopped listening but looked as if she was listening with love. She knew the woman was a fool. But perhaps the woman could help her" (Gordon 1985, 8). After she tells Helene she has nowhere to go, Helene suggests Laura accompany her to Selby: "In America the women do not want to take care of their children," she tells Laura. "They say they want to find themselves. I did not know that they were lost." The woman laughs and Laura laughs with her, "pretending that she understood" (10). Not surprisingly, when Laura's religious machinations fail to convert Anne or her children, she takes her own life—an idealized end to the New Right's crusaders.

Gordon's 1989 novel, *The Other Side*, takes another swing at the pro-motherhood faction. Although it has been called "mean-spirited" and "a blanket indictment of a people" (Fanning 2001), it is not so much an indictment as it is "a rather long-winded exploration of the sort of unhappy family that has long been in the forefront of Irish and Irish American writing" (Wall 1999, 37). This multigenerational novel traces the lives of elderly first-generation Irish American parents Ellen and Vincent MacNamara, their children, grandchildren, and great-grandchildren—all of whom have been psychically damaged by cruel, absent, or neglectful mothers. The title, a phrase used by immigrants referring to Ireland, suggests that this tale of neglect stems from Ellen's physically and psychologically absent Irish mother, who hid herself away because she kept having miscarriages: "She was nearly always pregnant, or getting over the loss of a child. But she was never whole with child" (Gordon 1989, 90). Her mother's absence contributes to Ellen's inability to nurture her own children, Magdalene, Theresa, and John, who perpetuate this behavior.

To frame the story, Gordon uses a familiar Irish trope: the gathering of the clan to await the death of the matriarch, Ellen. In developing the plot and exploring the mother's influence on her children and subsequent generations, Gordon expands on Elizabeth Cullinan's *House of Gold*, both in number of characters and by alternating points of view. However, in playing with the phrase "the other side," Gordon not only allows it to suggest the children's points of view but she also slyly develops the characters by picking from her own family tree. Practically every character exhibits traits of Gordon's maternal aunts described in her memoirs, *The Shadow Man* (1996) and *Circling My Mother* (2007). In other words, rather than indicting the Irish, Gordon is mostly damning the Italians while perpetuating the Irish penchant for family feuds.

In detailing the many characters peopling her life, Mary Gordon gets to tell "the other side"—her side—of the story. She is able to revenge the slights against her mother and herself and preserve happy memories of her bigoted father. At the same time, Gordon extracts "revenge" by refuting every stereotype perpetuated by the Heritage Foundation: in this novel, there are no successful marriages, no smooth courtships, no happy mothers. As such, this novel serves as the perfect illustration of Rebecca Du Plessis's (1985) theory that twentieth-century feminists examined and then delegitimized every sex-gender trope invented by man.

Despite these successes, some women felt that feminism had overplayed its hand. In 1984, Germaine Greer published *Sex and Destiny*, an unfortunate tome lamenting that feminism had superseded childbearing, a wholly unintended interpretation that led to subsequent "feminist complaints of the 1980s—involuntary singlehood, involuntary childlessness, loneliness" (Showalter 2009, 298). In 1985, Betty Friedan reiterated what she had first reported in *The Feminine Mystique*: young women once again felt guilty and alone, pressured to be superwomen on the job and in the home (Greene 1993, 12). The feminist Nancy Miller summed up these feelings when she wrote, "Choosing motherhood or refusing it has proven to be more complex than we feminists had bravely imagined in our consciousness-raising groups of the early seventies" (quoted in Showalter 2009, 299).

Such feelings are explored in Ellen Currie's *Available Light* (1986). The main character, Kitty, assumes that her lover, Jacques Rambeau, will desert her, and he does not disappoint. Currie advances the plot by presenting Kitty and Rambeau's points of view in alternating chapters where additional characters are introduced: Mick, Kitty's Irish mother; Eileen, Kitty's sister; and Dorinda, a pregnant wild child who tries to sleep with every man she encounters. Each character reflects a different side of motherhood. The stereotypical Irish mother, Mick constantly criticizes her daughters but loves them fiercely. When Kitty calls to bemoan Rambeau's absence, Mick consoles her, saying, "there's nothing to roar and cry about, no nothing, you'll do rightly." Longing for comfort, Kitty asks, "I will?" to which her mother replies, "Och aye . . . you little hooer, you wasn't new when he got you"— and hangs up the phone (15). Eileen so badly wants a child that she tolerates Gordon, her philandering husband, and eventually succumbs to hysterical pregnancy, stuffing her clothes to appear with child. Dorinda, the only character who *can* become pregnant, shows neither interest in motherhood nor concern for the fetus. She drinks, takes drugs, and sleeps around while seeking a buyer for her baby.

Available Light earned rave reviews. Maureen Howard called it "an extraordinary book, truly a fine work." It is all that. But it is also a thematic mess. Simultaneously, it reflects anti-feminist propaganda, which claimed that feminists could not be happy in a relationship, by tracing Kitty's worry before and misery after Rambeau leaves, yet questions the pro-motherhood stance promoted by the Reagan administration by illustrating various unfit mothers as well as concerned potential fathers. At the same time, Kitty is portrayed as an independent career woman who gradually grows stronger and happier without Rambeau. Then the plot comes full circle by providing a decidedly post-feminist conclusion: Kitty and Rambeau reunite and live happily ever after.

Conversely, Maureen Howard's *Grace Abounding* (1982) explodes 1980s propaganda about sexuality, education, and mother-daughter relationships, while *Expensive Habits* (1986) sends forth potent political messages regarding marriage, motherhood, and women's work. In *Grace Abounding*, Howard's decidedly unmerry widow, Maude Dowd, is horny. She so wants a man that she deliberately takes dark and dangerous back roads in the hopes that she will be stopped for speeding or her car will break down and she will be ravaged by a stranger. The plot periodically switches from straightforward narrative to fantasies such as seduction by a policeman, a "truck driver jacking me up" (4), sweaty teenage hitchhikers, gas station attendants, and a gift shop proprietor—who eventually becomes Maude's lover. But despite her plans for the future and pleas that he divorce, he abandons Maude, sneaking out of town without even a goodbye note.

Throughout this interlude, Maude and her teenage daughter Elizabeth essentially trade places. While Maude excitedly hides her affair, Elizabeth remains calm and responsible, doing her homework and practicing her singing each night. However, as Maude recovers her equilibrium and discovers her daughter's talent, Howard shows us how Irish American women survive: not with a man, but with education. Mother and daughter move to New York, where Maude attends Columbia to become a counseling psychologist while Elizabeth studies voice at Juilliard. In this environment they do not revert to their traditional roles; rather, they are "living like roommates" (90).

As the novel develops, Howard explores the dichotomy between her generation and her daughter's. After Elizabeth marries Gus, she gives up her singing career to be a housewife and mother. She and her husband are, her mother says, "hopelessly suburban": "She had paid me with silence. Sold out in Westchester. Gagged in her house with a lawn and trees, a baby. With her money and her husband, the corporation stud. Ungrateful child" (156). This is the life Elizabeth and her husband think they want—"as though we were about to live as an ideal family before the Second World War" (111). Elizabeth protests that she did not give up her music for her marriage, but the fact remains that she stops singing.

Mother and daughter come together over tragedy. After Maude has surgery for a "minor chalzion" she calls Elizabeth. Waking up, she is thrilled to find her daughter at her side. More delightfully, after drifting off again, she awakens to hear Elizabeth singing. "When it was done we smiled at each other foolishly, until she said, 'Stop that, Mother. Stop crying'" (159). Elizabeth sings a requiem for the dead, "a song that the reader recognizes as not only for those characters who have died (Elizabeth's father; a young patient of Maude's) but also for those selves that Maude and Elizabeth have left behind" (Durso 2008, 65).

Howard's acclaimed 1986 novel, *Expensive Habits*, expands on this theme by detailing the price women pay for fame and fortune. The protagonist, Margaret "Maggie" Flood, is a highly successful writer, tough, arrogant, and loud. Maggie is the dreaded feminist—twice married, divorced, fiercely independent, who spies on her husband's lover and flies to Mexico to get a divorce. Yet she is no caricature. As she freely admits, "I pricked my flesh with the sight of this woman to beg relief from what seemed a terminal wound—my life" (50–51). It wasn't the infidelity that hurt so much. "I saw that I had not been taken seriously and that broke my heart more than a peroxide blonde" (75).

As the novel opens, Margaret is suffering from heart disease. In this expansive iteration of Howard's stylized approach debuted in *Bridgeport Bus*, the novel ranges forward and backward, intermixing characters as well as snatches of novels and reflections scattered across five long chapters in which she retells and then recasts the story of her first marriage (and novel), undergoes a heart operation, and loses her son. In the final scene Margaret is challenged one last time: looking at the stars, she falls into a hole and breaks her leg. But she perseveres, dragging herself out of the hole, across the lawn, and up to the porch: "They could never call her in," she recalls. . . . She would not go, defiant, then dreaming on in the dangerous night air. Too smart for her own good. . . . [T]hey called, but she took her chances. She would not go in" (298). Maggie Flood personifies the strong feminist working woman of the 1980s. While independence is an "expensive habit," carrying both rewards and punishment, Irish American women would not relinquish it.

Yet the war on women continued. In a time when the divorce rate had risen from 44 percent in 1970 to 52 percent in 1980 (Woods 2005, 367) and the number of single-parent households continued to rise, Reagan's budget director decimated domestic spending, drastically reducing funding for WIC, the Women, Infants, and Children Program. Hundreds of thousands of families were thrown off welfare or faced reduced benefits, over a million people lost their food stamps, three million children no longer qualified for free school lunches, and 75 percent of all day-care centers had their budgets cut (Davis 1991, 439).

To accomplish their goals without appearing to beat up women, the men of the New Right employed two ingenious strategies: linguistic subversion and female "hit men." Instead of attacking women's liberation, they denounced feminists as "antifamily." Rather than be anti-abortion they became "pro-life" and "pro-motherhood." Hiding behind this linguistic subterfuge, they not only attacked practically every federal program assisting mothers but also lobbied "for every man's right to rule supreme at home" (Faludi 1991, 239). More insidious was the use of women against their own sex. Like turncoat Serena Joy in *The Handmaid's Tale*, working mother Phyllis Schlafly railed against the Equal Rights Amendment. Connaught "Connie" Marshner stuck her three children in day care because she was busy promoting the Family Protection Act. Then when she was dismissed after becoming pregnant with her fourth child, she switched gears and attacked women who used day care instead of staying home with their children!(Faludi 1991).

Mary McGarry Morris's first novel, *Vanished* (1988), uses role reversal to question these essentialist beliefs. Aubrey Wallace is a mentally weak white man; Dotty is a white trash teenager who has more or less kidnapped Aubrey by driving off with him in his truck. When he tells her they need to head back, Dotty runs away and returns with "a loaf of bread, a blue mason jar filled with dimes"—and Canny—a "baby girl with a pale pink ribbon in her yellow-white hair" (9). For five years, Aubrey, Dotty, and Canny travel around the country stealing and conning people out of their belongings. Although they appear as a family, Dotty is not the typical mother. She picks up men wherever they stay and she physically abuses Canny. When they stop at a county fair, Dotty has sex with a cowboy while his pal molests Canny. Aubrey is no help. Whenever he "tried to think about his dilemma, he would be seized with a helplessness so vast and so paralyzing" that he could not act (11). Aubrey is the demoralized "wife" who so fears being left that he is unable to protect his "daughter" from physical or sexual abuse. Some people, Morris suggests, are not fit to be parents.

Regardless of their politics, women began disappearing from public office after Reagan's election (Faludi 1991, 257). The number of women appointed to judicial positions fell from 15 to 8 percent; the number of women put forth for Senate confirmation also dropped. In the White House, the female staff was reduced by half. And even though 2.5 million women lived below the poverty line, Reagan cut their funding too. Granted, he did appoint a few women—most of them Irish American—to office. In 1981, Sandra Day O'Connor became the first female jurist on the Supreme Court. Reagan also appointed Jeanne Kirkpatrick to the United Nations, hired Peggy Noonan as his assistant and speech writer, and named Elizabeth Dole and Margaret Heckler to his cabinet (Davis 1991, 419–20). But they were not sufficient to stop the New Right juggernaut.

After Reagan won a second term, he eliminated the Coalition on Women's Appointments, the Working Group on Women, and the Federal Women's Program. After passing the Paperwork Reduction Act, the Reagan administration stopped collecting statistics on women's status altogether. Even the women who had supported Reagan's measures discovered that their jobs carried "inflated titles but no authority or required them to carry out the administration's most punitive antifeminist policies." Marjorie Mecklenburg had to enforce the "squeal rule"—a term coined by Irish American Mary Cantwell during her tenure on the *New York Times*—which required clinics to report teenage girls seeking birth control. Another woman, Nabers Cabaniss, was charged with ensuring that members of family planning clinics were fired if they "mentioned the word abortion." Jo Ann Gasper was assigned the job of eliminating domestic violence programs (Faludi 1991, 257–59).

When the Reagan administration wasn't fighting feminists, unwed mothers, and poor women, its cohorts tried repeatedly to take away their right to choose. Federal funding for poor women seeking abortions was eliminated, family-planning clinics found their funding cut by 25 percent, and support for international Planned Parenthood stopped altogether. Since efforts to repeal Roe v. Wade had failed on the national level, pro-life groups began focusing on individual state laws so that getting an abortion—especially for teenagers, the least-prepared of all mothers—would be more difficult. Valerie Sayers's *Due East* (1987) seemingly supports this stance. Fifteen-year-old Mary Faith Rapple is pregnant and the baby's father is dead, but she is determined to have the baby. Although the novel's denouement suggests that Mary Faith is a very mature fifteen, such a conclusion might strike some as unrealistic.[3]

More down-to-earth is Alice McDermott's second novel, *That Night* (1987). McDermott turns her literary clock back to the 1950s to remind readers how pregnant teens were treated at midcentury. A nameless female narrator recalls the events leading up to her teenage neighbor Sheryl's pregnancy and what happens after her mother sends her away to give up the baby for adoption—a common practice in the 1950s. Certainly marriage would not have solved Sheryl's problems, for she is too immature. Pressured by a nurse to look at the child, Sheryl finds it "incredibly small and ugly" (173). Upon returning from the hospital, she endures dinner with the family, then asks, "'Can I go?'" Up in her room, she applies heavy makeup, teases her hair, slips on some bracelets. "The sound of them, she knows, will reach the boys, make them turn away from their cars. She practices a slow, wise smile. She wants to love someone else" (175–76). Sheryl has learned nothing; she is too young to be a mother.

The 1980s saw abortion laws infantilizing women by requiring their husband's or parents' permission, initiating a twenty-four-hour waiting period, mandating that any abortion after the first trimester be performed

3. Sayers's second novel, *How I Got Him Back* (1988), revisits Mary Faith, now the single parent of four-year-old Jesse; however, the focus here is less on motherhood and more on various romantic entanglements of Mary Faith and her friends in Due East.

in a hospital, and requiring that doctors lecture about the potential dangers and show pictures of fetuses to dissuade women's decisions about their own bodies. Next, the anti-abortion movement targeted clinics through bombings, arson, death threats, and intimidation (Davis 1991, 459–60). During the 1980s, there were more than three dozen attempted bombings and acts of arson, with nine clinics targeted in 1984 alone (Martin 2011, 166). In response, feminist groups escorted pregnant women into clinics while feminist lawyers filed lawsuits. By 1989, their efforts began to pay off in the form of injunctions and court decisions. Ironically, Sandra Day O'Connor was the key vote in the decision *not* to revisit *Roe v. Wade* (Davis 1991, 463). Her decision may have been influenced in part by the huge pro-choice rally in Washington, DC, not to mention polls indicating that 63 to 74 percent of all Americans supported abortion rights (Martin 2011, 167–68).

Joyce Carol Oates addresses the abortion issue in *Solstice* (1985). Unlike her usual plots, which deconstruct male-female relationships, *Solstice* not only tells the story of the relationships between two females, but also represents the earliest Irish American novel to address the aftermath of abortion.[4] This theme marks Oates's first clearly articulated argument for a woman's right to control her body and her life. Similarly, in *You Must Remember This* (1987), only after the main character, Enid, has an abortion does she begin to respect her mother. Through this plot, Oates suggests that a loss of innocence is necessary to develop the "self-knowledge . . . necessary if Americans are to revise their conception of the family romance and to mature as a nation" (Daly 1996, 192). In this regard, Reagan's politics actually helped, for his war on women galvanized the very cohort he hoped to quash. By the end of his first term in 1984, it was women's votes that decided state elections; by 1986, women so swayed the vote that Democrats regained control of the Senate; by 1988, female Democrats influenced election results in forty out of fifty states (Davis 1991, 271–72). Thanks to women's votes, Reagan's congressional agenda was effectively derailed (Davis 1991, 430).

4. Although pregnant characters in previous twentieth-century Irish American novels considered abortion, they either rejected it, miscarried, or started their period.

A Gran Fury

The Reagan administration also inadvertently hastened the growth of the lesbian novel. Despite the spread of the AIDS pandemic, Reagan refused to act; during his first six years in office he refused even to utter the word "AIDS" in public. Consequently Burroughs Wellcome, the sole drug company authorized by the FDA to develop AIDS drugs, was able to get away with charging as much $10,000 annually for the use of the drug AZT, which no doubt contributed to twenty-five thousand AIDS deaths during that period (Martin 2011, 171–72). To bring attention to the epidemic as well as to government inaction, ACT UP began to engage in public demonstrations that combined civil disobedience and activism with theatrics. They hung the FDA commissioner in effigy, staged "die-ins," nominated a pig for president, and infiltrated the Republican National Convention. Using fake name badges, they somehow gained entrance to the Republican Women's Club, then stripped away their Republican "costumes" to reveal huge buttons reading LESBIANS FOR BUSH. But these people were deadly serious. ACT UP was an acronym for the AIDS Coalition To Unleash Power by fighting back against the Reagan administration's stonewalling. "To be a movement activist during Reagan/Bush," said one member, "was to work in the Resistance," for this was a "war to influence policy and widen the public space to live as lesbian, gay, and bisexual people" (Vaid 1994, xi).

As the decade progressed without noticeable progress on the AIDS front, ACT UP became more confrontational. In New York City, they held a protest in front of St. Patrick's Cathedral that drew forty-five hundred people. They chose this site because they believed the Catholic Church fostered homophobia, obstructed abortion rights, influenced the government's stasis, and was complicit in the lack of treatment for AIDS patients. Cardinal John O'Connor was specifically targeted thanks to his documented antigay stance as well as his role in convincing the Pope to reverse the National Conference of Catholic Bishops' stance on contraception, which led to *Humane Vitae*.

ACT UP was joined by visual artists and activists in Gran Fury. One of their posters used a pink triangle—the Nazi symbol employed to indicate homosexuals—reading "SILENCE = DEATH." Having captured the viewer's attention, the next lines read, "Why is Reagan silent about AIDS?

What is really going on at the Centers for Disease Control, the Federal Drug Administration, and the Vatican? Gays and lesbians are not expendable . . . Use your power . . . Vote . . . Boycott . . . Defend yourselves . . . Turn anger, fear, grief into action" (Martin 2011, 177–80). Subsequent posters, some displayed in the New Museum of Contemporary Art, railed against the Reagan administration's failure to act. One graphic representation featured pictures of the Nuremburg trials to equate the administration's inaction with American indifference, conservative commentators, and of course, Nazis and their collaborators. As co-organizer Marlene McCarty explained, "Gran Fury's goal was to deliver messages to the mainstream world in the most 'raw and rambunctious' way possible" (Martin 2011, 180–81).

Given the history of Irish American women writers, it is not surprising that they reacted to the Reagan mindset through an outpouring of creative works promoting and defending lesbian issues. In 1980, Peggy Shaw and Lois Weaver started putting on the Women's One World festivals; in 1983, Holly Hughes produced *The Well of Horniness*, a parody of Radclyffe Hall's lesbian novel, *The Well of Loneliness* (Bona 2004, 229). Between 1984 and 1987, when lesbian novels were coming out at a pace of twenty-three per year (Zimmerman 1990, 207), Irish American women contributed almost one half of this number.[5] Unlike the 1970s "coming out" novels, 1980s novels such as Maureen Brady's *Folly* celebrated the lesbian mother (Zimmerman 1990, 45). *Folly* (1982) reflects the tone of Reagan conservatism as well as lesbians' desire for normalcy. Rather than exploring steamy relationships, the importance of home is highlighted (Zimmerman 1990, 91–92). Home becomes a metaphor for the community of women (Faderman 1991, 280) as

5. Irish American lesbian novels published in the 1980s include: Maureen Brady, *Give Me Your Good Ear* (1981), *Folly* (1982), and *The Question She Put to Herself* (1987); Elizabeth Dean, *As the Road Curves* (1988); Nisa Donnelly, *The Bar Stories* (1989); Catherine Ennis, *To the Lightening* (1988); Evelyn Kennedy, *Cherished Love* (1988); Lee Lynch, *Toothpick House* (1983), *Old Dyke Tales* (1984), *Swashbuckler* (1985), *Home in Your Hands* (1986), *Dusty's Queen of Hearts Diner* (1987); Vicki McConnell, *Mrs. Porter's Letter* (1982), *The Burnton Widows* (1984), *Double Daughter* (1988); Diana McRae, *All the Muscle You Need* (1988); and Patricia A. Murphy, *Searching for Spring* (1987) and *We Walk the Back of the Tiger* (1988).

the female workers in this novel defy their corrupt bosses and leave to form their own company.

The theme of community runs throughout lesbian novels published in the 1980s. Valerie Miner's 1981 novel, *Blood Sisters*, recounts its failure among women in the Irish Republican Army, whereas her 1982 work, *Movement*, traces the gradual emergence of a feminist consciousness (Bona 2004, 232–33). Miner's *Murder in the English Department* (1982), *Winter's Edge* (1984), and *All Good Women* (1987), demonstrate the power of women's friendships. Nisa Donnelly's *The Bar Stories* (1989) reflects different aspects of the lesbian community, including alcoholism and recovery, as these women gather at Babe's bar for company and support. Similarly, Lee Lynch's *Dusty's Queen of Hearts Diner* (1987) serves as a locus for the novel's action, representing what Zimmerman refers to as the "Lesbian Nation" (1990, 218–19), while her essays in *The Amazon Trail* (1988)—ranging from "The Good Life," "Gay Lit," and "Gay Rites," to "Portraits and The Geography of Gay"—opened the closet door on that nation for all to see. *Mrs. Porter's Letter* (1982) and *The Burnton Widows* (1984), by Vicki P. McConnell, expand this notion. In the latter novel she shows gays and lesbians uniting to support each other in reaction to 1980s conservatism. As one character explains, "don't think we don't have our own network. . . . People with no civil rights have a historic bonding" (181).

Feminists played a key role in this growth. While complacent Americans napped, feminists protested in the streets and in print against the "radical dislocations, cruel injustices, and irreconcilable paradoxes that dominated the American scene in the Reagan-Bush years" (Kauffman 1993, xv). Although women's studies had been a part of the academy since the 1970s, in the 1980s their numbers doubled, with almost half of all universities offering course work (Martin 2011, 165). Feminists moved beyond simply "discovering" women in every field to questioning the male-dominated paradigms governing them and expanding their analyses to include related issues of race and class (Kauffman 1993, xviii). Mary Daly's *Pure Lust* (1984) addressed the ways male-created and male–dominated language oppressed women: "Women in academia are killed softly by 'his words,' by the proliferation of bland and boring texts, by the obligation always to return to elementary consciousness-raising (consciousness-razing)—[an] objective achieved simply enough by the requirement that males be admitted to Women's Studies classes. Women's Studies thus can serve the establishment of Boredom, becoming an agency of anti-Change, anti-Metamorphosis" (Daly 1984, 324).

Across the university, feminist scholars challenged the disciplines' canonical structure, arguing that objectivity was impossible and exposing the hard sciences' biases.[6] Irish American feminist analyses moved beyond the local and the national to the international: Josephine Donovan illustrated the breadth and depth of *Feminist Theory* by tracing its development from the Enlightenment through the twentieth century, Kate Murray Millet's *Going to Iran* publicized the "brutal suppression" of the country's women's movement, and Lin Farley publicized sexual harassment with *Sexual Shakedown*, while Robin Morgan's *Sisterhood Is Global: The International Women's Movement Anthology* analyzed the many ways terrorism targets women (Kauffman 1993, xx). Such works outraged rightwing critics, who showed their disdain by panning them (Kauffman 1993, 300–301). To call attention to this practice, Joyce Carol Oates published *(Woman) Writer*, which exposed the sexism of male publishers and reviewers.

During the 1980s, Oates also published nine novels and three collections of short stories.[7] These works mark a continuation of her changing focus first observed at the end of the 1970s. Rather than serving as vehicles for political commentary, these works are more introspective, reflecting

---

6. Judith Stacey and Barrie Thorne took on sociological research in "The Missing Feminist Revolution in Sociology"; Donna Haraway's "The Biopolitics of Postmodern Bodies" deconstructed the hard sciences; Gayle Rubin's "Thinking Sex: Notes for a Radical Theory of the Politics of Sexuality" urged feminists to recognize the effects of governmental interference on individuals' sexual lives. The subtitle to Trinh T. Minh-ha's essay, "The Language of Nativism," pointed out that anthropology had become "A Scientific Conversation of Man with Man," while Paula Treichler's "AIDS, Gender, and Biomedical Discourse" revealed that the "medical profession's negative stereotypes of the female body . . . put women at risk" (192).

7. Joyce Carol Oates's fiction published in the 1980s includes: *A Sentimental Education* (1980), *Bellefleur* (1980), *Angel of Light* (1981), *A Bloodsmoor Romance* (1982), *Last Days: Stories* (1984), *Mysteries of Winterthurn* (1984), *Raven's Wing: Stories* (1986), *Solstice* (1985), *Marya: A Life* (1986), *You Must Remember This* (1987), *The Assignation: Stories* (1988), and *American Appetites* (1989).

Oates's emerging feminist consciousness (Cologne-Brooks 2005, 90–91). This new direction is attributed partly to Oates's recognition that she needed to move beyond a focus on failure—the theme of her last four 1970s novels (95)—as well as her belief that "art has a moral role" (Oates 1981, 96). Given the political climate, it is therefore not surprising that Oates's historical works, *A Bloodsmoor Romance* (1982) and *Bellefleur* (1980), represent her first straightforward feminist novels (96). In addition, Oates continues her tradition of seeking community, expressed through female communal narrators speaking as "we." Even more specific to the themes dominating the 1980s, Oates's plots feature daughters who reject identification with their mothers because they are silent and powerless, until they realize that to be a whole person one must acknowledge her mother and build relationships with other women as well (Daly 1996, 125–28).

Oates's 1980s novels parody long-standing patriarchal traditions by mocking the family saga (*Bellefleur*), the gothic romance (*A Bloodsmoor Romance*), and the detective novel (*Mysteries of Winterthurn*). In each, the daughters escape familial (read paternal) repression and then serve as narrators to reveal the crimes of their fathers in personal versions of feminist resistance (Daly 1996, 138–39). In *Bellefleur*, one of the narrators is Germaine, the hermaphrodite daughter of Leah and Gideon Bellefleur, characters so enamored of each other than they argue over who is most beloved. But they are not the only egotists. Grandfather Vernon Bellefleur dominates this large extended family, making every decision his alone—one reason why the novel is "concerned with the repression of a feminist unconscious"—something its female characters are well aware of (Wesley 1993, 140). Indeed, as grandmother Della quickly cuts off Germaine's male genitalia at birth, she announces, "'Now it's what it was meant to be, what God intended. Now it's one, not two; now it's a she and not a he. I've had enough of *he*, I don't want anything more to do with *he*,'" and sweeps the penis and scrotum to the floor, exclaiming, "'here's what I think of *he*!'" (Oates 1980, 106).

Although the arch conservatism of the Reagan administration caught most feminists by surprise, its heavy-handed tactics inadvertently helped publicize feminist issues. Amidst a wave of *Rambo*-esque movies starring muscular male action heroes, the few with female stars generally presented a strong image. In *Alien*, the Irish American Sigourney Weaver's Lt. Ripley was tough, fearless, and persevering. Mary Tyler Moore, Geraldine Page, and Shirley MacClain once again knocked the sainted mother off her pedestal in *Ordinary People*, *The Pope of Greenwich Village*, and *Terms of Endearment*, respectively. Similarly, Meryl Streep exuded a powerful presence in *Out of Africa*, as did Sarah Connor (Linda Hamilton) in *The Terminator*, and the female stars in the ensemble piece, *The Big Chill*. Apart from *The Terminator*, these women made their male co-stars look weak in comparison. On the other hand, a number of vehicles painted women in a negative light. To members of the New Right, Glenn Close's character in *Fatal Attraction* represented the apotheosis of the feminist working woman, just as Roseanne Barr and Katie Segal's characters in the television shows *Roseanne* and *Married With Children* showed how annoying opinionated women could be. But in television land, older women were not threatening. Angela Lansbury's sleuth in *Murder She Wrote*, the matriarch Miss Ellie in *Dallas*, and the cast of *Golden Girls* were all beloved. Finally, coinciding with the rise of youthful third-wave feminists at the decade's end, Lisa Simpson appeared.

There were other points of light. Influenced in part by the activists Lynn Farley and Catharine MacKinnon, the Equal Employment Opportunity Commission (EEOC) expanded its definition of sexual harassment to include actions leading to an "intimidating, hostile, or offensive working environment" (Martin 2011, 158). The inclusion of such language eventually led to the Supreme Court's 1986 landmark decision that "sexual harassment constituted a form of Title VII sexual discrimination" (Martin 2011, 160). Despite the administration's agenda, the Family Violence Prevention and Services Act was passed by Congress in 1984, resulting in the establishment of 1800 shelters, hot lines, and support programs across the country (Brownmiller 1999, 277). As the decade progressed, so did these programs, moving from consciousness-raising to a systemized, organized infrastructure offering crisis intervention and legal aid (Martin 2011, 163). In the private sector, initiatives to support women also expanded. In 1985, Betsy Warrior published the first issue of the Battered Women's Directory (Brownmiller 1999, 274–75).

The lesbian community supported these initiatives (Faderman 1991, 249). Lesbian cultural feminists supported groups such as Women Against Violence and Pornography in the Media and Women Against Violence

Against Women, while Irish American lesbians further raised awareness through their novels. Patricia A. Murphy's *Searching for Spring* (1987), for example, addressed incest, a topic that emerged with surprising force in the late 1980s, most likely because it "has become the paradigm of patriarchal power, the ultimate abuse by the Father" (Faderman 1991, 213). Throughout this decade, lesbian authors also tried to place their characters further into the mainstream. Lee Lynch's *Toothpick House* (1983) draws on nature to suggest that lesbian love is natural (Zimmerman 1990, 81) and Nevada Barr introduces a lesbian Western in *Bittersweet* (1984), while Diana McRae's *All the Muscle You Need* (1988) is a detective story. Such works reflect the late 1980s desire for normalcy in that the lesbian protagonist is simply another character rather than a political statement (Zimmerman 1990, 227).

What is most striking about this decade is not the flowering of the lesbian novel, but rather the number of Irish American women coming out of/in this bouquet. While overall the emergence of lesbian novels partly corresponds with the growth of lesbian publishing companies during the 1980s as well as the controversy surrounding attempts to define "lesbianism" (Palmer 1993, 4), the appearance of Irish American lesbian writers also reflects a reaction to the political atmosphere denying AIDS while reifying marriage and motherhood. Traditionally, the American literary canon privileged family and heterosexual sex. In contrast, lesbianism had been presented as corrupting not only fertility, families, and fathers, but also language, for critics considered such works "barren" and "perverted" (Rohy 2000, 5). These women set out to challenge that mindset. In the process, they demonstrated that "Lesbian writing does not exist in a vacuum but is closely linked to the social and political circumstances which form its context" (Palmer 1993, 5).

It's Only a Pretty Custom

Following the turbulence that emerged from *Humana Vitae*, the 1980s became a time of rebuilding, both literally and figuratively, the Catholic Church. In New York City, the church was able to refurbish its image by helping the New Irish. During this decade, at least 40,000 Irish officially arrived in New York, although immigration advocates and the *Irish Voice* placed that number between 150,000 and 200,000. But because of the 1965

Immigration and Nationality Act, they arrived as illegal aliens unless they had family members to sponsor them. For the most part, they did not. The INS claimed that only 949 immigrants were awarded visas in 1982, 1,839 in 1986, and 25,412 between 1987 and 1990 after the immigration laws were loosened. However, most visas were awarded to the Irish who had previously arrived. Consequently, throughout the 1980s the majority of Irish immigrants lived "underground" and were paid "under the table." These immigrants were generally single men and women in their twenties with at least a high school degree. Ironically, more than a quarter left Ireland to escape the repressive lifestyle reinforced by Catholic dogma, yet it was the American Catholic Church that came to their aid (Almeida 2001, 62–63).

Project Irish Outreach, sponsored by the New York Archdiocese Catholic Charities, was created as a result of the 1986 Immigration Reform and Control Act to aid Irish immigrants ineligible for amnesty or visas. This office served as a resource for the New Irish, offering counseling and referrals to doctors, lawyers, employers, day care, and shelter. To aid in this task, the Irish government assigned priests to New York City parishes. Their job was not to proselytize, but rather to provide the support lacking due to the absence of extended family in the United States and to serve as trustworthy sounding boards to wary, undocumented aliens. In this regard, the clergy acted more as social workers than priests, providing counseling and sometimes free service at Catholic hospitals. Such activities underscored the strength of the Irish leadership still existent in the 1980s. As the Project Outreach founder Monsignor Murray, himself the son of Irish immigrants, said, such efforts were his attempt to repay the Irish for their contributions to the United States. But this outreach also reflected the positive side of Vatican II as the American Catholic church attempted to minimize the hierarchical distinctions between priests and laity (Almeida 2001, 102–7). Unfortunately, this olive branch did not extend to its disenfranchised and disenchanted female members.

After Vatican II, women religious had felt hopeful about the church. At their annual assembly in 1976, they focused on newfound feelings of empowerment; by 1978, they had developed a five-year plan to foster "study, prayer, and action on women's issues" (Weaver 1985, 86). This feeling quickly turned to dismay as the Pope repeatedly refused to acknowledge, let alone meet with, members of the Leadership Conference of Women Religious such as Sister Theresa Kane, Mary Luke Tobin, and Margaret Brennan. Consequently, the sisters turned inward, working together toward "renewal" within their communities. The Sisters of Charity of the Blessed Virgin Mary created their own democratic society. Led by Sister Tobin, the Sisters of Loretto developed a focus on social justice. The Maryknoll Sisters reversed their traditionally hierarchal missionary strategies to a "basic Christian community" model to better help the poor and oppressed. More radically, the Sisters of Mercy of the Union moved outward into politics in their efforts for change. Across the board, the more independent the sisters became, the more opprobrium they experienced from Rome (Weaver 1985, 97).

Formed in 1977, the goal of the Womanchurch movement was to help Catholic women escape the double bind of remaining in the church and thus repressing the need to question its treatment of women, or leaving the church and repressing their religious and cultural heritage (Weaver 1985, 64). In 1983, participants at the Womanchurch Conference, feeling their standoff with the Vatican had reached a crisis point, issued a statement calling for the church to admit that it had been "guilty of sexism, heterosexism, racism, and classism" (Martin 2011, 164). This conference provided a space for feminists in groups such as Chicago Catholic Women, Catholics For a Free Choice, the Institute of Women Today, Las Hermanas, and WATER—Women's Alliance for Theology, Ethics, and Ritual. WATER "became a kind of think tank and organizing center for the women-church movement," an initiative that almost led to a split between factions supporting Womanchurch and those supporting women's ordination. In fact, the conference agenda promoted the former, arguing that women's ordination merely "signified acceptance of a hierarchical church." Nevertheless, so many women believed in the goal of ordination that they refused to drop it despite the Vatican's declaration that "the ban on women's ordination was 'infallible'" (Ruether 2003, 10).

In the wake of this conference, the Irish American Mary Jo Weaver published *New Catholic Women: A Contemporary Challenge to Traditional Religious Authority* (1985) to underscore the church's historical misogyny as well as American Catholic women's desire to retain their cultural and religious heritage amidst a harmful and repressive environment. Less radical than Mary Daly, Weaver argued that the church needed to rethink its hierarchical structure, respect women's contributions, and recognize their frustration. To aid in change, she suggested that the feminist movement offered a positive model for governance through its respect for pluralism, democratic governance, and collegiality (Weaver 1985, 39)—elements that seemed to follow naturally from Vatican II.

Pope John Paul II did not support such changes. During the 1980s alone, he:

- reiterated his refusal to ordain women into the priesthood,
- no longer allowed priests to receive dispensations to become laicized,
- warned against taking the changes initiated under Vatican II too far,
- ordered priests to refrain from politics,
- threatened activist and independent orders of sisters, ordering them to conform or resign,
- attempted to expel females—directors, teachers, and students—from seminaries,
- tried to force sisters to wear religious habits,
- refused to allow altar *girls*,
- maintained his stance against birth control,
- ordered pro-choice nuns to retract their support of abortion,
- expressed support of traditional church teachings against homosexuality, and
- decried in vitro fertilization.

In other words, he attempted to counteract if not contravene the changes of the past decade (Seidler and Meyer 1989, 163–64).

The Pope's actions contributed to two different approaches in Catholic women's novels of the 1980s: "Visions of Reconciliation" and "Visions of Individualism." The former entails reconciling one's life experiences with the church's dictates, while the latter yields a "privatized Catholicism" in which individuals subordinate the church to their own desires (Gandolfo 1992, 144). Mary Gordon's *The Company of Women* (1980) reflects the first category. As usual, Gordon praises and faults the church only to come full circle by her conclusion.

Readers familiar with Gordon's memoir, *Circling My Mother* (2007), will recognize this novel as a homage to her mother, Anna. Widowed when Mary was seven, Anna Gordon raised her daughter among a company of women—friends she encountered each year as part of the Catholic Working Women's Retreat Movement. This group respected women's spiritual lives, brought similarly minded women together, and in essence provided a room of their own where they could get away from their families. Several times a year, the women traveled around the country to meet, attend Mass, listen to sermons and talks by the priests, and visit their friends. These retreats led to enduring friendships not only among some of the women but also with some of the priests.

This is precisely the situation in *The Company of Women*. The brilliant and doted-on Felicitas Maria Taylor is obviously Gordon's persona, just as Felicitas's mother Charlotte resembles Gordon's mother, Anna. The novel is divided into three sections. The first recounts young Felicitas's relationship with Father Cyprian and her mother's friends during their summer retreats. Cyprian represents the traditional church, for under his tutelage Felicitas learns that "woman is always a sexualized, inferior being. . . . For Cyprian, woman equals weakness, an inability to engage the true nature of the Catholic mysteries; to be orthodox one must be the opposite of womanish: manly" (Del Rosso 2005, 41).

Part 2 moves away from this company when Felicitas enters college. At first it appears that she has fallen for Cyprian's opposite—a man who is dishonest, profane, undisciplined, immoral, unfaithful—her professor, Robert Cavendish. Yet the aptly named Felicitas ("the ultimate antifemale martyr") has obviously internalized Cyprian's beliefs (Del Rosso 2005, 42). When Cavindish tells Felicitas he is "hoping to become her lover," she replies, "It would be the greatest honor in the world" (Gordon 1980, 114). To spend more time with him, she moves out of her mother's apartment and into the one Robert shares with two other women—a situation that parallels the servile relationship her mother and her friends share with Cyprian (minus the sex). When, inevitably, Robert tells her, "'It's just not working,'" Felicitas begs, "'Just tell me what I'm doing that you don't like and I'll change it'" (197). When he says the problem is her belief in monogamy, she immediately sleeps with a boy downstairs and gets pregnant.

Part 3 recounts the aftermath: Seven years later, after considering and rejecting abortion,[8] Felicitas has had her baby and decided to marry Joe, a man she does not love, because he will take care of her and her daughter. This action, as well as the novel's denouement, counter the belief that Felicitas "emerges as a more sophisticated and independent thinker, particularly with respect to the subordination of women in the church" (Labrie 1997, 257). Although Gordon has been castigated by critics for her depiction of the Roman Catholic Church, in this novel, at least, she emerges "ostentatiously Catholic."

Writers who maintain visions of reconciliation try to retain their individualism without rejecting the church. Under this category, the 1980s saw three strong novels and two very weak ones. Among the latter, Kathleen Ford's *Jeffrey County* (1986) and Diana O'Hehir's last literary effort, *The Bride Who Ran Away* (1988), basically toe the party line: marriage and motherhood are idealized goals to be obtained at almost any cost. More impressive and considerably more sophisticated are Caryl Rivers's *Virgins* (1984), Susan Minot's *Monkeys* (1986), and Elizabeth Cullinan's *A Change of Scene* (1982). Like Rivers's memoir, *Aphrodite at Mid-Century* (1973), *Virgins* details the influence of the Catholic Church, parochial education, and the incipient feminist movement on the mindset of teens during the Eisenhower administration. This confluence leads to reflections on the necessity of remaining a virgin as well as the conflict between marriage and a career. When the main character, Peggy, complains, "'sometimes I wish we weren't Catholic. It's so *hard*,'" her boyfriend Sean replies, "'Well, we are. We just have to be better than other people because we have informed consciences'" (Rivers 1984, 86). Conversely, Rivers's subsequent novel, *Girls Forever Brave and True* (1984), which follows up on the characters fourteen years later, exemplifies visions of individualism. The younger characters try to conform yet rebel against what they view as "the absurdities

8. As she makes clear in "Abortion: How Do We Really Choose?" Gordon is pro-choice; nevertheless, in this essay and "Abortion: How Do We Think About It?" it is equally obvious that Gordon is cognizant of the personal, logical, and theological aspects involved in making that choice.

occasioned by attempting to deal with modernity through authoritarianism" (Gandolfo 1992, 144).

Elizabeth Cullinan's *A Change of Scene* (1982) conveys a similar theme. Ann Clark, Cullinan's persona, has moved to Ireland to escape her messy personal life—an affair with a married man, explored in Cullinan's earlier collections, *Yellow Roses* and *In the Time of Adam*. As Ann says in chapter 1, "unlike most of my friends I wasn't about to move into marriage. I was in love, but the man was already married, unsatisfactorily but firmly, or so it seemed to me, for I'm a Catholic, though this man made me question what I'd previously taken for granted about religion and everything else—leaving me emotionally stranded in the process" (1982, 3). This bildungsroman traces Ann's exploration of Ireland and herself as she makes new friendships, enjoys new relationships, learns what she wants out of life and where she belongs. Eventually she meets Michael Flynn. Because her friends warn her off Michael, she balances her interest by going out with other men, viewing her willingness as a favor, but (like Mary McCarthy's Meg Sergant) hoping she meets none of her friends when she's out with them (Cullinan 1992, 199). What gives her pause is a priest's advice. When he asks if Michael will marry her, she responds quickly, "'He'll marry an Irish girl.' It was the first time I'd said that to myself or to anyone else."

"'Then drop him,'" the priest replies. 'Don't waste your time. . . . And make it definite'" (Cullinan 1992, 275). And so she does.

Cullinan is one of the few Irish American female novelists expressing a relatively positive outlook during this decade. Perhaps because of their Catholic backgrounds, but more likely because of the political climate, Irish American women writers of the 1980s rarely allowed a utopian vision to flourish. In fact, a number of novels seem to suggest a third category—visions of independence, or results of a life without spiritual guidance—in which characters often fall victim to the double standard, with the sexually adventurous abandoned if not punished. In this regard, the protagonists once again parallel their 1880s precursors, for the New Woman of that age was also "the nervous woman," a trait that can be found in many of the 1980s fictional mothers. But whereas the former exhibited these traits via "anorexia, neurasthenia, and hysteria" (Showalter 1990, 40), the latter suffer from depression or alienation. This should come as no surprise, for "throughout much of Irish American literature, reality seems to be not an option but simply the hand dealt. Given those limits, despair is avoided either through escapism—in particular into alcoholism—through faith, or by imbuing reality . . . with imaginative richness so that phenomena originally perceived as limits or boundaries take on greater significance than merely the limitations of real life" (Jacobson 2008, 124).

In Diana O'Hehir's *I Wish This War Were Over* (1984), a negligent mother escapes into alcoholism, leaving behind her seventeen- and nineteen-year-old daughters Clara and Helen. This novel stands out, not only for its heroine's evolution from "familial bondage to self-definition" (Fanning 2001, 333), but also for its inclusion of a female alcoholic. For the Irish Catholic woman, alcoholism is considered a sin because it causes her to be unreliable if not unable to fulfill her obligations of motherhood. Consequently, pain and guilt are compounded (Dezell 2001, 133). Such is the case in this novel, which ends in the ultimate escape—suicide. Tess Gallagher escapes by placing her characters in a setting nontraditional for Irish Americans—the Pacific Northwest. In *The Lover of Horses* (1986) she explores the power of memory and imagination, the loss of language, the effects of mistranslation, the need for faith, and their effects on identity (Ryan 2008). Ann Beattie's novels *Falling in Place* (1980) and *Love Always* (1985) interrogate the angst of this generation. But Jean McGarry's *Airs of Providence* (1985) and Tish O'Dowd Ezekial's *Floaters* (1984) best exemplify this malaise.

Floaters describes life as a Catholic girl growing up in midcentury America. Like so many Irish American protagonists of the 1980s, the narrator is an "abandoned" child in that her mother—referred to throughout as "the fat woman"—is distant. Her aunts are of no help, for they are mired in their roles as housebound baby makers, producing as many as twelve children, mourning their premature deaths, and often descending into mute alcoholism as a result. Fanning dismissed the novel as "slanted toward the negative" (2001, 330). But women's lives in the 1950s were not always positive. Moreover, Ezekiel redeems herself once the narrator finally wends her way to adulthood. As she matures she realizes that "Something had made her [mother] sad and savage and had defeated her so that she wanted sometimes, like Sampson, to bring all the world down around her" (1984, 168).

In the novel's closing chapters the narrator plumbs the depths of her mother's depression, describing her as "so wrapped up in her own melancholy that she could neither see nor hear me" (Ezekial 1984, 232). Contrary to Fanning's assertion that Ezekiel's persona converts to Judaism out of revenge, she writes that she married her Jewish husband because she "was young and dumb and didn't know much and . . . partly because he wasn't loud or boorish and occasionally dangerous the way [her Irish American brother] sometimes got when he'd been drinking" (203). Religion is not the problem. "We seldom fought. Instead, that tedious voice of his wore me down—abraded the edges of my being, shut me down and caged me in. Inside, I grew small and lonely and quiet and found it increasingly difficult to breathe" (211). Taking her problems to a psychiatrist, the narrator receives typical pre-feminist advice: "to the degree that I wasn't contented with my life and wanted more, I was rejecting my role as a woman . . . furthermore, I should learn to derive my pleasure and satisfaction from watching others grow" (213).

Jean McGarry's *Airs of Providence* continues in this vein. The characters' lives are unsatisfactory, inadequate, and unrewarding, their families "eaten up by the same problems of isolation, loss, and emptiness" (Lee 2008, 221). *Airs of Providence* is divided into two sections. The first features eight unrelated short stories describing "people who are dead, dying, sick, and hoping and planning to die" (Lee 2008, 222); the second presents seven interrelated stories recounting the lives of April and Margaret Flanaghan, who feel alienated from their environment as well as their religion. Similarly, McGarry's *The Very Rich Hours* (1987) details the very unhappy life of Anne Marie Kane. Divided into eight chapters or "hours," the book follows Kane throughout her formative years from child to coed to wife as she grows increasingly alienated from family and friends.

Unlike these novels, Susan Minot's *Monkeys* initially seems ostentatiously Catholic. When it appeared in 1986, the *Chicago Tribune* blurb gushed, "Striking and original. . . . Few novels have so powerfully displayed the collective unity and joy of family life." Clearly, the reviewer had not read many Irish American women's novels, or closely read this one. *Monkeys*, the name Rosie Vincent applies to her brood—"seven of them one right after another" (Minot 1986, 61)—tells the story of the Irish Catholic Vincent family's interactions. Early on, there are hints that Mr. Vincent is an alcoholic, as he periodically disappears or passes out. When the children finally confront him about his drinking, he agrees to quit, but minutes later pops open a beer. Mrs. Vincent, "Mum," says and does nothing about this; her role is to bear children. This is most tellingly revealed shortly after the birth of the last child. As Mrs. Vincent prepares to nurse the baby, Caitlin and Sophie "saw it—that wild look—only this time there was something added. It was aimed at them and it said: There is nothing in the world compares with this. The eye was fierce. The baby stayed fast. There is nothing so thrilling as this. Nothing" (73).

Apart from Mr. Vincent's alcoholism, marriage and motherhood seem great. The seven children rarely squabble; when they get into trouble, there are no consequences. Even Mrs. Vincent's death is introduced offhandedly: "Caitlin and Delilah are blabbing away in the kitchen. . . . The girls never stop talking, worrying about their boyfriends, worrying about Dad, always having fits—especially since their mother died" (Minot 1986, 109). The fact that the older girls take over their mother's job of cooking, cleaning, and caring for their father and brothers does not mean all is well; rather, it reflects a continuation of the patriarchal hierarchy. Through this plot, Minot seems to imply that the Catholic structure perpetuates the traditional sex-gender system: "the reproduction of these relations in consciousness, in social practice, and in ideology turns especially on the organization of family, kinship, and marriage, of sexuality, and of the division of all sorts of labor by gender" (Del Rosso 2005, 1). This message only grows darker in Minot's subsequent novels.

The convergence of second-wave feminism with the post-Vatican church practically ensured the emergence of women's fiction about the American Catholic experience. The result was a second model of the Catholic novel in the 1980s, "one of personal process" or as Andrew Greeley termed it, the "personalist movement." Not surprisingly, in this model personal needs override religious beliefs (Gandolfo 1992, 157). Elaine Ford's novels, *The Playhouse* (1980) and *Missed Connections* (1984), are somber looks at young women's attempts to escape the vicissitudes of family life. Likewise, Maura Stanton's short stories in *The Country I Come From* (1988) are told from the point of view of a daughter in a large Irish Catholic family. "The Palace" recalls the narrator's experience at her cousin's wedding. What is supposed to be a fairy tale event actually exposes woman's lot: the narrator is accosted by an exhibitionist in the basement, stumbles into rooms of hot tired women doing the hotel laundry, and recoils from her aunts' envy and exhaustion. Disillusioned, she realizes, "I knew even less about everything than I ever had" (Stanton 1988, 57).

"John McCormack" extends disillusion to the church. First the narrator learns that her visiting uncle is a recovering alcoholic; next, she and her siblings witness the recovery of a drowned body. To comfort the children, their uncle suggests praying for the dead woman and lighting a candle for her soul. But when they arrive at the church none of the candles are lit and the parish priest orders them to leave so he can lock the doors. When they do finally light a candle, the priest tells them to put it out because it's a fire hazard. "'I know you lit it for a soul. Very nice. But it's not the candle that counts, it's the prayer behind it.'" When the uncle persists, saying, "'I always thought it was the candle, Father,'" the priest retorts, "'It's only a pretty custom'" (Stanton 1988, 69).

These Catholic-centered works hint at the role of the church in the late twentieth century. Although American Catholics were willing to identify with their faith, they made their own decisions "in matters of conscience" (Labrie 1997, 268). Such actions suggest that the personalist revolution had gained ground among American Catholics, no doubt a reaction, in part, to the church's intransigence with regard to women's rights. The result, at least among women writers, is a sense that "recent American Catholic fiction writers have been unable to propose a 'viable new paradigm'" (277) in which to reconcile feminism with Catholicism. Instead, the Catholic faith has increasingly been relegated to "a pretty custom," a remembrance of things past.

To paraphrase Mark Twain, the 1980s reports of feminism's demise were greatly exaggerated. Despite the heavy-handed attempts of the Reagan administration, the women's movement actually expanded in number and emphasis, moving into mainstream politics, recognizing the need for diversity, and supporting women's rights. "The second wave maintained enough headway to avoid death by discouragement, and it was in no danger of expiring from a surfeit of success," writes the historian Flora Davis. Nevertheless, by the end of the 1980s, "it was clear that feminism would be around for a long time to come" (Davis 1991, 472).

This decade marked the point at which women's writing began to be recognized and respected, supported by millions of female readers, explored by feminist scholars, and reflecting the impact of feminism (Showalter 2009, 467). Of course, Ronald Reagan helped. Thanks to his war on women, the banshees once again banded together to refute the administration's anti-feminist messages. Not all women should be mothers, nor should lesbians be denied the right. Teenagers should not be forced to take on motherhood, but working mothers should not be punished for supporting their families. Through their novels they argued that women—and mothers—were as multifaceted as feminism and Catholicism.

5

The 1990s

Fin de Siècle

"You get set like that with a guy, and happy, and you turn into one of those little wooden dolls, one of those awful smiling nodding ones with springs for necks." She began to bounce her head up and down in imitation. "You turn into a pea brain."

—Jacqueline Carey, *Good Gossip*

Thanks to the tireless efforts of feminist groups, the 1990s began on firm footing. At the national level, Washington, DC, was full of PACs and women's coalitions. Internationally, feminists were working toward peace, welfare rights, and health care for women with AIDS. This decade saw growth in women's art shows, women's studies programs, hotlines for abortion and domestic abuse, and shelters for the homeless. Females also made significant inroads into traditionally male careers such as law enforcement, medicine, and the law (Davis 1991, 492–93).

Women were beginning not only to recognize their rights but also, and more important, to fight for them. In September 1991, sexual harassment entered the national spotlight. First the Tailhook scandal hit the airwaves after eighty-seven female and seven male Navy retirees complained of sexual assaults and harassment at their annual reunion in Las Vegas. Next, the country watched Anita Hill testify against Clarence Thomas before Congress. After observing male politicians' crude questioning of Ms. Hill, the National Organization for Women was flooded with members and women began running for political office in record numbers. As the nation raised its consciousness, the number of sexual harassment suits filed with the

EEOC doubled—and women actually began to win (Brownmiller 1999, 293). Three years later these issues again dominated the headlines when it was revealed that President Bill Clinton had had sexual relations with the twenty-two-year-old intern Monica Lewinsky. Subsequently, even women's magazines, the barometers of popular culture, began featuring articles on sexual harassment.

Women were making advances in other arenas as well. In 1992, the "Year of the Woman," Hillary Rodham Clinton became the first, First Lady to have a career to put on hold during her husband's presidency. The Clinton cabinet included Janet Reno, the first female attorney general; Madeleine Albright, the first female secretary of state; and Ruth Bader Ginsberg, the second woman to join the Supreme Court. As of 1993, women were allowed in combat. In sports, women's softball debuted at the 1996 Olympics, and in 1999 the U.S. women's soccer team won the World Cup. Reflecting Irish Americans' political diversity, the Democrat Patty Murray was one of four women elected to the United States Senate, followed by the Republican Kay Bailey Hutchison a year later. From 1993 to 1998, Jean Kennedy Smith served as U.S. ambassador to Ireland, where she played a major role in the Good Friday Agreement (Almeida 2006, 561). In *Irish America's* "Business 100" listing of the most successful Irish Americans in the country, Margaret Duffy, the audit partner at Arthur Andersen, was the sole woman among New Yorkers (Almeida 2001, 93).

Within the Kennedy family alone, Kathleen Kennedy Townsend was elected Maryland's lieutenant governor, Courtney Kennedy Hill worked as a human rights activist, Rory Kennedy achieved acclaim for her documentary films, Carolyn Kennedy Schlossberg became a legal scholar and attorney, and cousin Maria Shriver gained fame as a television personality. Eileen Collins was the first woman to pilot the space shuttle; in 1999, she became the first woman to command one. That same year, Kathleen Sullivan had the honor of becoming the first woman to head Stanford Law School. As increasing numbers of women melded work with philanthropic activities, Mary Pat O'Connor inaugurated the Brigid Award luncheon to recognize Chicago's professional women "whose lives and work reflect the sense of justice, generosity, and compassion" exemplified by St. Brigid of Ireland (Dezell 2001, 90).

Indeed, the 1990s witnessed a burgeoning Irish popularity. In 1993, Notre Dame and New York Universities established the first endowed centers for Irish Studies; by 1996, twenty-six universities offered Irish Studies courses. Such increases reflected not only the widespread existence of Irish immigrants, who comprised 18 percent of the U.S. population, but also the desire of newly suburban Irish Americans to retain their ethnicity (Dolan 2008, 305–6). In keeping with Irish American women's history of academic achievement, this decade saw the publication of significant scholarly works. Doris Kearns Goodwin published a second edition of her biography of Lyndon Johnson in 1991; four years later, *No Ordinary Time* (1995), which described the partnership between Theodore and Eleanor Roosevelt during World War II, came out, followed a year later by *Character Above All: Ten President*, and her memoir, *Wait Till Next Year*, in 1998.

The religious theologian Mary Jo Weaver published *Springs of Water in a Dry Land: Catholic Women and Spiritual Survival Today* and was promptly awarded the 1993 Midwest Book Achievement Award for "Best Religious Book." Two years later, the tenth-anniversary edition of her groundbreaking work, *New Catholic Women: A Contemporary Challenge to Traditional Religious Authority*, came out. This was followed by two politically oriented edited collections: *Being Right: Conservative Catholics in America* (1995) and *What's Left? Liberal American Catholics* (1999). Unlike many anthologies, these were collaborative efforts; each section emerged from working groups and expert critiques before being submitted for publication (Weaver 1995, x). During this period, realizing that "wherever [she] went, the rules for gender inequality still applied" (McGoldrick 1994, 222), the fourth-generation Irish American Monica McGoldrick moved from family therapy per se to a more specific focus with *Women in Families* (1991), *You Can Go Home Again* (1995), and *Re-Visioning Family Therapy: Race, Culture, and Gender in Clinical Practice* (1998).

In literature, the 1990s were hailed as the "feminization of the literary market" thanks to an "absolute burgeoning of first-rate women writers" (Showalter 2009, 495). This area was dominated by Irish American women. Alice McDermott's *Charming Billy* (1999) won the National Book Award for Fiction. *Time Magazine* listed Mary McGarry Morris's *A Dangerous Woman* (1991) as one of the "Five Best Novels of the Year," as did the

American Library Association Library Journal. Morris's *Songs in Ordinary Time* (1995) was equally popular: it made the *New York Times* "Best Sellers" list, was featured on Oprah's Book Club, and became a TV movie. Eileen Myles's co-edited book, *The New Fuck You*, won the Lambda award in 1996, while her poetry won again in 1999. During the 1990s, Anna Quindlen, Maureen Dowd, and Gail Collins were awarded Pulitzer Prizes for their columns in the *New York Times*, as was Eileen McNamara for the *Boston Globe* (Dezell 2001, 115). The memoirist Lucy Grealy won numerous awards for her poetry as well as the Whiting Writer's Award in 1995 (University of Iowa); in 1998, her best friend and biographer, Ann Patchett, was short-listed for the Booker Award. But no one could top Joyce Carol Oates. During the 1990s alone, Oates earned the PEN/Malamud Award for Excellence in the Art of the Short Story, the *Boston Book Review's* Fisk Fiction Prize, the Bram Stoker Award, and the Rea Award for the Short Story. She was also co-winner of the Heidemann Award for one-act plays, twice-nominated for the Pulitzer, and a contender for the PEN/Faulkner Award, the National Book Critics Circle Award, and the National Book Award.

Irish women were also recognized for their work in drama and television. Anna Manahan and Marie Mullen won Best Featured Actress and Best Actress awards, respectively, for Martin McDonagh's *Beauty Queen of Leenane* (1998). On television, *Northern Exposure* had strong-willed Maggie O'Connell, *Murphy Brown* centered around the eponymous single mom and star reporter, *The X-Files'* co-star was the Irish Catholic FBI agent Dana Scully, MD, and Emmy-winner Rosie O'Donnell was a favorite daytime talk show hostess. Considering that as late as 1990, Irish American women outnumbered their male counterparts by 30 percent, the presence and accomplishments of these women should come as no surprise (Dezell 2001, 110).

Roles for women in specifically Irish films were more reflective of their heritage. In *The Crying Game* (1992), Miranda Richardson played a murderous IRA member. *The Playboys* (1992), *The Snapper* (1993), and *Circle of Friends* (1995) protested the Irish Catholic law prohibiting extramarital sex (Almeida 2001, 87). The 1993 film, *In the Name of the Father*, Jim Sheridan's Oscar-nominated version of the trial of Gerry Conlon and the Guildford Four, starred Emma Thompson as tough-minded Gareth Peirce, the lawyer who defended them. *Some Mother's Son* (1996), co-written by Tony

George and Jim Sheridan, starred Helen Mirren and Fionnula Flanagan as mothers who try to save their sons' lives during the 1981 hunger strike in Northern Ireland's Maze Prison.

In a decade dominated by action movies starring steroid-fueled muscle men, a few women's movies nonetheless stood out. *The Piano, The Wide Sargasso Sea, The Age of Innocence, Portrait of a Lady, Shakespeare in Love, The Cider House Rules,* and *Girl, Interrupted* reminded viewers of the rights women had won regarding marriage, mental health, and abortion. Other films featured strong women determined to make it in a man's world. Sigourney Weaver's Lt. Ripley reappeared as feisty as ever in *Alien 3,* while Frances McDormand's portray of the pregnant female cop Marge Gunderson was one of the bright lights in *Fargo.* Jodie Foster portrayed a valiant FBI agent in *The Silence of the Lambs* and Cameron Diaz played a doctor in *There's Something about Mary,* while Susan Sarandon and Gina Davis shot a would-be rapist and refused to go quietly in *Thelma and Louise.* The divorcées in *The First Wives Club* got revenge on their philandering husbands, whereas in *Get Shorty,* Rene Russo was clearly the brains of the outfit. Of course, not every movie offered positive images. *Pretty Woman* tried to make prostitution look fun, while *Basic Instinct's* Sharon Stone and Juliette Lewis in *Natural Born Killers* most likely scared every man in the room.

Actually, the dearth of such negative films is somewhat surprising, considering that every period of feminist success has been followed by a backlash. Just as the Reagan administration made it socially acceptable to criticize feminism in the 1980s, early successes in the 1990s were once again followed by hostile responses later in the decade. Indeed, the anti-feminist backlash of the 1990s paralleled the strategies of a decade earlier. Critics used "the very hard-earned *gains* of the feminist movement against women; women's successes [were] turned around as the very reasons for women's *losses*" (Ferguson, Katrak, and Miner 1996, 50–51). This backlash was not without consequence.

Whereas the decades prior to 1990 reflected a predominantly feminist stance among Irish American women writers, the 1990s suggest a more refracted sensibility. Mary Gordon's memoir, *Shadow Man* (1997), moves away from women's issues to describe her search for the truth about her father; moreover, rather than continue her feminist themes, Gordon uses this tract as a way to extract further literary revenge against her maternal aunts. Although loyal second wavers such as Maureen Howard, Joyce Carol Oates, and Anna Quindlen continued writing feminist novels, the previously neutral or uncommitted—like Tess Gallagher, Alice McDermott, Bobbie Ann Mason, and Beth Lordan—tended to subsume feminist issues by featuring both male and female protagonists, a tendency suggesting movement beyond "women's writing" per se. Overall, this mixture of genres and messages reflected the "postmodern concept of hybridity" (Showalter 2009, 501–5)—something Irish Americans have practiced for years.

Equally important, such mixed messages again typified the fin de siècle. As in the 1890s, novels of the 1990s suggested the state of mind accompanying the century's end illustrated through deliberate breaks with literary conventions. Even as most Irish American women's novels promoted feminist themes and issues, they could be further categorized by their use of nontraditional structure, nonchronological narratives, and multiple points of view; nontraditional themes, almost all of them featuring divorced or unhappily married women rather than traditional conclusions ending in marriage; and nontraditional mores, usually in the form of violence and/or sexual anarchy. This chapter illustrates the prevalence of these traits throughout the decade.

Fractured Fairytales

Maureen Howard's *Natural History* (1992) epitomizes the fin de siècle practice of nontraditional themes and structure. Instead of chronological narratives told from a single point of view, the timeline is fractured, recounted by multiple narrators. Such strategies exemplify the end of a century, which in turn has become associated with a "myth of the temporal that affects our thought about ourselves, our histories, our disciplines." Thus crisis and change at the fin de siècle are "more intensely experienced, more emotionally fraught, more weighted with symbolic and historical meaning, because we invest them with the metaphors of death and rebirth that we project onto the final decades and years of a century" (Showalter 1990, 2).

Of course, Maureen Howard was unconventional long before century's end. Like her previous novels, *Natural History* is semi-autobiographical, nonsequential, and highly experimental. The main characters are fictionalized versions of Howard's parents residing in her hometown of Bridgeport,

Connecticut; their children, James and Catherine Bray, personify Howard and her brother. Like Eavan Boland, Howard uses cartography to establish a sense of place. Like absolutely no one else, Howard evokes present and past through stylistic experimentation.

The heart of the novel, "Museum Pieces," is bookended with chapters under "Natural History," which tell James's and Catherine's stories as they reflect on their childhoods and the paths of their adult lives. "Museum Pieces" includes eight chapters: four narratives and four experimental pieces. Among the latter, "Closet Drama" relies on one of Howard's favorite tropes—a play—to round out the story of James's life. "The Lives of the Saints" recalls Catherine's youthful infatuation with the saints as well as James's travels to County Mayo while filming a movie about the Irish Revolution. Most daring, "Screenplays" relies on jump cuts in time and place, moving from present and past and from "fantasy to reality" (Fanning 2001, 365).

The longest and most experimental section is "Double Entry": "In the beautiful concept of double entry bookkeeping, the debit and credit must always agree; no inaccuracies or altered circumstances are permitted" (Howard 1992, 220). The debit side (left page) is full of poetry, quotations, pictures, illustrations, cartoons, and historical tidbits; it is balanced on the credit side (right page), with a narrative about present-day Bridgeport recounted first by James as he considers making a film about a murder case involving his father, and then by Catherine who encourages him. Overall, Howard attempts to create "as full a picture as possible, historical and personal at once, of the connectedness over time of a city and its people, of Bridgeport and this novel's characters and author" (Fanning 2001, 366). Bridgeport is evoked as an archetypal city that, despite its fading glory, retains its "heart— a term that includes a sense of ethnicity still present among third-generation Irish Americans" (367).

Traditionally, Irish identity centered around "nationalism, Catholicism, and either language (in Ireland) or Democratic Party politics (in the United States)"—all of which were challenged in the second half of the century (Almeida 2006, 556). Jacqueline Carey's first novel, *Good Gossip* (1992), illustrates the role of language. This novel could just as easily be called *Good Craic*, for it is full of Irish Americans who love to talk—about themselves and about one another. The narrator, Rosemary, is friends with Susannah

and Harry Tierney, Dee Kilmartin, Liz Quirk, and Eileen Finney, New
Yorkers in their early thirties, each of whom is allotted at least one chapter.
Given the resurgence of Irish popularity in the 1980s and 1990s in New
York City, upstate New York, and along the eastern seaboard, this setting
is only logical (Dezell 2001, 60). Each chapter can stand alone, but taken
altogether the reader gets a sense of these characters' interrelationships as
they talk about their lives and loves in a contemporary novel of manners.
Their stories convey the social scene as well as women's fairly secure status
early in the decade.

Outraged that her boyfriend wants her to vacation with him, Eileen, a
playwright, exemplifies these women's independence: "'You get set like that
with a guy, and happy, and you turn into one of those little wooden dolls,
one of those awful smiling nodding ones with springs for necks.' She began
to bounce her head up and down in imitation. 'You turn into a pea brain'"
(Carey 1992, 76). Eileen is happy being single. In fact, when she meets a man
who Rosemary describes as "just like you," she replies, "Well, that's not very
interesting, is it?" (132). These women are savvy in the ways of love. "We
were more amusing when we got off on a tangent about the unfair techniques used by our own lovers: silence, feigned objectivity, reexamination of
long-forgiven sins, unflattering comparisons to much-loved or much-hated
parents" (157). Eventually they marry, but on their own terms. Liz Quirk
agrees to marry after her fiancé promises to keep a separate residence. Tina
Fleck marries a man ten years her junior. When Rosemary decides to marry,
she does not descend into romanticism: "Once upon a time I'd assumed
husbands and wives would know everything about each other. By the time
Anthony and I decided on a wedding date, I realized this was unrealistic. . . .
I knew, after all, how scary it was to pick out one person to marry; it was as
if you had to pick out only one self to match. And how can you be only one
person, when you have the whole world in your head?" (180). This postmodern view of marriage capsulizes early 1990s attitudes among the younger
generation of Irish Americans, particularly the influx of New Irish, many of
whom were "younger and more sophisticated" than their forebears (Dezell
2001, 60).

Tess Gallagher's short stories evoke a nontraditional sense of place for
Irish American writers: the Pacific Northwest. Her characters are similarly

nontraditional—eco-feminists—whose concerns about the rape of the environment, exemplified in stories of loggers, are intertwined with tales of male dominance over women. The stories in *At the Owl Woman Saloon* (1997), narrated by omniscient males and females, center around humanity versus nature. But the pervasive message is dark: "Shelly had the all-encompassing sensation that places of refuge were thinning out across the face of the planet. Soon enough, if a human impulse fixed its mark on a creature, it would be found and destroyed" (91–92). But it is the humans who are lost, wounded, or blind. Even darker is Beth Lordan's *And Both Shall Row* (1998). In this collection of short stories and a novella, Lordan treats the woes of men and women almost equally. Like Howard, she develops her characters by drawing on their memories to flesh them out and move the plot along. Since all but the novella had been previously published, it is easy to trace a growing pessimism as the decade progresses.

Jean McGarry's *Home at Last* (1994) is no lighter. A young boy witnesses his father's suicide. Two girls lose their father to a heart attack. Wives cope with disappointing husbands. Each story is different but the themes remain the same—sadness, disappointment, and alienation. *Gallagher's Travels* (1997) continues on this note. McGarry's protagonist, Catherine Gallagher, wants to leave home and make her way in the world. But wherever she works, she encounters the same sexist attitudes exemplified by "ever more trivial . . . moronic assignments." In this case, Catherine exhibits a sense of agency: she simply quits her job and drives away. "It wasn't a tragedy; it was just the end" (McGarry 1997, 221–22).

Susan Minot's third novel, *Evening* (1998), is a fine example of fin de siècle narrative. As she lies in her deathbed, Ann Lord recalls meeting the love of her life, Harris Arden, as well as her three subsequent husbands. These memories are intermixed with the worried solicitousness of Ann's adult children, her friends, and her nurse, as well as jumbled stream-of-consciousness, morphine-induced recollections. The gathering of the clan around the dying matriarch is a familiar Irish American plot device reminiscent of Elizabeth Cullinan's *House of Gold* and Mary Gordon's *The Other Side*. Although her children's comments suggest Ann is similarly detached—"I think she's gotten sweeter. . . . I wouldn't go that far. . . . It's just the drugs" (Minot 1998, 166)—her life does not revolve around religion. It revolves around men.

A disjointed narrative, *Evening* is a bittersweet tale about love and romance. Attending the wedding of her best friend, Ann meets Harris Arden, who introduces her to the pleasures of the flesh. When she learns that Harris is engaged, Ann repeatedly vows to have no more to do with him, but after a couple of kisses she changes her mind, believing everything will turn out all right. Despite three marriages and even as she lays dying, Ann holds on to his memory. She never outgrows her romanticized beliefs, preferring to believe Harris would return to her if only he would change his mind, when in actuality he was only toying with her. As he says after checking on his pregnant fiancée, "he remembered the weeping of the other one [Ann] and how he could not reassure her. Well there was only so much a person could do" (Minot 1998, 233). This novel serves as a cautionary tale: women should not give in to their romantic versions of love, nor should they believe that the men in their lives will remain true simply because of sexual attraction. Indeed, when Minot's first novel, *Monkeys*, and her collection of short stories, *Lust*, are viewed along this continuum, the message grows even darker. Neither love nor lust is lasting; men will go on as they have because they can, because women do not learn from their mistakes. Obviously, this theme is more universal than Irish or Irish American.

In the decade following Bloody Sunday, the popularity of the Irish rose to almost epidemic proportions in the United States, evidenced in part by the Clinton administration's diplomatic efforts culminating in the Good Friday Agreement in 1998. At the same time, Irish Americans' identity was growing more diffuse. Starting in the 1980s, the influx of the New Irish had diluted the melting pot, so to speak; this cohort, along with second- and third-generation Irish Americans, was more interested in economics than politics. Yet this interest itself caused a rift. Assimilated Irish Americans were increasingly middle to upper middle class, having "distinguished themselves in several arenas, including politics, the Catholic Church, business, literature, education, entertainment, law, medicine, and sports" (Almeida 2006, 560–62). They no longer lived in ethnic conclaves; they had moved out of the cities into the suburbs. Although they were therefore in a position to help the often-impoverished New Irish, they were not of a mind to do so. Conversely, the New Irish came from a more advanced Ireland than the earlier immigrants; consequently, they felt no need to become

"Irish American." Rather, they saw themselves as commuters, not immigrants (Wall 1999, 563).

Valerie Sayers' *The Distance Between Us* (1994) offers a "history" of this fluctuating landscape. Moving from the 1960s through the late 1980s, this novel is a bildungsroman depicting the lives of Irish Americans set within their insular but gradually disintegrating communities, thanks in part to the influx of drugs. On the other hand, Lisa Carey suggests the ambivalence experienced by the New Irish in their new environments as well as the continued tradition of independent female Irish immigrants. Whether Carey is alternating between characters or from present to past, this shifting point of view helps reconcile misunderstandings and sad, mysterious deaths while exploring feminist themes regarding identity and independence.

Carey's first novel, *The Mermaids Singing* (1998), interweaves the closely related memories, stories, actions, and mindsets of three generations of Irish and Irish American mothers and daughters—Cliona, Grace, and Grainne—as they move between Ireland and America. Each woman rebels against her mother; each generation is angrily independent, afraid of being her husband's prisoner yet waiting for him to save her. However, Grainne's aunt warns, "Waiting doesn't always get you what you want. Sometimes, it's the waiting on a thing that causes it to pass you by . . . you're best not depending on the man to make the first move" (Carey 1998, 199–201). As the novel closes, Grainne reiterates this lesson, noting that in Ireland "the women adore the men, but only pretend to depend on them" (257).

Louise Moffett, the heroine of Maureen Howard's *A Lover's Almanac* (1998), is no less independent. Angry when her carefree lover, Artie Freeman, treats his proposal of marriage as a farce, Louise casts him out and continues living alone in New York. Although the heartache affects Louise's work as an artist, Artie is bereft. Howard contrasts this contemporary love affair to the missed opportunities of Artie's grandparents, Mae Boyle O'Connor and her husband, Cyril, moving from Lou and Artie's present to their and their families' pasts as Artie tries to learn who fathered him. To illustrate the lovers' pangs as they count the days apart and as "a dumb way of saying what's on [their] mind," Howard intersperses illustrations and tidbits from the *Farmer's Almanac*; quotations from Virgil, St. Augustine, Emerson, Donne, and Wallace Stevens; and Cyril's journal entries and letters

(84). For Louise, art underscores woman's power to create the world. She takes what might be viewed as sentimental artifacts and turns them into something that will "force observation, destroy nostalgia" (11), knowing that such backward looking can only conceal the truth and contaminate life (Durso 2008, 73). Yet Howard herself includes instances of her own artistic awakening (Fanning 2001): listening to Wagner's *Ring* cycle on the radio and later, commenting on the influences of Twain, Hawthorne, and Cather: "*sentences, whole paragraphs . . . which I knew to be grand,* la vrai chose, *even when I did not understand the jokes, the parables, the writers' passion for words or their passions*" (Howard 1998, 224).

Like many traditional novels, Artie and Louise eventually reunite; in fact, as the novel comes to a close, Louise is nursing their newborn infant. But once he falls asleep, she returns to her first love. Walking home from the art supply house, baby in tow, she escapes the present to dream of future artistic endeavors wondering—like Howard—"what will it come to?" (270).

Sexual Anarchy

Feminist waters were further muddied with the 1992 arrival of Hillary Clinton as First Lady. Hillary's activism elicited both "boiling resentment and . . . adoring worship . . . symptoms of contemporary feelings about feminist intellectuals" (Showalter 2009, 322). When she asserted that women in the 1990s wanted not only "a right to have control over our own destinies, and to define ourselves as individuals; but where we also acknowledge that, whether it's biological or social, women want to be part of relationships as well," conventional wisdom might have agreed. Instead—in yet another example of fin de siècle misogyny—Hillary was viciously castigated. Like the 1990s, the 1890s were believed to be a period of "sexual anarchy." In England and France, women called for equality via movements that "challenged the traditional institutions of marriage, work, and the family." As a result, many men viewed women as maddening aliens, while the women considered such males self-pitying conservatives trying to defend an "indefensible order" (Showalter 2009, 7).

Mary McGarry Morris's novel, *A Dangerous Woman* (1991), paints a picture of alienation with the story of Martha Horgan, or "marthorgan" as the local children call her. Martha has never fit in. Apparently suffering from

Asperger's or Tourette's Syndrome, "all her tics and rituals were only parts of other things, engine-revving incantations against fear and failure" (Morris 1991, 50–51). With Martha, as with all her flawed heroines, Morris points out the misunderstandings and indignities women—especially women who speak out or refuse to conform—must endure. Martha's life is hell, often of her own making, but also the result of victimization by men. As a teenager, local boys trick her into the woods, where they tear off her clothes and threaten to rape her. Yet in a fine display of the double standard, when the incident is reported, the story is reversed. "Martha had somehow asked for it, . . . she had brought it on herself with her attractive figure and her peculiar ways" (Morris 1991, 8).

The novel's action resumes fifteen years later, but the victimization continues. First Martha is fired after her accusation of stealing is used against her. Next her sister's handyman seduces and impregnates her. When she goes to tell her girlfriend, the woman's boyfriend will not let her in. Mistaking his manhandling for a sexual advance, Martha grabs a knife, stabs him to death, and blood-covered, staggers down the street. When her pregnancy begins to show, the authorities try to force her to admit she was raped. Finally her seducer confesses that he was drunk and took advantage of her. "But Martha won't call it that," he says. "She thought it was love. And maybe it was" (Morris 1991, 357). That is all she needs.

Martha survives. Moreover, like Maureen Howard's Mary Agnes Keely, she does so with the realization that "it was no great sin to be, at last, alone" (Howard 1961, 309). Morris's Marie Fermoyle is another oddity—a divorced woman in a Catholic community rife with sexual anarchy. Adultery, extramarital sex, teenage sex, and worst of all, sex with a priest flourish among the many characters in *Songs in Ordinary Time* (1995). Daughter Alice is the neediest. Lacking her mother's approval and her father's presence, she looks for love from other outcasts and finally finds it with the family priest. But like Martha Horgan, Alice is strong. Despite the priest's weepy pleas, she breaks off the affair and goes away to college. Like all of Morris's female characters, these women are survivors.

It is probably no coincidence that this novel emerged during the revelation of widespread sexual abuse among priests. Although the Pope expressed dismay about the damage done to children, he was equally worried about the impact of these revelations on the church. Similarly, many bishops responded either by sending the miscreants to be "rehabilitated," blaming the media, or absolving themselves, since priests were considered "independent operators." Despite conservative estimates revealing that abuse had occurred at the rate of 375 minors per year over the previous forty years (that's 15,000 victims), only 10 percent of priests considered this a significant problem. Likewise, although parishioners found the practice deplorable, they did not leave the church; rather, they blamed the Vatican for not dealing with the problem more forcefully (Dezell 2001, 180–81).

Mary Jo Weaver's edited collection, *What's Left?* (1999), addresses these and other social issues. In "Resisting Traditional Catholic Sexual Teaching," she points out that unlike its weak-kneed stance on priestly pederasty, the church has had no problem laying down the law to gays and women about sexuality, homosexuality, abortion, divorce, and remarriage. Whereas parishioners generally accepted ecclesiastical mandates regarding birth control pre-Vatican II, the debacle of *Humana Vitae* led them to view subsequent encyclicals as patriarchal and paternalistic, denying women "moral agency." Yet rather than leave the church, for many dissent became "a necessary (if not painful) part of their Catholic identity" (91). As a result, Catholics for Free Choice (CFFC) was formed. CFFC supported the radical notion that sex was not just for procreation, questioned whether a celibate clergy could or should speak knowledgeably about sexual matters, and— as in Weaver's 1985 *Catholic Women*—faulted the church for ignoring the rights and needs of women, particularly sexual freedom and freedom of choice (92).

But Anna Quindlen's 1994 novel, *One True Thing*, suggests that the church was not the only institution punishing sexually independent women. When the novel opens, Ellen Gulden, an outspoken, goal-oriented feminist, is working in New York; however, she is soon coerced by her father into moving home to care for her cancer-ridden mother. Ellen leaves the job she loves because her father, whom she emulates and adores, demands it—even though he refuses to ask his sons to come home from college, to hire a nurse, or to participate in his wife's care-giving. When Ellen objects, he has the nerve to accuse her of being heartless, "something many people said George Gulden had never had at all" (30).

Initially, the novel juxtaposes Ellen's efforts to continue her job while working in and from the home. She begins to respect the mother she once dismissed, to realize how selfish and unfeeling her father is, and to recognize these same traits in herself. This coming of age comprises the first half of the novel. After her mother dies, Ellen is arrested for her murder. In practically every case, men view women as the enemy: Ellen's father refuses to visit her in jail or to post bail; her boyfriend tells prosecutors Ellen wished her mother were dead; the prosecutor does his best to damn her. Women are her primary supporters. While awaiting the grand jury hearing, a former teacher posts bail, gives her a home, and loans her money for a lawyer. For this the teacher is rumored to be a lesbian. But ultimately, women persevere. As the novel closes, Ellen remarks, "someday I will tell my father [what caused her mother's death] although there is a great temptation to leave the man I once thought the smartest person on earth in utter ignorance" (385).

The anti-feminist backlash was furthered by the very people who most loudly proclaimed their patriotism—the white male members of the Heritage Foundation. Whereas the 1980s saw this cohort claiming reverse discrimination (against themselves), in the 1990s their targets were Others— "immigrants, gays and lesbians . . . women and children" (Faludi 1991, 52). Unfortunately, these attitudes were not limited to the Heritage Foundation.

In 1992, Cardinal Joseph Ratzinger (who went on to become Pope Benedict XVI) issued *Some Considerations concerning the Catholic Response to Legislative Proposals on the Non-Discrimination of Homosexual Persons*, which essentially *supported* discrimination. This missive, which reaffirmed his 1986 letter suggesting that homosexuals possessed "a more or less strong tendency ordered toward an intrinsic moral evil," resulted in some priests refusing communion to homosexuals (Weaver 1999, 99–101). In Boston, as late as 1999, women were still excluded from Boston's Clover Club and the annual St. Patrick's Day parade was "off-limits" to gays and minorities (Dezell 2001, 40). Likewise, in New York City, members of the Ancient Order of Hibernians, with the support of the Catholic Church, barred LGBT people from the parade—a move resulting in the establishment of the Irish Lesbian and Gay Organization—whose members rejected the conception of Irishness as white, male, Catholic heterosexuals (Cochrane 2010, 117–18). Not coincidentally, the 1990s saw the beginning of research on the sexual harassment of homosexuals in the academy, which revealed multiple examples of homophobia throughout the decade. To fight back, lesbians began to come out, speak out, and publish stories of their harassment.

Lesbian novels also reflected the fin de siècle mindset. In late nineteenth-century art, female lovers were depicted as mirror images of each other (Dijkstra 1986). In literature, the "divided self of the fin-de-siècle narrative . . . solved [homosexuals'] social and sexual problems by neatly separating mind and body, good and evil, upstairs and downstairs" (Showalter 1990, 118). Likewise, late twentieth-century lesbian writers defended themselves by exiting the closet via metaphorical side doors, following their foremothers' footsteps by devising "aesthetic strategies" to underscore their alienation from traditional literary genres (Gilbert and Gubar 1989, 218). In Eileen Myles's case, this division is literally represented through the fictional character of "Eileen Myles."

In *Chelsea Girls* (1994), Myles's persona is an alcoholic. Her alcoholism is a result of a genetic predisposition inherited from her father as well as a common "side effect" arising from conflicts about her sexual orientation.[1] In no particular order, Myles describes her bouts of drinking supplemented with a range of drugs; her lifelong feelings of displacement and inferiority; and warring feelings of homophobia and lesbianism. With discussions of tampons ("crammers") and menstruation, sexual liaisons and orgasms, Myles embodies sexual anarchy. But she leavens these rants with vignettes describing her father's death, shopping with her mother, or the little things you do when you're in love. Although the harsher stories are compelling (like watching a train wreck), the soft ones make you like her.

Myles's descriptions of sex are graphic, too graphic to report here. In "Popponesset," she describes being gang-raped but blames herself for being drunk. She often seems self conscious, guilty, or apologetic—and vulnerable: "I only know in the midst of passion she would always betray me like pleasure was a hook she used to throw me. I was just a poor fish" (Myles

---

1. Jean Swallow's 1983 study, *Out from Under: Sober Dykes and Our Friends*, found that "38 percent of lesbians are alcoholics and another 30 percent are problem drinkers" (Faderman 1991, 282).

1994, 77–78). And she is hooked: "it seemed that every time a woman kissed me and touched me was like something that had never happened before. Still it's like that. Kind of a shock. . . . With a woman I felt whole, not different. . . . I was willing to sacrifice all for that moment" (269–71).

Growing up in an Irish Catholic family at midcentury, it is not surprising that Myles suffered from depression and feelings of rejection. In "1969," she writes: "I was going down to get some coffee and the Boston Globe to make me be something. Everything I did was something to fix me. With all my heart I was trying to be dead. . . . The attention of women was softer and more pleasing [than men's], but I didn't know there was anything you could do with those feelings. The best solution I ever arrived at was to try and control myself and be dead. . . . I wasn't normal, I never would be (Myles 1994, 107–17). Such feelings echo those expressed by Radclyffe Hall's heroine, Stephen Gordon, who laments that "the loneliest place in this world is the no-man's-land of sex" (quoted in Gilbert and Gubar 1989, 218).

Of course, Myles had been warned. The Vatican's 1988 *Letter to the Bishops of the Catholic Church on the Pastoral Care of Homosexual Persons* stated that homosexuals should "expect increasing violence directed against them when they advocated publicly for civil legislation to protect their behavior." This letter's "un-Christ-like hatred" against homosexuals paralleled its treatment of women, a stance evident since the Reformation. Then, in 1992, the Vatican's new Catholic catechism pronounced that homosexuality was not a choice and that gays and lesbians should not be "unjustly" discriminated against—a stance that anticipated the 1994 decision by the American Psychological Association that homosexuality was "neither mental illness nor moral depravity" (Peters 2003, 179). These mixed messages were reflected in Irish American women's gay and lesbian novels.

Ann Patchett's *The Magician's Assistant* (1997) demonstrates both the humanity and the tragedy surrounding the AIDS epidemic in a story of a woman who loved, and lived with, a gay man, exploring their relationship and the aftermath of his death from AIDS. Dorothy Allison and Stephanie Grant deal with the issue metaphorically. In her 1998 novel, *Cavedweller*, Allison indirectly explores sexuality, drawing on the metaphor of spelunking to represent her character's exploration of lesbian tendencies. Grant uses similar strategies. Her 1995 novel, *The Passion of Alice*, might be viewed as a modern version of Rudolph Bell's *Holy Anorexia*: "holy anorexia—broadly defined to include all historically relevant types of self-starvation by pious women—has existed for centuries in western European society and is but one aspect of the struggle by females striving for autonomy in a patriarchal culture" (Bell 1985, 86). In other words, "anorexia was agency for women in the Middle Ages" (21). Taking a more modern approach, *Catholic Girlhood Narratives* posits that one of the factors contributing to anorexia is "sexual suppression." Certainly suppression of homosexual desires would fall into this category (Evasdaughter 1996, 8).

When the novel opens, Alice has been hospitalized at a treatment center for people with eating disorders following cardiac arrest induced by severe malnourishment. In the prologue she explains that "anorexics differentiate between desire and need. Between want and must" (Grant 1995, 2). These young women find agency in their ability to recognize their desire and control it. But Alice begins to lose control after meeting Maeve Sullivan, one of the overeaters. In the process of making Alice aware of her body, Maeve ignites desire. When their love affair founders, Alice stops eating; however, when she realizes that Maeve will not come back to her, Alice is furious. In the process, she comes to an important realization: "After all this, after all the wanting and not wanting and trying-not-to-want, desire itself was a disappointment. It lacked agency. I had been afraid of it so long without realizing how ineffectual it could be. . . . Desire was a choice I could make or not. Nothing more" (256).

With this, Alice realizes that she had in fact already made that choice: she had not only decided to love a woman, but also to love one as imperfect as Maeve. Somehow, this epiphany provides the impetus to return to life. If the key to anorexia is controlling desire, but desire is ineffectual, then it is not to be feared. Obviously, this conclusion simplifies a complex psychological condition.[2] Nevertheless, in this fin de siècle novel, anorexia is representative of the divided self "neatly separating mind and body, good and evil, upstairs and downstairs" (Showalter 1990, 118). When Alice realizes that she loves women and that desire is not to be feared, this division disappears.

2. As Marya Hornbecker demonstrates in *Wasted*, insight is not a cure.

Blanche McCrary Boyd's persona deals with her emerging recognition of homosexuality by relying on symbolic renaming and misidentification amid a haze of alcohol and drugs. Such artistic strategies represent "the most notably original form of the lesbian novel to emerge [since] the late 1980s," for in their focus on "*speaking* ourselves out of oppression, of ending silence as a path toward liberation," such writers aided "the development of lesbian culture" (Zimmerman 1990, 212–15). Since her first novel, *Nerves*, was published in 1973, Boyd's fiction illustrates the gradual development of lesbian novels described in *"Romancing the Margins"? Lesbian Writing in the 1990s*. Like other works in this genre, Boyd plays with the concept of lesbian identity (Griffin 2000, 1). Whereas *Nerves* suggested the protagonist's growing dissatisfaction with heterosexual relationships, *Mourning the Death of Magic* found the heroine ultimately exploring her homosexuality. In the conclusion of *The Revolution of Little Girls* (1991), Boyd's persona, Ellen Larraine, finally comes out.

This is not an easy transition. Throughout the early months of her first stable relationship, she is tortured by hallucinations of three little girls. These hallucinations resemble the Dr. Jeckyll/Mr. Hyde phenomenon in the 1890s. During the sexually repressive and restrictive Victorian age, it was impossible for women to lead a double life. Although lesbian tendencies were recognized in the early twentieth century, as late as post–World War II, psychoanalysis posited that women's "transgressive desires" merely resulted in feelings of guilt. Men might act on their feelings, but women could not. Instead, they were diagnosed as suffering from a split personality. However, like Boyd's hallucinations, studies of multiple personalities revealed that women were more likely to possess at least three. As Elaine Showalter explains, "In the United States especially, duality always seemed insufficient to . . . cope with the conflicts in women's roles that were a major factor in the American phenomenon of multiple personality" (1990, 119–21).

In her 1995 memoir, *The Redneck Way of Knowledge*, Boyd revisits many of the settings, characters, and incidents originally discussed in her fiction. This approach illustrates Teresa de Lauretis's description of lesbian writing in the 1990s: "the writer struggles to inscribe experience in historically available forms of representation, . . . each writing a rereading of (one's) experience" (quoted in Griffin 2000, 1). Such intertextuality typifies feminist fiction of the 1990s, whose strategies also include mixed genres: meta-fiction, self-reflection, parody, fantasy, and irony. These methods are particularly specific if not essential to lesbian fiction, whose authors keenly feel the "lack of an authorized/authentic script for the articulation of lesbian desire" (Andermahr 2000, 15). With her 1997 novel, *Terminal Velocity*, Boyd draws on these strategies to articulate her persona's burgeoning desire. This novel is clearly intertextual. Many of the details first recounted in her memoir reemerge in this and earlier novels, making it easy to trace the parallels. Moreover, the graphic sex scenes suggest that Boyd rejected the notion of eliding lesbian sexuality observed during the 1980s and 1990s (Griffin 2000, 5). Although the 1990s novels of Irish American lesbians are full of such scenes, they were devoid of love, contributed nothing to the plot, and may have contributed to the demise of the lesbian novel (Zimmerman 1990, 224).[3]

Feminism was also threatened by its own. Within the academy, some feminist scholars took external rejections to heart and began a period of "self critique" marked by the rise of theory. Strongly influenced by the work of Michel Foucault, feminist scholars moved away from critiques of larger social institutions to a more intense focus on the body, the subject, and subjectivity (Ferguson, Katrak, and Miner 1996, 29). In a surge of self-reflexivity, scholars such as Charlotte Brundson began to question the duality between the terms "femininity" and "feminism," clearly demarcating the beginning of third-wave feminism (evidenced in the popularity of the Riot Grrls). Rather than reflecting outwardly on bodies of oppression, too often feminist reflection moved inward, focusing on internal divisions instead of the need for political change. As feminism became more institutionalized, the movement shifted further toward theory, with academics postulating that theory was superior to action, a stance that oversimplified and denigrated second-wave

---

3. Mary Jo Bona's discussion of "Gay and Lesbian Writing" refutes this stance. Such works proliferated in the 1990s, thanks to the development of gay and lesbian presses (e.g., Alyson, Naiad, Seal, and Firebrand); the development of special series among academic presses, for example, Columbia University's "Between Men/Between Women," Duke's "Series Q," and NYU's "The Cutting Edge"; and the growth of gay and lesbian literary journals such as *James White Review* and *Common Lives/Lesbian Lives* (2004, 212).

activism. Consequently feminism became "more of a 'career' and less identi-fiable as oppositional politics." This tendency inadvertently created a parallel professional track intent on "trashing feminist work" rather than working toward change (Whelehan 1995, 128–32).

In 1994, the rightwinger Christina Hoff Sommers published *Who Stole Feminism? How Women Have Betrayed Women*. Although she declared her-self a feminist, she used the book to attack her so-called sisters. She labeled some women "gender feminists—angry, strident, and intellectually bank-rupt," and others "equity feminists—who care about equality for women but refuse to look at the world through gender-colored lenses" (Ginsberg and Lennox 1996, 187). The former, she maintained, had become the gate-keepers for Women's Studies programs, while the latter were viewed more favorably because they contributed "to a grander conservative agenda"—arguments dismissed as "largely anecdotal" and "simplistic" (187–89).

An unfortunate example of this mindset is Gabrielle Donnelly's *The Girl in the Photograph* (1998). At first, this appears to be a feminist mystery novel, for the plot traces Allegra O'Riordan's efforts to learn more about her mother, who died when Allegra was only three. Allegra is a liberal who dislikes the church's stance on women and whose two best friends are gay men; she has a strong voice, essential for her work as a stand-up comedienne; she is sexually liberated, having had numerous relationships and defiantly taking the Pill. All of these traits combine to carry her from Chicago to San Francisco in search of the truth about her mother. However, upon learning the truth—that while engaged to another man, her mother had an affair with a priest whose guilt led him to commit suicide—Allegra damns her. Her mother, she exclaims, "deserved to go to hell. . . . To be so thoughtlessly wicked, so wantonly destructive; to stumble so lightly into wickedness her-self, and then to lure another to follow her, yes, hell, or whatever stood for it in that unknowable world beyond this, hell and for all eternity was what [she] deserved, if any did. Allegra hoped she was there; she thought she must be there" (Donnelly 1998, 300). This reaction not only negates Allegra's feminist beliefs, but also returns woman to her archetypal role as the weak one, the temptress, the doom of man.

Sommers, Katie Roiphe, Naomi Wolf, and Camille Paglia propagated the myth that feminism was not empowering, but rather reduced women to victims. Roiphe argued that "rape is a natural trump card for feminism. Arguments about rape can be used to sequester feminism in the teary province of trauma and crisis" (quoted in Showalter 2009, 318). Similarly in *Fire With Fire* (1993), Wolf blamed women for their own oppression, citing "the culture of competition between women" (quoted in Whelehan 1995, 140). Two Irish American memoirs refute this stance: Martha Manning's memoir *Undercurrents* (1994) and Lucy Grealy's *Autobiography of a Face* (1994) are prime examples of how such pressures lead not to oppression, but rather to depression and suicide.

In *Black and Blue* (1998) Anna Quindlen similarly attempts to reveal the effects of domestic violence and quash the post-feminist tendency to blame the victim by tracing the genesis of abuse. Quindlen tells the story of Fran Benedetto, alternating between efforts to escape her husband Bobby, a violently abusive New York City policeman, and delving into their early relationship to explain why women stay and how hard it is to escape. Fran finally gets away thanks to a women's "underground railroad." But eventually Bobby finds her, beats her yet again, and kidnaps their child. Fran tries to rebuild her life without him, but the doubts never disappear. The last thing she tells us is, "Everyone says that, that I did the right thing, that I shouldn't look back, that I had no choice. Maybe they're right. I still don't know" (300).

Novels by Dorothy Allison and Joyce Carol Oates further expose the fallacy of this position. Such works were necessary. According to Teresa de Lauretis, as long as no terminology existed for "'family violence' medical professionals usually ignored the causes of a patients' injuries, returning wives and children to their abusers, thereby perpetuating domestic violence." This lack of attention, fostered by "gender neutral language," was particularly harmful to victims of incest since it obscured the fact that with incest and child sexual abuse, "92 per cent of the victims are female and 97 per cent of the assailants are male" (1989, 242). Similarly, Judith Fetterley called for such works, arguing that "the traditional canon of literature also constitutes a form of violence" in its reification of male authors and masculine values (quoted in M. Daly 1998, 206).

An example of the female gothic, Dorothy Allison's *Bastard Out of Carolina* (1992) tells about growing up—and surviving—as a victim of physical, psychological, and sexual abuse. In this, survival is the key, for Allison prefers to focus on her character's strength (Bona 2004, 233). Throughout the 1990s, Joyce Carol Oates also wrote about "victims and victimizers" (Cologne-Brooks 2005, 175). Although she recognized victims of both genders, like Allison, Oates prefers to focus on her characters' strength—mentally disturbed Kathleen Hennessey in *The Rise of Life on Earth* (1991), a fictionalized version of Mary Jo Kopechne in *Black Water* (1992), female gang members in *Foxfire: Confessions of a Girl Gang* (1993), incest and child abuse in *First Love* (1996), date rape in *We Were the Mulvaneys* (1996), gang rape and domestic violence in *Man Crazy* (1997), and the loveless life of Marilyn Monroe (and in some ways, Princess Diana [Cologne-Brooks 2005, 216ff]) in *Blonde* (1999). Although Oates has been criticized for her dark visions of violence against women, she justifies her approach by the fact that these issues must be explored—and exposed (Showalter 2009, 498).

The fin de siècle also marked the novelistic emergence of the sexually androgynous half female, half male, described as possessing a "man's brain and woman's heart" (Showalter 1990, 60). This describes the main characters in Karin Cook's *What Girls Learn* (1998) and Oates's *We Were the Mulvaneys* (1997). Although the theme of rape is a constant in her works, *Mulvaneys* stands out as a powerful exploration of its impact. Corrine Mulvaney, mother of four, fails to fulfill her sacred obligation of motherhood when she casts out her daughter Marianne after she is raped so as to "save" her husband Michael from incipient alcoholism fueled by grief. When Michael confesses, "God help me, I can't bear to look at her," overnight Corinne spirits away their seventeen-year-old daughter, abandoning her with a distant aunt, failing to discuss the decision with her children, refusing to allow Marianne to visit, and rarely visiting her. The punishment for the mother's sin is suggested by the past tense title (*We Were the Mulvaneys*), for what had been a happy family disintegrates. First the oldest son, Michael Jr., moves out; next, Patrick goes away to college.

Throughout, Patrick's experiences are mirror images of Marianne's. Both begin college yet remain isolated from family and friends. While Marianne sporadically attends classes, she takes on the appearance of a young boy, cutting off her hair and wearing baggy clothes to appear asexual. Patrick, meanwhile, lets his hair grow long to indicate his disregard for society.

Fueled by their individual demons, Patrick and Marianne eventually drop out of college and lose contact with their family for years. Their primary difference lies in how they deal with the rape: Protestant Marianne finds solace in the Catholic Church, where she learns to pray and grows serene, whereas Patrick plots revenge. However, when he decides only to humiliate rather than kill the rapist, the two halves are fused. "After I left that day, Easter Sunday, remember?—it all just drained out of me. Like poison draining out of my blood. Like I'd been sick, infected, and hadn't known it until the poison was gone" (Oates 1999, 453).

We Were the Mulvaneys concludes on an ironic note. As the family reunites after years of estrangement, the siblings notice a change in their mother. Her previously unruly head of red hair has been tamed; her formerly plain face looks pretty. Then Corinne introduces her new friend—Sable— who had come into her life "like a hurricane . . . with her brassy hair newly cut in a virtual flattop" (Oates 1999, 437, 441). The two co-own a business and share a home. While the nature of their friendship remains slightly ambiguous, Corinne's choice of partner seems congruent with the tendency of fin de siècle novels to feature nontraditional heroines whose identities are far from static, if not marked by sexual anarchy.

This state is exemplified in Mary Gordon's three novellas, *The Rest of Life* (1994), each of which tells the tale of a lost love; it is personified by Monica Szabo in Gordon's *Spending* (1998) and Frannie Thorstin in Susanna Moore's *In the Cut* (1995). Gordon's Monica is a fifty-year-old divorced female artist in search of a muse—not just for inspiration and financial support, but also for sex. She finds him in "B," a man who takes care of all her needs. As Monica's art improves, so does her sex life. After their first encounter, Monica awakens the next morning exclaiming, "I couldn't remember how many times we'd had sex, and it wasn't even eleven o'clock in the morning" (Gordon 1998, 43). Sex is spotted throughout the novel. But apart from Monica's occasional concern that she might be literally selling herself, these encounters are lighthearted—unlike *In the Cut*.

Susanna Moore's novel is easily the most graphic example of the decade of Irish American heterosexual anarchy. Frannie and her friend Pauline are both sexually independent women, and for this they must pay. As the novel opens, Frannie watches strangers having sex and keeps watching even after the man notices her. Unbeknownst to her, this becomes the scene of a sex crime and so she meets detective Malloy, who is investigating the case. Soon they are engaging in such descriptive sexual acts that Joyce Carol Oates calls them "powerful, shameless," and Bret Easton Ellis, the master of the obscene, was shocked (Wadler 2007). Frannie enjoys everything Malloy does to her; indeed, her need for love is so great that she feels no embarrassment even when he seduces her in the precinct's interrogation room. Frannie's life revolves around sex: her research focuses on sexual street slang, she and Pauline regularly meet for drinks at a strip club, she tries to seduce one of her undergraduate students. She willfully puts herself in harm's way, walking the New York streets or riding the subway in the middle of the night. Frannie may be a professor, but she is not very smart.

Although Frannie's behavior places her far beyond mainstream heterosexual Irish American fiction, it positions her firmly within the fin de siècle paradigm. With its scenes of sex and violence, anarchy and alienation, *In the Cut* epitomizes "extreme female gothic" (Showalter 2009, 497).

The novel also recalls the late nineteenth-century belief that women were indistinguishable, illustrated in artists' works featuring identical women peering at their images in mirrors and pools.[4] Frannie and Pauline are two of a kind, literally dying for love, for whatever Frannie attributes to Pauline describes them both. Pauline refers to herself as a slut. She speaks "resignedly of her inability to find true love" (Moore 1995, 29). Listening to the detectives speak disrespectfully of women, Frannie recalls that "Pauline says they have to despise us in order to come near us, in order to overcome their terrible fear of us" (51). Later, Pauline "claims completely disingenuously to fuck only married men because she prefers to be alone on the holidays" (65). Reflecting their "cougar" status, she and Pauline agree that "the best lovers . . . are men who have been seduced when they were boys by older women" (67). When Pauline says dreamily, "I can remember every man I ever fucked by the way he liked to do it. Not the way I liked to do it," Frannie agrees. She is interested in "The After," "an expression [she] learned from Pauline"

---

4. To view the full extent of this misogyny, see Bram Dijkstra, *Idols of Perversity* (1986).

regarding men's ability to pull away emotionally after sex (86). Thus it should not be surprising that Pauline and Frannie must be punished, both killed in the same way by the same man.

Elaine Showalter notes that feminism was "problematic for women in the 1990s." It raised women's expectations without the means to fulfill them. But how could it? Neither philosophy nor ideology has that ability. Nevertheless, "feminism can help us accept the struggle and resist regression into victimization, infantilization, or revenge" (Showalter 1997, 105). In this, Irish American women novelists played a strong role.

Unhappy Marriages, Bitter Divorcées

Fin de siècle novels represented change. Prior to George Eliot's death in 1880, Victorian novels reflected gender characteristics as a series of binary opposites, with the female possessing the lesser or negative traits. But after Eliot's death, fin de siècle narratives discarded their traditional structure, particularly closure ending in marriage (Showalter 1990, 17–18). This trend is especially evident in the works of Irish American women, for practically every 1990s novel dwells on unhappy marriages or bitter divorcees. Anna Quindlen looks at the Scanlan family's marriages in her first novel, *Object Lessons* (1991), while also inscribing the end of insular, ethnic communities in the early 1960s. In fact, this cultural breakdown is one factor in the family's ongoing squabbles. Quindlen reinforces this message in Connie Scanlan's closing advice to her daughter about marriage: "it's not just a man. It's your house, your kids, your family, your time, everything. Everything in your life is who you marry" (318). Ann T. Jones underscores this message in *A Country Divorce* (1992). Set in Ireland during the 1930s, Jones tells the story of confirmed bachelor Morgan Riley's marriage to Minnie Vaughn, who neglects to tell him she is pregnant by another man. Needless to say, when the truth is revealed, the marriage is over. Susanna Moore's third Hawaiian novel, *Sleeping Beauties* (1993), which includes scenes of domestic violence, reiterates these messages: marry your own kind.

Even in the 1990s, attitudes toward marriage and divorce reflected Irish American women's conflicted relationship with the Catholic Church. Despite reservations about the church's dictums, 85 percent of American Catholics continued to attend Mass regularly and millions were outraged at Sinead O'Connor's symbolic shredding of the Pope's picture on *Saturday Night Live*—even though she did it to protest the Irish prohibitions on contraceptives, abortion, and divorce (Almeida 2001). At the same time, 90 percent of American Catholics refused to support the ban on artificial contraception and the majority disagreed with the bar on divorce (Dezell 2001, 163). Thus it is somewhat surprising that in novels describing abusive spouses and unhappy marriages, many characters remain unhappily married; less surprising is the fact that among those who divorce, the children suffer.

In Jean McGarry's *The Courage of Girls* (1994), Loretta Costello St. Cyr is married to the domineering Daniel. Although he swears he loves her, Daniel continually demeans her, then is surprised that she remains "like a corpse" when they have sex (17). Although Loretta leaves him for awhile, she eventually returns. There is no hint that their lives will be different, but Loretta will persevere, for—in a line echoing Maureen Howard's *Facts of Life*—she has decided "just to resign myself to nothing" (81). Susan Minot's novels continue this sad song. In her second novel, *Folly* (1992), Lilian Eliot Finch (like Edna Pontillier in the *The Awakening*) is confined by the strictures proscribing women's behavior. Since *Folly* is set amidst World War I, just eighteen years after *The Awakening*, these mores are not surprising, especially in staid Boston society. Like Mrs. Pontillier, Lilian awakens when she experiences sexual desire for the enigmatic Walter Vail. But after Walter goes off to war without a word, Lilian marries Gilbert Finch. Lilian's folly is in holding on to her infatuation with Vail throughout her marriage until finally, at middle age, she sees the man for what he is.

In developing her plot, Minot appears to draw on Mary McCarthy's *The Group*. Although Minot is not primarily concerned with skewering her characters, she too exposes the emptiness of lifestyles centered around childcare and homemaking. As in *The Group*, Minot's novel traces the lives of Lilian and her girlfriends as they fall in love, marry, flourish or fail, with Lilian (like McCarthy's Kay Petersen) at the center. Since only one of Lilian's friends has attended college, their aspirations are not so high as McCarthy's Vassar graduates; nevertheless, over the course of the novel Minot exposes similar themes: alcoholism, depression, adultery, and man's inconstancy. Lilian has learned to tolerate it, but her friend Irene cannot. Increasingly drunk, she (again, like Kay Peterson) appears to commit suicide. In a conclusion reflecting the fin de siècle tendency away from the closure of a happy marriage, the novel's final pages find Lilian vowing to stay with Gilbert. Nevertheless, she says: "I don't have to like it, and if you come right down to it, I won't. But at least I won't moon after things. My parents did not raise me to behave like a fool" (278).

This message is echoed in Eileen Fitzgerald's *You're So Beautiful* (1996). Throughout, Fitzgerald's characters reflect on their past and present lives, conjure violent revenge scenarios, and fantasize about escape. All are realistic, for none reach satisfactory conclusions; they simply end, a strategy that reinforces the sense that they are trapped, their only escape through death or dreams. In *Lies of the Saints* (1996), Erin McGraw similarly deconstructs marital relationships. In "Blue Skies," for example, Ray and Constance struggle with the aftermath of alcoholism—sobriety and distrust, respectively—taking a realistic look at the damage a suspicious spouse can wreak on a relationship as well as the difficulties of letting go and rebuilding. In *House Work* (1994), Kristina MacGrath underscores the impact of the church on unhappy marriages. The schizophrenic Guy Hallissey cannot cope with his wife, his three children, or even his furniture, which he believes is moving. When Guy's illness escalates into carousing, wife Anna takes the children and leaves—an unsanctioned act in the days before divorce and working wives. "'Mrs.,' said Father Rawley. He would consider excommunication. 'Your place is with him,' he told her, 'He's a good man'" (74).

Bobbie Ann Mason's 1990's books also focus on marriage. Her memoir, *Clear Springs* (1998), pays homage to her mother, an orphan raised by her aunt's family. Details from this work appear in practically every novel. *Feather Crowns* (1993) is set in the rural Kentucky of Mason's grandparents and extended family, thus reminding readers of the harsh, hard scrabble lifestyle of tobacco farmers. *Spence + Lila* is a fictional version of Mason's parents' marriage, set (like Maeve Brennan's) in the same house—a foursquare, built by her father—outside Mayfield, Kentucky, where Mason grew up. Again like Brennan, the novel includes specific factual details, such as her mother's decision to work outside the home as well as the characters' superstitions and unschooled patois reflecting a "lowland Scots" heritage (Mason 1998, 38). In these settings she pursues timeless feminist themes: the guilt of sexual desire, the community of women, the demands of motherhood, the burden of grief (and concomitant guilt) on a relationship, the need for communication, and the effort necessary to make a marriage work.

Motherhood and, more subtly, abortion are addressed in Ann Patchett's *The Patron Saint of Liars* (1992). In a 2011 interview with *The Guardian*, Patchett mentioned that she had no desire to have children. "I never wanted children, never, not for one minute, and it has been the greatest gift of my life that even as a young person I knew. . . . Children are wonderful but they're not for everybody" (Rustin 2011). *The Patron Saint of Liars* explores this conundrum. Rose Clinton is married to a man she does not love, so when she becomes pregnant she leaves him because she believes she would not be a good mother, traveling to St. Elizabeth's Home for Unwed Mothers to put her child up for adoption—which does not trouble her as much as the prospect of leaving once she has given birth. Fortuitously, the home's groundskeeper proposes and agrees to raise the child as his own. The novel's last section describes the impact of Rose's unmaternal feelings on her daughter, Sissy. "We'd never gotten along," Sissy notes. "It wasn't that we fought, exactly. We hadn't even progressed that far. . . . The unspoken pact was that we ignored each other" (249). Although this is uttered casually, it is clear that Sissy misses her mother's love. Using multiple points of view, Patchett explores both the physical and psychological sides of maternity. Jacqueline Carey's second novel, *The Other Family* (1996), similarly reinforces the edict against divorce by looking at its effects—anger, depression, and drugs—on the children. As the abandoned daughter Joan Toolan says, "Once upon a time the center of my life had been firm. . . . All this came unmoored when our mother left us" (Carey 1996, 12–13). When her cousins' family similarly disintegrates, they echo her anger: "'How did you stand it when your parents split up?' Budge asks. 'I wish they would both die'" (185). Although this is a novel with a strong comic sense, its message about marriage and mothers comes through strongly.

Alice McDermott's *At Weddings and Wakes* (1992) and *Charming Billy* (1999) offer up more unhappy marriages. In the former, she uses a member of the third or fourth generation of Irish immigrants to deconstruct her family members' unhappiness. The narrator is one of the Dailey children—a daughter, like most of McDermott's narrators—who listens to her mother, aunts, and step-grandmother and observes their angry, eventually tearful interactions. As in her previous novels, McDermott fractures timelines, moving between present and past to develop a fuller picture, but also "to support more largely thematic concerns regarding the impact of time on memory and the story-making that is not only memory's key function but also a hallmark of the Irish American literary tradition" (Jacobson 2008, 123).

These images emerge throughout the course of the Dailey children's biweekly, day-long summer treks with their mother from the suburbs into New York City, highly detailed reversals of the Irish emigration as they move "west to east" (McDermott 1992, 55), from the New World back to the Old as personified by their aunts and grandmother. Behind each woman lies a sad story. Their grandmother, Momma Towne, married the aunts' father only to have him die within the year, so she "quickly became not merely a stranger to resent and accommodate but the only living adult to whom they were of any value" (27). Capitalizing upon these circumstances, Momma Towne quickly takes on the characteristics of the "martyred, manipulative Irish mother" (Dezell 2001, 104). Aunt May, a former nun, finally marries and then dies four days later. Aunt Agnes is an executive secretary who, lacking a husband or a vocation, has devoted herself to studying "the finer things" and "in her misanthropy . . . found all else, all the soiled, dull, and tasteless things about humankind, somehow appalling" (McDermott 1992, 111). A spinster, Aunt Veronica has descended into alcoholism.

But the children's mother—the only married sister—suffers the most. Each visit begins with her usual laments. "But who thinks of me?" (25). "He's not the man I married. . . . I'm not having the kind of life I wanted" (34–35). The plaints escalate until, mixed with late afternoon cocktails, the arguing begins, each woman believing her life the worst, and ends with sobbing. "Too many women in too small a place, they would say later . . . or, later still, too much repression, too much pity, too much bad luck. And then finally, convinced they'd hit the mark at last, too much drink" (124). The enervating Old World ends with the husband's arrival. Although he has been the object of scorn throughout the day, only he can save them—a dynamic that clearly parallels the housewife's malaise described by Friedan in *The Feminine Mystique*.

This novel marks the last of McDermott's explicitly feminist works. Henceforth—perhaps as she moved into middle age, perhaps in a reflection of the nation's anti-feminist move toward the fin de siècle—her novels grow darker yet more hybridized. Also set in New York's Irish American community, McDermott's *Charming Billy* (1999) traces the relationships between Billy and his long-suffering wife, Maeve; between Billy and the supposedly deceased Eva; between the narrator's father, Dennis, and his first wife Claire; between Dennis and Maeve; and between the narrator's grandmother and her two husbands, Uncle Dan and Mr. Holtzman—framed by the community's mourning of Billy's death by telling stories of his life. In this case, death and disintegration are due to the "Irish flu"—alcoholism—a disease more prevalent among Irish Americans than among the Irish themselves, presumably as a means of preserving ethnic identity. Despite the church's general sanction of drinking, its concomitant "grim theology of fear" has perpetuated such strong feelings of guilt and self loathing that among members of Alcoholics Anonymous they are distinguished as CIA, "Catholic Irish Alcoholic" (Dezell 2001, 118–24).

"Charming" Billy never gets that far. Billy is not a hero nor is his death heroic—on the sidewalk, his stomach bloated, his skin discolored by cirrhosis—yet he is fondly and sentimentally recalled. A more likely hero is Dennis, Billy's cousin and best friend who repeatedly drags him home and carries him to bed. But Dennis is also something of a cad. Although he matures to become a responsible husband and father, early on he seduces Eva's sister Mary with promises of marriage, treats her disrespectfully after she succumbs, and then breaks his promise after learning that Eva has married someone else. Perhaps the most heroic character is Dennis's father, Uncle Dan, the streetcar driver who gave dozens of newly arrived "Paddys" a home until they could afford their own. These characters are all engaging, but the female characters are equally interesting.

The majority of the narrative is told by Dennis's married daughter, Mrs. West. Unlike her Irish and Irish American predecessors (such as Mary Gordon's Isabel Moore), Mrs. West makes a conscious decision *not* to be "the girl child wedded to the widowed father." She goes away to college instead of attending a local university and "took only short breaks during the summer so that my father would know I had a life of my own. . . . Self-sacrifice having been recognized as a delusion by then, not a virtue" (McDermott 1999, 153). After she marries, she and her husband move to Seattle. In other words, both her name and locale identify her as representative of third-generation Irish Americans—much like McDermott herself—determined to assimilate, firmly rooted in the "West."

Billy's widow, Maeve, demonstrates a modicum of agency. Although she had been "the girl child wedded to the widowed [alcoholic] father" (153), Maeve actively pursues Billy until he catches her. But after she marries Billy her independence disappears as she slips even deeper into co-dependency. She enables Billy's drinking, calling Dennis to help carry him in, cleaning up after him, enduring "a thousand and one moments she would never recount, things he had said to her, terrible things he had done, ways she had seen him (toothless, incoherent, half-clothed, bloodied, soiled, weeping) that she couldn't begin to tell"—including the time "he had her by the throat" (182–83). Because this revelation is followed by a description of Billy's weepy contrition, it becomes a throwaway line, quickly buried beneath fonder reminiscences.

Maeve suffers not only Billy's alcoholism but also comparisons to Eva, his former fiancé. To many of their friends, Eva's tragic death is the reason Billy drinks, although Dennis (and the reader) know better. Eva is an example of agency gone wrong. Although she never professes her love for Billy, she accepts his engagement ring. Then she returns to Ireland, marries another man, and uses the money Billy sends for her return passage to buy a gas station for her husband. When Billy discovers her duplicity thirty years later, Eva is still running the business. Through her character, McDermott symbolizes the disappointment felt by some Irish American immigrants toward Ireland as well as the sentimental view held by others. Eva's sister Mary represents a more realistic view as well as a more positive example. As a teenager, she emigrates to America alone and finds work as a nanny. Upon learning her sister has deceived Billy, she cuts all ties; eventually she earns a college degree, becomes a teacher, and remains in the States. Mary personifies the young Irish female immigrants who comprised the majority of America's teachers in the early twentieth century (Nolan 2004).

Considerably more complex and stronger-willed is Dennis's mother, known as Mrs. Holtzman, representative of the Scots-Irish immigrants. An orphan, she is farmed from relative to relative, supporting herself at a bakery until she quite pragmatically decides to escape by marrying Dan Lynch.

After he dies, she meets and marries Holtzman—not for love, but because of his financial holdings. Mrs. Holtzman sees through the Irish sentimentality: "She could dismantle a pose with a glance and deflate the most romantic notion with a single word . . . and she sought truth so single-mindedly that under her steady gaze exaggeration, self-delusion, bravado simply dried up and blew away, as did hope, nonsense, and any ungrounded giddiness" (McDermott 1999, 45–45). She is clearly the toughest character in the novel; however, by contrasting her with the Irish Catholics, her toughness becomes equated with hardness and so she appears less than them.

In these couples' relationships and the Irish American community's gathering, we find feminist themes of connection, community, and hope for the future. Ironically, these emerge out of a narrative formed around drunkenness, deception, and domestic violence. While such opposites suggest that the title is not to be taken literally, they could also be interpreted as the Irish preference for fiction over fact. Adding to these dichotomies are role reversal—using a female rather than a male storyteller—as well as the interwoven themes of faith and sentimentality (Hagan 2010, 217–18). Billy clings to his faith to assuage Eva's loss, yet his belief in her has always been romanticized. Dennis leaves the church after his wife's death, but maintains his devotion to Billy. His mother, the formerly pragmatic Mrs. Holtzman, develops faith in her dying days. In the novel's closing pages, the narrator explains, "Their faith—all of them, I suppose—was no less keen than their suspicion that in the end they might be proven wrong. And their certainty that they would continue to believe anyway" (243). Such schizophrenia provides an apt metaphor for the century's end.

✳

America's struggles with feminism in the 1990s reflected previous fin de siècle upheavals: "The death throes of a diseased society and the winding down of an exhausted culture . . . the breakdown of the family, the decline of religion, the women's liberation and gay rights movement; the drug epidemic; and the redefinition of the humanities" signaled—at least to the right wing—"a waning culture" (Showalter 1990, 1–2). But embedded within these portents lay a positive message, for all signs of doom were linked to the growth of feminism, a contradiction familiar to the unruly feminist movement. Just as the 1890s were viewed optimistically by first-wave feminists, the 1990s ended with a determination among second-wavers to hold fast to their "quest for personal autonomy and quality" (Segal 1999, 229).

By the end of the twentieth century, women's novels were no longer monolithic tales, as their stories expanded along with their world views. From "sex wars" to sex change, from new versions of the family romance to "altered definitions of the erotic," the fin de siècle female novelist addressed new theories regarding the social construction of gender and the mutability of identity, as well as the impossibility of closure. In sum, second-wave feminists took traditional themes, plots, and characters beyond canonical (male) conventions and made them their own. Such changes underscore "the magnitude of the societal disruptions associated with the evolution of feminism in this century" (Gilbert and Gubar 1989, 360–76).

6

The New Millennium

End of an Era?

> There was this attitude of, "Oh, we don't need to hire women anymore." It was almost like throwing a switch and we were back in the 50s. Across the country I was seeing what I saw decades ago.
> —Susan Faludi, *The Terror Dream* (2007)

For many Americans, the al-Qaida attack on 9/11 marked the end of an era. Although the Taliban had bombed American targets before and George W. Bush had been warned they would strike again, 9/11 made the terrorist threat a reality. In the aftermath, research abounded on Arabs, Muslims, and Islam; terror and terrorism; and to a lesser extent, the impact on health and safety. But 9/11 also brought about some surprisingly contradictory changes:

- Although the U.S. government was the Taliban's target, the Bush administration responded by attacking women's rights.
- While some pundits reacted with a return to the church, others believed 9/11 marked the end of an era for Catholics.
- Whereas a grateful public embraced Irishness as personified by the New York police and firefighters, New Irish emigrants were suddenly personae non grata.

Even more surprising was the response of Irish American women writers. Rather than fighting the latest feminist backlash, their novels and short stories reflected the nation's schizophrenia. As women became the targets of post-terrorist rage, a wave of post-feminist romance, detective, and fantasy novels emerged featuring upper-middle-class spunky Irish American heroines who overcame all the odds only to marry. As the media urged women to return to domesticity, formerly feminist writers began championing home and hearth, marriage and motherhood. In response to the devotional revolution, some second-wave feminists who had criticized the church began proselytizing. Others simply sidestepped the issue. Following the logic of Emma Donoghue, who defended her historical novels by noting that "'new' material . . . is often best delivered to a wide readership in what seems like comfortingly old-fashioned forms" (quoted in Moloney and Thompson 2003, 175)—a number of Irish American second-wavers retreated to memoir and historical fiction.

Nevertheless, as the decade progressed, loyal second-wavers continued to remind readers that women's rights were fragile, while angry third-wavers—clearly tired of being viewed as delicate flowers—loudly proclaimed their independence by revealing a generation of young women suffering from anger, depression, and low self-esteem. Finally, as the nation tired of Bush-era greed, dishonesty, and warmongering, Irish American women writers drew on their long tradition of satire to remind readers that there was more to life than money and that these women, at least, had had enough of post-9/11 intimidation.

Pushing Feminism off the Map

According to Susan Faludi, many of the nation's pundits and leaders viewed the collapse of the Twin Towers as "a symbol of the nation's 'emasculation.'" Analyses of post-9/11 dreams revealed men's fixations on "the dreamer's shame" whereas women's dreams dwelled on the fear of "masculine violence invading [their] lives" (2007, 9–11).[1] Unfortunately, they were right. As the sociologist Barbara Finlay recounts, immediately after taking office, George Bush—like Ronald Reagan—had begun removing liberal women from administrative positions and dismantling feminist gains. Shortly after his inauguration, he started "restructuring units whose missions affect women, changing enforcement of policies that protect women, appointing conser-

---

1. See also Kelly Bulkeley, *Dreams of Healing* (New York: Paulist Press, 2003); and James Gibbons, "The September 11 Dream Project," http://www.hungryghost .net/dream/dreampjtinnit.html.

vatives to policy positions, and redefining missions of women's programs"
(2006, 13). Although Bush was praised for his high-profile female appointees—such as Secretary of Labor Elaine Chao, Secretary of Agriculture Ann
Veneman, Secretary of the Interior Gale Norton, EPA Director Christine
Todd Whitman, and Communications Director Karen Hughes—Chao,
Veneman, and Norton were conservatives, and Whitman soon resigned in
frustration. Like Reagan and Bush senior, George W. Bush's percentage of
white female appointees overall hovered at about 25 percent; black women
appointees were even scarcer (Tessier 2002).

The Bush administration also ignored women's input regarding female
appointees, thus nullifying a quarter century of political progress (Finlay
2006, 14). Although she was a Republican, the Irish American Roselyn
O'Connell, president of the National Women's Political Caucus (NWPC)
and chair of the 2001 Women's Appointments Project, publicly and repeatedly expressed dismay about the administration's failure to recognize women,
lamenting, "It's a signal that we're just not that important" (Tessier 2001,
n.p.). Indeed, within weeks of Bush's inauguration, the Interagency Council
on Women, the Equal Pay Matters Initiative, and the White House Office
on Women's Initiatives and Outreach were eliminated. Luckily, attempts to
close offices of the Women's Bureau of the Department of Labor, the Wom-
en's Educational Equity Act programs, and the Women's Military Advisory
Committee were unsuccessful, as were efforts to halt federal workers' contraceptive coverage and weaken Title IX. Nevertheless, in every case the agencies' funding was cut, and in many instances Bush cronies were appointed to
run women's agencies, while information was either omitted or disinforma-
tion posted on women's reproductive health sites (Finlay 2006, 15–23).

If the Towers had not been attacked, the public and the media might
have taken issue with these actions. Instead, the nation succumbed to "a
symbolic war at home, a war to repair and restore a national myth . . . our
fixation on restoring an invincible manhood by saving little girls" (Faludi
2007, 13). The press not only capitulated, but also took the mission a step
further, crowing that the tragedy "pushe[d] feminism off the map" and her-
alding "the return of the manly man" and his partner, the devoted homemaker. Such attitudes led feminist historian Susan Faludi to write: "Of all
the peculiar responses our culture manifested to 9/11, perhaps none was

more incongruous than the desire to rein in a liberated female population. In some murky fashion, women's independence had become implicated in our nation's failure to protect itself" (2007, 20–21).

In the immediate aftermath of 9/11, a wave of Irish American trade novels took that attitude a step further by implying that feminism was no longer necessary. Post-feminist writers conflated Bush-era neoconservative politics pertaining to gender and sexuality with more progressive movements, arguing either that feminism had been attained and was now a matter of common sense, or that feminism had been attained but should be repudiated (McRobbie 2007, 28). These novels valorized "female achievement within traditionally male working environments and the celebration of surgical and other disciplinary techniques that 'enable' (i.e., require) women to maintain a youthful appearance and attitude in later life" (Tasker and Negra 2007, 1–2). Such beliefs perpetuated the racist, ageist, and classist distinctions characteristic of patriarchal thinking, for clearly not every woman was able to maintain such a lifestyle.

Although post-feminism values individualism, "this formulation tends to confuse self-interest with individuality and elevates consumption as a strategy for dealing with those dissatisfactions that might alternatively be understood in terms of social ills and discontents."[2] Post-feminist culture assumes and promotes equal educational opportunities as well as "freedom of choice with respect to work, domesticity, and parenting; and physical and particularly sexual empowerment" (Tasker and Negra 2007, 2)—again, rights fought for by feminists and now assumed to be givens. These in turn lead to the assumption that rather than needing to work, women might merely *choose* to work, yet another example of post-feminist culture generally excluding women of color or lower social class. Equally troubling is the post-feminist "othering" of feminism—the assumption that it is difficult, shrill, and restrictive.

As might be expected from nonliterary works aimed at the general public, early twenty-first-century Irish American mystery and romance novels

---

2. Recall George W. Bush's advice to go shopping to overcome the trauma of 9/11.

reflect many of these assumptions. Since the writers are of Irish American descent, the female leads are white, educated, and at least middle class. In this they are representative of their generation: "college educated suburbanites who disagree with Church teachings on social issues" and are more likely to associate "IRA" with their retirement accounts than with their ancestors (Dezell 2001, 35). These heroines are "vital, youthful, and playful while [their] opposite number, the 'bad' female professional, is repressive, deceptive, and deadly" (Tasker and Negra 2007, 9).

Among the mystery writers are Karin Ficke Cooke,[3] Diana O'Hehir, and Nevada Barr, whose female sleuths are seemingly free to stop work at the first hint of homicide to track down the perpetrator. Among the romance novelists, Sarah Dunn's and Kristin Hannah's heroines fall into the "Sex in the City" category of independent young women looking for love in New York. Megan McCafferty focuses on teenage angst, a white middle-class luxury as well as a staple of post-feminism's "chick lit" youth fetish. The heroes in Christina Dodd's "Darkness Chosen" series are usually upper-middle-class shape-shifters. Similarly, Christine Feehan writes about vampires, who generally do not hold jobs. Vampires are, however, almost always white and they are timeless, yet another element of post-feminism. Post-feminist writers are obsessed with youth and temporality; vampirism takes care of that (Wearing 2007). All of these characters remain firmly entrenched within a post-feminist sensibility that does not reject feminism so much as ignore it (Tasker and Negra 2007, 21).

The unfortunate epitome of post-feminist novels is J. Courtney Sullivan's *Commencement* (2009), mistakenly considered by some as the twenty-first-century counterpart to Mary McCarthy's *The Group*. Structurally there are a number of parallels. Both novels feature a group of young women, best friends in college and as adults. Both narratives move from past to present, between Smith and Vassar, respectively, and life in New York, settings generally requiring characters to be white members of the upper class. As in *The Group*, *Commencement*'s chapters alternate between a group of friends—in

---

3. Karin Ficke Cook's mysteries should be distinguished from Karin Cook's coming-of-age novel, *What Girls Know*.

this case Bree, Sally, April, and Celia—and the novel begins with Celia's anticipation of Sally's postgraduation wedding, just as *The Group* begins with Kay's. One of the characters, Bree (like McCarthy's Lakey), is a lesbian who only belatedly accepts her sexuality. Like McCarthy's Polly, Celia is the only Catholic and ultimately the most positive character; like McCarthy, she is also an atheist and an aspiring novelist.

But *Commencement* is not *The Group*. Whereas the women in *The Group* are torn between their feminist aspirations and the confines of reality, the women in *Commencement* take feminism for granted. As Sally says: "They recognized that they were the first generation of women whose struggle with choice had nothing to do with getting it and everything to do with having too much of it—there were so many options that it felt impossible and exhausting to pick the right ones" (Sullivan 2009, 139). This line sounds like the perfect entrée for a bit of Irish American satire, but *Commencement* takes itself seriously. It is not a satire, nor does Sullivan mimic her friends' conversations or situations. Although some critics maintained that they were "strong, warmly believable three-dimensional characters" (Maslin 2009, 25), apart from their names and varied familial concerns, all but April sound identical. Indeed, some statements verge "on the banal" (Russo 2009, 8). In her blurb for *Commencement*, Gloria Steinem compares Sullivan to McCarthy, noting that Sullivan "adds a new feminist generation." Nevertheless, she continues, these characters "make clear that the feminist revolution is just beginning"—again!

Among the four women April is the only practicing feminist, yet she is dismissed as a radical. Through April's story important women's issues— rape, domestic abuse, prostitution, genital mutilation, and sex trafficking— are raised. But "even most Smith feminists thought she was too strident, which was really saying something" (Sullivan 2009, 38). After graduation, Sally marries Jake, jettisons plans for medical school, and has a baby. Her constant chatter about their connubial bliss causes Bree—who had been planning her wedding since age fifteen—to snap. "The extent of Bree's disappointment shocked her. It felt almost physical, like a broken rib poking through the skin, so that every time her thoughts twisted this way or that, a horrible pain spread through her whole body" (54). She feels the pain because she is in love with Lara, but "she still wished for a normal life, for the kind of love that would please her parents" (77), a story line perhaps familiar to other women in that situation.

Meanwhile, April begins working for Ronnie Munro, a militant feminist who insists on April's complete obedience—to the point of faking her own death—and then uses the news to promote her latest documentary about prostitution, a story line the *New York Times* critic Maria Russo dismisses as "preposterous": "It reads like a parody of Andrea Dworkin-style, all-men-are-rapists feminism, and yet the novel is too earnest and timid to question the blinkered viewpoint April develops" (2009, 8). Although the girls acknowledge that Ronnie is crazy, her self-interest and disregard for April's well-being cast feminist activists in a negative light. Indeed, "Ronnie was the sort of icon you loved if you were a militant, and loathed if you were just your average run-of-the-mill feminist" (Sullivan 2009, 267).

Celia Donnelly (the author's persona) is the lucky one. Initially, she worries about finding a man so she can quit working and write novels, but slowly she starts to question that path. "Marriage wasn't security. . . . Nor did it necessarily mean happiness" (Sullivan 2009, 211). Eventually she realizes "There was a very real possibility that no one was coming to save her. She would have to make her own plan. If she wanted to someday leave her job and write books, then she'd have to write books to do it, not wait around for some hedge fund guy to finance her fantasies" (213). Similarly, Sullivan published her first novel while writing for *The New York Times*.

But the *Times* critics were fairly critical of their colleague: "This undertow of denial and avoidance is unfortunate in a novel with so much verve, making it feel overly tame, as if Sullivan wants to soothe and reassure her characters rather than letting them face the truths that might have elevated *Commencement* into a league with . . . that paragon of women's college novels, *The Group*" (Russo 2009, 8). Indeed, *Commencement's* failure to interrogate the characters' behavior or even to question it via satire places it firmly within the post-feminist category.

Recall that post-feminist culture valorizes "female achievement within traditionally male working environments." Bree is a lawyer, Celia is a writer, Sally wants to be a doctor, and April is a lackey for the documentary filmmaker Ronnie. These are upper-middle-class positions unavailable to many women. Post-feminism values individualism, but "this formulation tends to confuse self-interest with individuality"—and everyone but April has her own interests at heart. Post-feminist culture assumes and promotes equal educational opportunities, but it also believes in "freedom of choice with respect to work, domesticity, and parenting; and physical and particularly sexual empowerment"—again, rights fought for by feminists now taken for granted. Rather than needing to work, post-feminist women like Sally and Bree *choose* to work—or not—when prostrate with grief. Finally, post-feminism assumes that feminism is difficult, shrill, and restrictive—traits that characterize April and Ronnie Munro.

Despite her personal disregard for feminism, Mary McCarthy not only exposed societal inequities but also opened the door for future Irish American feminist novels. In contrast, Sullivan's novel reveals a complacent feminism, which is just another term for post-feminism. These characters are more interested in their own lives than those of women in less comfortable environments; indeed, Sullivan's women worry more about April's feminist activities than the problems she tries to expose. Worse, there is no sense of satire or irony in Sullivan's rendering of their concerns. Feminism no longer merits attention.

With the 2000 election of George W. Bush, a version of this mindset had already begun to emerge among the conservative Right, but 9/11 somehow gave it legitimacy. Although most people dismissed Jerry Falwell's proclamation that "the pagans, and the abortionists, and the feminists, and the gays and the lesbians helped [9/11] happen," his message was soon promoted by mainstream mouthpieces (Faludi 2007, 22; Finlay 2006, 3). Denouncements of feminism might be expected from the Bush administration, but soon respected pundits such as Jonathan Alter and Jonathan Turley not only took up the cry but also attacked any women brave enough to offer counter opinions. Journalists and intellectuals such as Susan Sontag, Katha Pollitt, Barbara Kingsolver, and Naomi Klein were publicly castigated as Taliban supporters simply for expressing their wish that war be avoided and cooler heads prevail (Faludi 2007, 29–30). In *George W. Bush and the War on Women*, a study that demonstrates the many parallels between the Bush and Reagan administrations, the sociology professor and feminist scholar Barbara Finlay joins Faludi in calling out Bush for fomenting such behavior, noting that the mainstream media were so enmeshed in the administration's jingoism that they not only let such comments pass but also failed to "analyse his actions critically and ignor[ed] contradictory evidence" (Finlay 2006, 3).

Female commentators were not the only targets. By 2004, the nation's mindset reflected the post–World War II antiwoman propaganda reported by Betty Friedan and Susan Hartmann. First, female writers disappeared from the nation's editorial pages. Within a week of 9/11, only 5 of 88 op-ed pieces in *The New York Times, The Washington Post,* and *The Los Angeles Times* carried female bylines. Although women writers had never dominated these pages, in *The New York Times* their numbers dropped from an average of 22 percent before 9/11 to 9 percent in the weeks following, whereas *The Washington Post* featured only seven women out of 107 editorials. Even *The Nation* was in league: the October 8, 2001 issue was all-male (Faludi 2007, 35–36). As the Irish American journalist Caryl Rivers observed, "If you're a regular reader of [*The Atlantic*], which I am, you'd think that some sort of plague had decimated the female population. Between December 2001 and December 2002, for example, I found 38 major articles by men and seven by women. . . . The essays were even worse. During this period, I found 41 essays by men and two by women. Or to be precise, two essays by the same woman. For the *Atlantic*, Margaret Talbot represented all of womanhood" (2003).

The "shunning" of women in the media continued for several years. From January through June 2002, over three-quarters of the Sunday morning talk shows "featured *no* female guests." By 2005, women were still missing on the editorial pages of major newspapers, comprising only 10.4 percent of the bylines at *The Washington Post* and 16.4 percent at *The New York Times* (Faludi 2007, 37). As late as 2006, women were still grossly underrepresented. In a *New York Magazine* special issue, "What If 9/11 Never Happened?" featuring responses from eighteen pundits, only two women were represented—the Irish American historian Doris Kearns Goodwin and the Slate correspondent Dahlia Lithwick—and they received considerably less space than their male counterparts (Heilemann 2006). Just as the Bush administration had managed to ignore the plight of the poor and minorities, women's rights were now "largely dismissed as being unimportant or insignificant by mainstream opinion leaders" (Finlay 2006, 4).

When women tried to call positive attention to their patriotic efforts, such as the documentary *The Women of Ground Zero,* they were disregarded.

As Brenda Berkman notes, "'I've been a firefighter for 20 years and I've never seen the contributions of women firefighters, police officers and paramedics so completely ignored. Suddenly we've become invisible." Even worse was the reaction to the film. The noted liberal jurist Jonathan Turley actually accused the filmmakers of mining the tragedy "for aggrieved heroes who would carry a banner of division" (quoted in Faludi 2007, 81–82). When the movie was released across the country, many people were outraged, most notably New York City firefighters. Although the department hired 308 new recruits to replace those killed in the Towers, not a single one was female. Similar backlash was evident among police officers. Said the first female police chief in Portland, Oregon, "There was this attitude of, 'Oh, we don't need to hire women anymore.' It was almost like throwing a switch and we were back in the 50s. Across the country I was seeing what I saw decades ago" (quoted in Faludi 2007, 85–86).

Despite the three-to-one ratio of male-to-female deaths in the Towers (Faludi 2007, 3), the media focused on the female victims. They ignored the women who walked down the stairs of the World Trade Center, the women who worked the day of the tragedy, the women who returned to their jobs after burying a family member. Instead, they singled out the 9/11 widows who "were at home that day tending to the hearth, models of all-American housewifery" (Faludi 2007, 93). This message was promulgated not only by the Right, but also by the mainstream media and representatives of the Left. An article in *The New York Times Magazine*, for example, suggested that the attacks made single women want to marry and married women want children. *Time* magazine announced that in the aftermath of the attack, Americans were returning to "our oldest values," among them "homecoming and housecleaning" as well as "couples renewing their vows," while *Time* magazine reported that matchmakers were overwhelmed with clients (Faludi 2007, 117, 122).

These headlines were reinforced by the nation's retailers. Just as post–World War II marketers emphasized labor-saving appliances for stay-at-home wives forced out of their jobs, advertisers were now advised to "dust off their old commercials and jingles . . . banking on the theory that post-9/11 Americans would want to retreat to fifties-era domesticity" (Faludi 2007, 135). Fashion reinforced the message by designing "Crisis Couture"—described by *The Washington Post* as "softer, without the hard edges and S&M sexuality of recent years." As recently as May 7, 2009, a *New York Times* article noted that post-9/11, "child-women were bowed and baby-dolled up to resemble decorative Easter eggs: newly and uptightly pregnant (a paragon of marital fidelity), half-crippled by feminine weakness and excess luxury, declawed and wholly dominated by the unstoppable twin libidos of war and Wall Street. Men's wear, in the meantime, flew its most ruthless semiotic pirate flags: pinstripes and camouflage—merciless prints altogether deaf to feminine pleading and blind to the suffering of tots. Clothing, in a symbiotic reflection of the times, told us that the men were to *have their way*" (Wilson 2004, E4, original emphasis).

Some Irish American women writers took this to heart. Pre-9/11, Mary McGarry Morris's novels featured tough but misunderstood heroines. The eponymous heroine in *Fiona Range* (2000) exemplifies the traditionally strong Irish American woman (Gott 2008, 172). Fiona is persistent, self-aware, and honest to a fault—perhaps Morris's most positive and successful heroine. But in *A Hole in the Universe* (2004), Morris's main character is Gordon Loomis, a slightly backward man convicted of murder. The novel traces Gordon's clumsy reacclimation to life outside prison, including his relationship with Delores Dufault. Delores is the real heroine of this book, but it is the desire for a family that drives her. This reification of family grows more profound in Morris's next novel, *The Lost Mother* (2005). Set during the Depression, Thomas and Margaret are themselves greatly depressed by the disappearance of their mother, Irene. Throughout, the children long for her return. In fact, this longing becomes a refrain. Margaret "didn't care if they stayed poor and had to live in a tent forever so long as they could be together again" (Morris 2004, 2). Thomas sobs, "His mother was gone, his house. . . . And here he sat bawling in their shadows because his whole life had changed and he couldn't do a thing to make it better" (18–19). Despite a happy ending—which includes a loving stepmother—the children never forget their mother. "For how could any of us not? . . . Even if you make that conscious effort, there is still the longing, the almost primitive need. In the marrow, the blood, the genes. What is so very amazing then is how she could walk out on her children and then betray them" (270).

Anna Quindlen's *Rise and Shine* (2006) represents another strong reaction to 9/11. Rather than continue her string of twentieth-century feminist novels such as *One True Thing* and *Black and Blue*, Quindlen explores what happens when the TV celebrity Meghan becomes so immersed in her career as a television talk show host that she is gob-smacked when her husband leaves her. A subplot concerns Meghan's sister, Bridget, a social worker in a long-term, happily childless relationship with an older man. Yet the novel concludes with Meghan leaving her job and finding love with a longtime admirer and Bridget happily pregnant. Unlike Quindlen, Beth Lordan and Bobbie Ann Mason have never written overtly feminist novels; however, they definitely move away from women's issues in their twenty-first-century works. In *But Come Ye Back* (2004), Lordan takes a retired Irish American couple to Ireland where they find new romances before they reconcile. The plot of Bobbie Ann Mason's *An Atomic Romance* (2005) falls right into the post-9/11 mindset regarding the need to marry and bear children. In fact, as the novel closes the main character actually thinks, "Something about the scene was like the unreality of a movie ending . . . the warm, phony wrap-up" (Mason 2005, 265). *Nancy Culpepper* repeats this message. As *The Chicago Tribune* blurb puts it, this novel "honors our ideas of home, and the efforts we make to keep it safe, to remake it and to find it again."

Following a string of feminist novels—as well as the recession—Jacqueline Carey[4] began catering to the public interest with *It's a Crime* (2008). In the tradition of Irish American women writers, Carey was perhaps the first to capitalize on the trend of developing chick lit heroines who "cope with recession woes" (La Perla 2004, E1).[5] Although *Chick Lit* (2005) authors

4. The novelist Jacqueline Carey shares her name with the historical romance writer Jacqueline Carey, author of the Kushiel fantasy series.

5. In keeping with the tradition established by Irish American women writers, Carey was the first to publicize the recession through her fiction. She was quickly *followed*, in 2009, by Tatiana Boncompagni's *Hedge Fund Wives*, Wendy Walker's *Social Lives*, Sarah Strohmeyer's *The Penny Pinchers Club*, Michelle Wildgen's *But Not for Long*, Karen Weinreb's *The Summer Kitchen*, and Jill Kargman's *The Ex-Mrs. Hedgefund*.

Mallory Young and Suzanne Ferris defend these works as "real women responding to real-world situations" the fact remains that independence emerges only after the money runs out (LaPerla 2004, E10). But Carol Gilligan represents the most dramatic reversal. Whereas her 1982 study, *In a Different Voice*, initiated feminist research on the psychology of women, the main character of her 2010 novel, *Kyra*, attempts suicide when her lover leaves and ultimately abandons her job and her career as an architect to follow him to Europe.

Summing up this trend, Faludi writes, "The myth of American invincibility required the mirage of womanly dependency, the illusion of a helpless family circle in need of protection from a menacing world. Without that show of feminine frailty, the culture could not sustain the other figment vital to the myth, of a nesting America shielded by the virile and vigilant guardians of its frontier" (145).[6]

The Devotional Revolution

In a 2008 essay, the theologian Paul Elie pronounced the twenty-first century the end of an era for Catholics. In the aftermath of 9/11, with the discovery of sexual predators and complicit bishops, Catholic culture was in disarray. You could see it in their writing: Catholic writers were "riven by the tension between 'an attraction to the holy and the disbelief in it,'" a stance that had driven them to be "more critical than creative." Rather than create new fiction, they "work[ed] with materials already at hand, using journalism, memoir, essay, narrative history, and historical fiction to make our story fresh and strange." Both the church and Catholic writers were "in arrested development together" (Elie 2008, 14–16). Recent Catholic history supports that view.[7]

---

6. Lest Faludi be dismissed as another radical feminist, it should be noted that five out of seven reviews from major news outlets found her research impressive and persuasive. Moreover, while the *Washington Post* reviewer David Greenburg suggests that Faludi's fears of feminism's demise would likely be disproven by the 2008 election of Hillary Clinton, it is now obvious that Greenburg was mistaken.

7. Little has changed since then: this charge was repeated as recently as 2012 in Kurt Anderson, "You Say You Want a Devolution?" *Vanity Fair*, January.

In his encyclical *2004 Letter to the Bishops of the Catholic Church on the Collaboration of Men and Women in the Church and the World*, the then-Cardinal Joseph Ratzinger "demeaned feminist theory as inimical to the common good of the church, the family, and society [and] argued against women's ordination," in the process revealing not only hostility to women but also to their accomplishments over the past four decades (Sister X 2009, n.p.). Such hostility ignored the argument that contemporary women could be both feminists and good Catholics (Cummings 2006). Indeed, a month later the Vatican decided to investigate the Leadership Conference of Women Religious. "Evidently the Vatican is concerned that the LCWR has not been forthcoming about the magisterium's teachings regarding the ordination of women, the relation of the Catholic Church to non-Christian religions, and the 'intrinsically disordered' nature of homosexual acts," wrote Sister X (n.p.).

The Vatican was not concerned with the nuns' quality of life, the diminishing number of women religious, or even its priestly predators and the $2 billion in related lawsuits; instead Rome worried that feminism might run rampant within the convent. Moreover, its "secretive, unfriendly, and one-sided" visitations suggested that among leaders of the Catholic Church, women were still not trustworthy. Its visiting "team" included no women and precluded the opportunity for any sisters to review the results. Most telling, Sister X so identified herself because she feared "disciplinary action" for speaking out. Meanwhile, as local dioceses ensured that retired priests received housing, medical care, and pensions, retired sisters were sometimes literally left out in the cold—yet the priests' caretakers were almost entirely female.

Ironically, while priests retain major positions of authority, women workers now run the American Catholic Church, comprising 80 percent of parish workers and roughly half of all diocesan, administrative, and professional posts. Women are the teachers and principals in the Catholic schools and the caretakers for the increasingly elderly population of Catholic sisters. At the post-secondary level, women are the administrators who have taken the lead in making higher education accessible for ethnic minorities. These women do not necessarily want to be priests. And while they might prefer that the Vatican change some rules, they are not put off by its intransigence. Rather, they choose what guidelines they will follow and ignore the others—as well as the Vatican (Dezell 2001, 177–85).

Eileen Myles's nonfiction novel, *Cool for You* (2000), reflects this mind-set with a vengeance. Like many of her twenty-first-century contemporaries, in particular the tradition practiced by lesbian writers (Zimmerman 1990, 50–51), Myles rejects the traditional narrative. In *Cool for You* she resists convention by blending genres and presenting herself sometimes as narrator, sometimes as character. This duality allows her to develop traditional Irish American themes of isolation and the paradox of memory, recounted in ironic and mocking tones, while at the same time exploring generally verboten issues surrounding sex and sexual identity. Myles herself is a hybrid, half Polish and half Irish American, Irish Catholic and lesbian, sometimes middle class and sometimes lower class, depending on the severity of her father's alcoholism. Needless to say, alcoholism is a staple of Irish and Irish American writing, but here too Myles blurs boundaries, describing her father as a "better" alcoholic than others, kind and loving rather than angry and loud. Perhaps because of this she tends to identify more with him than with her mother, who in turn perpetuates the stereotype of the distant Irish matriarch.

But Myles's primary targets are sexism and the church. In a scattershot style, she touches on various examples of the mistreatment of women—nuns, young girls, elderly ladies, her grandmother, herself—by the males in her life and the masculine hierarchy of the church. "I've often thought of a female Christ. Mostly the world can't take it . . . because of what a meaningless display female suffering simply is. If you belittle us in school, treat us like slaves at home, and finally, if you get a woman alone in bed just tell her she's all wrong, no matter what sex you are. . . . I mean if that's the way it usually goes for this girl what would be the point in seeing her half nude and nailed up? Where's the contradiction? Could that drive the culture for 2,000 years? No way. Female suffering must be hidden, or nothing can work. It's a man's world and a girl on a cross would be like seeing a dead animal in a trap" (Myles 2000, 15–16).

This degree of anger is unique among Irish American women writers. At the opposite extreme is Caitlin Macy's satire, *The Fundamentals of Play* (2000), which owes a great deal to Evelyn Waugh's *Brideshead Revisited*. But whereas Catholicism doomed the Brideshead progeny, in *Fundamentals* Catholicism is the hero's salvation. As in *Brideshead*, Macy's characters are privileged members of the upper class, attending the same private high schools and private colleges. These characters parallel the roles set out by Waugh. The narrator and "poor" friend is George Lenham. Playing the part of the wealthy drunken best friend is Chat Wethers. The much-sought-after love interest is the coolly uninterested Kate Goodenow. Waugh's American Rex Motram and winner of Kate's hand is Harry Lombardi, a "foreigner" to this set in that he has chosen to drop out of college. "Kate would cotton to that fact—his dropping out—as much as I had. It was something new in her world, at least new in her New York world" (Macy 2000, 85). Just as Waugh's novel takes place before World War I changes society, *The Fundamentals of Play* is set in the early 1980s immediately prior to the Wall Street explosion inaugurated by the World Wide Web.

But the Irish American Macy reverses the religious onus. Whereas *Brideshead's* adamant Catholicism bred guilt and hypocrisy among the Brideshead offspring and served as an obstacle to the daughter's marriage to the divorced Motram, the Episcopalian New Yorkers of *Fundamentals* ridicule Harry for being Catholic. After he drunkenly monopolizes a conversation, George muses, "most people would have started apologizing for talking too much. But perhaps when confession is a part of your religion, it is only natural to want to run through the whole guilty spiel in front of an audience" (Macy 2000, 193). When Harry discovers that a casual encounter has resulted in the girl's pregnancy, he immediately takes responsibility and breaks off his engagement with Kate—who immediately snags another blue-blood and marries him the day she was to wed Harry. In this novel, it is the non-Catholics who come off poorly. As George says to Harry, "'You're going to be quite the martyr . . . I hate religious people'" (Macy 2000, 256–57).

More typical is Alice McDermott's *Child of My Heart* (2002). Written in response to the trauma of 9/11, the novel exemplifies Elie's fear that Catholics had developed an "attraction to the holy and the disbelief it." At the same time the novel suggests Irish Americans' disillusion with the Bush administration's profiteering, warmongering, and usurping of civil rights. As such, the novel can be viewed as a farce—especially after one realizes that the narrator is not an innocent fifteen-year-old girl but rather a middle-aged woman looking back on the summer of her deflowering (Hagan 2010, 191). Indeed, although McDermott moves away from her traditional theme of faith, recognition of this narrative voice leads to the realization that this is not about the innocence of childhood and the purity of nature. A modern-day bildungsroman, it traces the coming-of-age of Theresa, attained by losing her virginity and her young cousin, Daisy, in a single summer.

Whereas McDermott's previous works were set in Manhattan and Long Island, *Child of My Heart* moves out of the city to the safety of the Hamptons. Because this is an alien social milieu and her parents commute daily to the city, Theresa seems displaced in this rural, albeit beautiful, setting, which stands in stark contrast to the prevailing theme of death. Unlike McDermott's *Charming Billy*, here death is presented not as a cause for celebration of the afterlife but as stark and inevitable. After one of the neighbors' cats, Curly, is killed, Theresa recalls, "It was not Curly anymore, that lifeless thing Debbie had cradled, not in my recollection of it. It was the worst thing. It was what I was up against" (McDermott 2002, 169). Nor does Daisy's death lead to reflections on eternal life; rather, reflecting on its imminence, Theresa has "a flash of black anger that suddenly made me want to kick those damn cats off the bed and banish every parable, every song, every story ever told by me, about children who never returned" (179). Nature has supplanted religion; love and morality have been displaced by dispassionate curiosity, if not cynicism.

In this McDermott was an outlier, for a surprising number of Irish American writers returned their characters to the church after 9/11. In fact, her 2006 novel, *After This*, represents a cautious step in that direction. Like many Irish American post-9/11 novels, *After This* goes back in time—in this case, to post–World War II—to trace the growth of a family as it moves through the rest of the century and its changing mores. This setting allows McDermott to explore issues of sexuality, moving from a young Catholic couple's marriage through sex, childbirth, and child-rearing, and then through the daughter's unwed pregnancy and consideration of abortion, gently illustrating the illogic of the church's stance in the process. McDermott examines the cultural expectations surrounding motherhood and the restrictions of patriarchy, reprising early themes of family, parenthood, and Catholicism while demonstrating the many changes that have occurred in the church and society. Ultimately she concludes that while many things have changed, the basics remain the same: family is important; faith conquers grief.

This should come as no surprise, as such movement has historic parallels, particularly among the Irish. As Emmet Larkin explains, prior to the famine, "The growing awareness of a sense of sin already apparent in the 1840s was certainly deepened as God's wrath was made manifest in a great natural disaster that destroyed and scattered his people. Psychologically and socially, therefore, the Irish people were ready for a great evangelical revival" (1972, 639). This revival occurred after the famine when attendance at Mass increased from 33 percent in 1840 to 90 percent by 1850. Part of this increase was attributed to the Vatican's insistence on improving the morals and the examples set by the priests (just as it did following the pedophilia coverups in the late twentieth- and early twenty-first centuries). This "devotional revolution . . . provided the Irish with a substitute symbolic language and offered them a new cultural heritage with which they could identify and be identified and identify with one another" (649).

Pre-9/11, the American people were already suffering from a sense of guilt and trauma. Post-9/11, the cultural historian Diane Negra notes that Irishness—as well as a return to the church—was "mobilized to stave off an anxious, traumatized perception of American identity" (2006, 365). In sum, the devotional revolution was just as true of twenty-first-century Irish Americans as it was for nineteenth-century Irish. Following 9/11, church attendance increased by 25 percent, while 64 percent of Americans said religion was "very important" (Zelizer 2002, n.p.). Among American Catholics, weekly attendance at Mass rose from 33 percent in September 2000, to 36 percent by January 2001, to a high of 39 percent by February 2002, after which it declined to the previous average (CARA 2005). This return is reflected among Irish American women writers who prior to 9/11 were more likely to criticize than to embrace the church.

Erin McGraw's *The Baby Tree* (2000) takes on the church's stance regarding abortion and female clergy. The heroine, Kate Gussey, is a Methodist minister married to her second husband and living at the buckle of the Bible belt, southern Indiana. Obviously, Kate's character is designed to make a political statement. If she were Catholic, she could not be a priest, divorced, *or* remarried. Throughout, Kate's inner turmoil is foregrounded, thus positioning the book within the genres of the feminist novel and Irish American private lives. At the same time, Kate's external actions as pastor and protector of her flock cross the boundaries into the traditionally Irish American male arena of public life. Kate carries on the role of the priest who perceives "religion as an active force, literal as well as symbolic, in their lives" (Fanning 2001, 326). Indeed, in her "insistence on life's religious import and [her] avowed moral purposes," Pastor Kate continues the pattern established in the works of Andrew Greeley, Father John Roddan, John Boyce, William McDermott, and John Talbot Smith (316). Yet none of these men would be likely to defend a young woman's right to choose—and that is the crux of *The Baby Tree*.

But whereas *The Baby Tree* questioned the church's stance on female ministry and abortion, McGraw's post-9/11 collection, *The Good Life* (2004), finds solace in the institution. Perceiving her mother as the cause of her problems, Tracy (a recurring character) religiously reads her daily affirmations and writes best-selling psychobabble prescribing self-love exemplified in the mantra, "I have nothing to apologize for" (McGraw 2004, 107). However, when she is called home to help care for her mother, Tracy finds the affirmations childish against her mother's barrage of guilt trips. Ultimately, Tracy finds peace after attending Mass, where she weeps uncontrollably and forgives her mother. This response—recounted much more humorously than this rendering—sounds suspiciously like a return to the church, or at least an awareness of the need for faith in a higher power.

Lisa Carey's *In the Country of the Young* (2000), whose plot is reminiscent of Toni Morrison's *Beloved*, deals more with myth than religion as the ghost of a young Irish girl teaches a contemporary man to love. Conversely, Carey's *Every Visible Thing* (2006) suggests the negative effects of leaving the church as well as the positive effects of return. In the aftermath of their eldest child's disappearance, the Furey family is thrown into disarray. Too depressed to function, Mrs. Furey takes to her bed while Mr. Furey, a rising star at Boston College because of his research on angels, rejects those values. Throughout their parents' turmoil Lena and Owen, the two remaining children, fend for themselves. Lacking parental guidance as they move into adolescence, they search for identity in the hope that it will provide them answers. Ultimately it does, but not until the family rekindles its faith.

This resolution offers an interesting allegory for twenty-first-century Catholicism. As in Joyce Carol Oates's *We Were the Mulvaneys*, when a woman fails to fulfill her sacred obligation of motherhood, the entire family suffers. Yet even as they fall away from their faith, the church remains with them and guides them back to the fold. The novel's conclusion (as well as its title) suggests the role of faith in this reconciliation: *Every visible thing in this world is put in the charge of an angel* (Carey 2006, 305).

Confirming Elie's prediction, many Irish American women approached these themes laterally "using journalism, memoir, essay, narrative history, and historical fiction to make our story fresh and strange" (Elie 2008, 15). The first decade of the twenty-first century saw more than the average from Irish Americans. In 2005, Mary Gordon published *Pearl*, a Christian allegory set in Ireland. The pure and perfect martyr, Pearl is the daughter of Maria and (ostensibly) Joseph. Gordon's second memoir, *Circling My Mother* (2007), takes readers back to the glory days of the Catholic Church when priests were treated like kings. In 2009 she goes all the way with her nonfiction work, *Reading Jesus: A Writer's Encounter with the Gospel*, in which she ponders the contradictions and ambiguities raised in the books of Matthew, Mark, Luke, and John. The Pulitzer prizewinner Madeleine Blais's memoir, *Uphill Walkers* (2002), covers the same period but in a loving, humorous tone as she recalls the task faced by her widowed mother in raising and supporting her five girls, as well as the role of the church in keeping their heads above water. So does Maureen Waters's *Crossing Highbridge* (2007), in which she describes growing up as a girl in Brooklyn's Highbridge area in the 1930s and her gradual disillusionment with the church.

Like their Irish counterparts, Irish American women used memoir not only to establish their identity but also to place it within the context of their changing culture (Grubgeld 2004, xi). Indeed, the burgeoning of Irish American women's autobiographies following 9/11 suggests a setting parallel to that described by Shane Leslie in his 1916 memoirs: "the suicide of a civilisation called Christian and the travail of a new era to which no gods have been as yet rash enough to give their name" (quoted in Grubgeld 2004, xx). In *I Myself Have Seen It* (2003), Susanna Moore once again returns to Eden—her home state of Hawaii—to explore its vanishing past and avoid dealing with the sullied present. In her second memoir, *Light Years: A Girlhood in Hawaii* (2009), Moore focuses on her personal story (which bears great resemblance to her first three novels), interweaving this account with the books that helped make her a writer.

Other memoirs center around a key figure in the authors' lives. Tess Gallagher's *Soul Barnacles* (2000) is a hybrid memoir/biography that traces the relationship with her husband Raymond Carver through letters, interviews, journal entries, and excerpts from his work. Kathleen Finneran's *The Tender Land* (2000) revisits the relationship with her institutionalized brother to better understand her own life. Jennifer Finney Boylan takes on two roles as she describes her transformation from male to female in *She's Not There* (2003). Ann Patchett recounts her friendship with Lucy Grealy in *Truth and Beauty* (2004), while Kelly Corrigan recalls her father in *The Middle Place* (2008). Jeannette Walls demonstrates how she managed to escape the influence of her family in *The Glass Castle* (2006) and then goes further back, performing "an act of literary ventriloquism" (Jiles 2009) by retelling (and sometimes recasting) her family's genesis through the voice of her grandmother in *Half-Broke Horses* (2009).

Memoirists look at the past to better understand the present. Novelists, on the other hand, might set their works in the past to escape the present. The poet Alice Fulton's first novel, *The Nightingales of Troy* (2008), tells the stories of the Garrahan women in Troy, New York, as they move through the twentieth century, to demonstrate how women's lives and responsibilities remain unchanged. Likewise, Lisa Carey's *Love in the Asylum* (2004) begins in the present at a northeastern asylum where patients Alba and Oscar meet and fall in love. Carey furthers our understanding of Alba by adding a third story, hidden in the asylum's library, where she discovers letters from a woman to her son after her husband committed her. These letters suggest women's lot in the early twentieth century as well as the parallels with the twenty-first. One letter notes, "We are made to walk in lines here. Lines of naked women shuffling toward the showers, lines marching over the fenced-in grounds for daily exercise. A circus procession of exhausted women, constantly moving in one straight line" (52–53). As writers such as Charlotte Perkins Gilman clearly demonstrated, crossing the line is grounds for commitment.[8] Through reading this woman's memoirs, Alba comes to

8. See also Phyllis Chesler, *Women and Madness*; Rebecca Shannonhouse, *Out of Her Mind: Women Writing About Madness*; Denise Russell, *Women, Madness,*

understand her problems, herself, and her father's role in her commitments. At the same time, this novel reminds readers of man's renewed, if not ongoing, control over women.

Erin McGraw's second novel, *The Seamstress of Hollywood Boulevard* (2008), based on the real-life story of her grandmother, Bess McGraw, also goes back in time. *Seamstress* tells the story of Nell Plat's marriage at age fifteen to an abusive husband, her escape from him and their two baby girls. Although twentieth-century Irish American women's novels moved from depicting loving mothers to exposing controlling matriarchs, before 9/11 none had featured a mother literally abandoning her children. In the twenty-first century, McGraw deconstructs and then resurrects this paradigm. Even though she could not bond with her first two children, Nell is a loving mother to her third child, Mary, and she gradually learns to love the others. Reprising Irish American themes, McGraw plays with the concept of ethnic doubling. With husbands one and two, Jack and George, she reincarnates Dr. Jeckyll and Mr. Hyde. Among Nellie's daughters, doubles abound. McGraw also fuses two Irish American traits—private and public lives. In her early collections, women were either discontented stay-at-home moms or frustrated single working women. With *The Seamstress of Hollywood Boulevard*, we see a conflicted but ultimately loving mother and strong working woman.

Stephanie Grant also steps back in time with *Map of Ireland*. Whereas her 1992 novel, *The Passions of Alice*, sublimated homosexual desire through anorexia, *Map of Ireland* relies on pyromania as a metaphor for Ann Ahern's lesbian desires. This novel is set in South Boston in 1974 when the city began forcefully desegregating the public schools, much to the chagrin of the Irish Catholics living there. Historically communal and resistant to interlopers—especially nonwhites—Irish Americans living in South Boston and Charlestown rioted over integration.[9] These political disparities pro-

---

and Medicine; Susan J. Herbert, *Questions of Power: The Politics of Women's Madness Narratives.*

9. Tim Meagher puts this into perspective, however, by noting that thanks to economic success, many Irish Americans had already left the neighborhood by this

vide the demographic context for Grant's novel. Conversely, through a plot set in Boston centering around adoption and reconciliation between black and white families, Ann Patchett's *Run* (2007) suggests that the Irish have moved beyond this era.

Run is a mesmerizing novel starring Tip and Teddy Doyle, black brothers adopted by former Boston mayor Bernard Doyle and his wife, Bernadette. Although she dies before the action begins, this novel is very much about matriarchal power, for her influence flows throughout; likewise, although the boys' birth mother has been absent throughout their lives, her decisions impact their futures (Patchett 2007, "P.S.," 7). Initially their adoption is viewed as a back story, recalled as their characters are developed—one skinny and serious, the other slumped and scattered. Then tragedy strikes. As Tip starts to cross the street during a snowstorm, he is knocked to the ground. "Immediately he heard the sound of another hit and then another" (39). His savior has pushed him out of the way of an oncoming car only to be struck herself, much to the horror of her eleven-year-old daughter, Kenya. The rest of the novel traces the tangled aftermath.

Patchett describes the plot as "Joe Kennedy-meets-the-*Brothers Karamozov* [for] it is a story about a father who is trying to raise one of his sons to greatness" (2007, "P.S.," 5). At the same time, it is a story about family and communal loyalties—"the family of community, and the family of country, and the family of responsibility." Written in the years following 9/11, *Run* calls for more of that. As Patchett sees it, Doyle is saying to his sons, "You have a responsibility to the world. You can't have received so much, and be willing to only follow your own heart's desire" ("P.S.," 9).

Communal Loyalties

9/11 marked the end of an era for Irish Americans. Prior to that date, "popular culture equated Irishness with a re-essentialized, simplified epistemology

---

point, thus suggesting that such insular communities were more or less anachronisms. Outside of Southie, Democratic Irish American congressmen were instrumental in promoting the Civil Rights Act and open housing bill, which infuriated denizens of the old community and led to their defection from the party (2005, 231–32).

. . . as pleasingly anachronistic." But after the tragedy, Irishness—personified by members of the NYPD and FDNY—became code for whiteness and
innocence, which generated "counternarratives of innocence and virtuous
heroism . . . [that] cast men as heroes or villains and largely reduced women
to the role of mourners" (Negra 2006, 365) and thus somehow reduced
Americans' anxiety.

This feeling was not necessarily shared by some elements of the Irish
American diaspora. Although they might have later regretted their choice,
more Catholic Irish Americans voted for George W. Bush than for John
Kerry in the 2004 election, even though Kerry himself was a practicing
Catholic. As the *Irish Voice* reported, Catholics preferred Bush over Kerry
by a margin of 52 to 47 percent. This further shift toward the Republican
Party confirmed the growing affluence of Irish Americans; at the same time
it underscored the fact that "Irish American" was no longer a static identity,
but rather "fluid and mobile" (Cochrane 2010, 8–10)—a fact evidenced in
the growing number and variety of Irish American women's novels. More
troubling, particularly given the Irish American support for Bush, was the
impact of 9/11 on more recent Irish immigrants. Even though none of the
9/11 hijackers had been in the United States illegally, the Bush administration focused its attacks on immigrants, a move that negatively impacted Irish
American relations (Cochrane 2010, 85).

Thanks to the Bush administration's "zero tolerance policy," resulting
in the swift passage of the Patriot Act and establishment of the Department
of Homeland Security, immigration laws were so tightened after 2001 that
Irish emigrants felt not just unwelcome, but squeezed out. Groups ranging from the Ancient Order of Hibernians to the Irish American Unity
Conference viewed these actions as detrimental to Irish Americans, a fear
confirmed with the expansion of Homeland Security's Bureau of Customs
and Border Protection Act, which suddenly allowed INS officials to deport
undocumented people without benefit of a hearing by an immigration judge.
Although this law was not aimed at Irish emigrants, many were caught and
some were held at gunpoint, manacled, and imprisoned with hardened criminals before being deported (Cochrane 2010, 88–90). Given the backlog
in immigration hearings, some people were incarcerated for months. And
although the Irish Lobby for Immigration Reform lobbied intensely, it was

ineffective largely because Irish Americans no longer held the political clout wielded by their forebears (97–102).

No longer a melting pot, America's post-9/11 enforcement of immigration restrictions meant that undocumented Irish emigrants found it practically impossible to obtain citizenship, let alone a driver's license. As recently as 2004, Jack Irwin, the assistant to New York governor George Pataki, lamented: "People are up in arms and the Emerald Isle Emigration Center is at the forefront of trying to do something about it. Hopefully it will be squared away because you have a tonne [*sic*] of people affected by it, there could be 100,000, it is not just the Irish, it is every ethnic group" (quoted in Cochrane 2010, 94). Irish American groups lobbied against these restrictions, but they were no match for the Bush administration's terror-driven rules. And while the Irish government generally applauded this anti-terrorist stance, its younger citizens, who had been raised to value neutrality and thus abhorred even the violence in Northern Ireland, were firmly antiwar and demonstrated against the invasions of Afghanistan and Iraq (Cochrane 2010).

Internationally, the United States' reaction to 9/11 initially impeded peace talks with Sinn Fein and the IRA. Prior to the attacks many Irish Americans tended to support the IRA, but the crumbling Towers put an end to that. This anti-terrorist/anti-Sinn Fein feeling only increased among members of the Bush administration after Sinn Fein leader Gerry Adams visited Cuba and one of his representatives, Niall Connolly, was arrested while visiting Columbia. Irish American relations further deteriorated in 2003 after Adams denounced the Bush administration's invasion of Iraq. They worsened in 2004 following a series of "terrorist" events in Ireland: the IRA was blamed for a £26 million robbery of the Northern Bank in Belfast and the murder of Robert McCartney. The IRA's threat to hunt down and kill McCartney's murderer (suspected to be one its own) did not help, nor did a plan for Gerry Adams to visit the United States to meet with Senator Ted Kennedy and Congressman Peter King, for both snubbed him (Cochrane 2010, 76). Although the perpetrators in both cases were arrested, the IRA was blamed, Sinn Fein was considered "guilty by association," and Washington began to repudiate its Irish allies, even refusing a visa for Sinn Fein's Rita O'Hare, director of its Washington headquarters.

Yet there was a positive side to this imbroglio: thanks in part to pressure from Irish Americans, Gerry Adams persuaded the IRA to halt military activity and limit itself to politics, which resulted in voluntary disarmament and ultimately reestablishment of the Good Friday agreement in May 2007. Still, resentment remained. The Irish (like most of the world) deplored the actions of the Bush administration, viewing the United States as "quasi-fascist" (Cochrane 2010, 78).

Amidst this wave of resentment and recrimination, second- and third-wave Irish American women remained faithful to their feminist roots. This sense of "communal loyalty . . . a sense of commitment rooted in the concrete community" is distinctively Irish American: "the conflict between such communal loyalties and the values and circumstances of the American environment—values of individualism and circumstances of economic abundance and racial and ethnic diversity—has been the central dynamic of the history of the Irish in America" (Meagher 2006, 610). Historically, Irish Americans exceeded Americans of other ethnicities in "sociability, localism, trust, and loyalty" (Dezell 2001, 75). Although this trait has been faulted for the failure of earlier generations of Irish American *males* to move up the economic ladder, this was never a problem for their female counterparts. It was the women—"the mothers and aunts, the teachers, the nuns—who brought the wild Irish into the modern world" and the middle class (Dezell 2001, 89). As the previous chapters have demonstrated, Irish American women had the motivation and desire to get an education, find a job, move up, and get out. And while Irish American male writers may have characterized this desire as "shallow, lightheaded, and easily bedazzled by the frivolous" (Meagher 2006, 623), it enabled Irish American women to attain financial, political, and intellectual independence. At a time when so many Americans blindly followed the anti-feminist propaganda spewed by their leaders, Irish American women rejected such essentialist nonsense.

Ann Beattie's *The Doctor's House* (2002) may be her most Irish American novel, for it explores the icy domineering matriarch, the problems caused by alcoholism, the impact of the past on the present, and "lives affected by extremes of dissipation [and] profligacy . . . the . . . inability to express love and compassion in private; [and] a penchant stylistically for . . . satiric modes" (Fanning 2001, 3). Beattie tells the story of a dysfunctional family from three points of view: a son, a daughter, and their alcoholic mother. Through disparate stories covering the same events, it becomes clear that their behavior stems partly from mistreatment by the doctor (the children's egotistical, promiscuous father), but even more so because of neglect by their self-centered, irresponsible mother. Jacqueline Carey's *The Crossley Baby* (2003) also questions the post-9/11 reification of marriage and motherhood. When Sunny and Jean's unmarried sister Bridget dies, leaving behind eighteen-month-old Jade, it is assumed that homemaker Sunny will take the child. But Jean, a highly motivated workaholic, surprises Sunny and everyone else when she decides to keep the baby. This decision and its aftermath provide the novel's narrative focus, for both women believe the other is wrong. As such, the novel inscribes characteristics of traditional Irish and Irish American feuds (Carey 2003, 295).

Susanna Moore's *The Big Girls* (2008) utilizes journalistic techniques by drawing on current statistics as well as interviews with female prison inmates. Their stories bring to light the nation's sexist, racist, prison-sentencing guidelines. The majority of women in prison are there because they were raped, abused, assaulted and fought back, or possessed drugs. According to the Bureau of Justice, although "female inmates largely resemble male inmates in terms of race, ethnic background, and age . . . women are substantially more likely than men to be serving time for a drug offense," while approximately 50 percent "reported prior physical or sexual abuse" (Snell 1994, n.p.). Such statistics support Elie's prediction about the use of journalistic information in the twenty-first century while underscoring ongoing sexual discrimination, as well as the need for third-wave feminism. Thus this novel once again demonstrates Irish American women writers' facility at rendering feminist literary history.

Elaine Ford, Jean McGarry, and Joyce Carol Oates also remind us that feminism is still necessary. The short stories in Ford's *The American Wife* (2007) focus on the drawbacks of traditional sex roles, including the "feminine mystique" still experienced by housebound mothers. As early as 2002, Jean McGarry's *Dream Date* was exploring disappointing male/female relationships, while *A Bad and Stupid Girl* (2006) emphasizes the importance of female friendships. Joyce Carol Oates reprises these themes throughout her seventeen novels between 2000 and 2010. Many of these—such as *Faithless*

(2001), *Beasts* and *I'll Take You There* (2002), *The Tattooed Girl* and *Rape: A Love Story* (2003)—focus on a daughter's ability to survive the loss of her mother. With *Mother, Missing* (2005) and *After the Wreck I Picked Myself Up, Spread My Wings, and Flew Away* (2006), Oates explores mother-daughter relationships, whereas *Black Girl, White Girl* (2006) and *The Gravedigger's Daughter* (2007) examine feminist themes of race, class, and identity. In *My Sister, My Love* (2008) she draws on the Irish penchant for satire as she deconstructs the American love affair with celebrity. With a nod to Alice McDermott, the plot and setting of *A Fair Maiden* (2009) share a resemblance to *Child of My Heart*—although with the usual dollops of Oatesian suspense. Regardless of theme, Oates can never be charged with a lack of creativity.

Nor can Maureen Howard. *Big as Life* (2001) is the second of a quartet of novels expounding on art and nature, preceded by *A Lover's Almanac* (set in winter), followed by *The Silver Screen* (a summer novel), and ending with *The Rags of Time* (in the fall). Set in springtime, *Big as Life* features three sections—April, May, and June—each of which offers stories of hope and renewal set within a distinctly Irish American context. In "April," Marie Claude goes back and forth in time as she considers the possibilities of a new relationship; in "May," the Irish immigrant Nell Boyle draws on the past even as she learns to move forward by observing her Irish American family; in "June," Howard revisits Lou and Artie from *A Lover's Almanac*, goes further back to recast the marriage of John James Audubon, and then returns to the present to illustrate the influence of nature on her own works. What makes these works Irish American, as well as particularly apt, given the post-9/11 anti-feminist propaganda, is Howard's ongoing theme that we cannot afford to mythologize, sentimentalize, or live in the past (Durso 2008, 73). Rather, we need to "force observation, destroy nostalgia" (Howard 2001, 11).

Granted, *The Silver Screen* moves back in time, to the late 1920s when "talkies"—movies with sound—were coming into being. In this, as in many of her previous novels (particularly *Grace Abounding*), Howard is concerned with the development of a woman's voice, and with it, agency and independence. However, in this series Howard moves away from her usual persona. Rather than featuring a version of herself at this stage of her life, her heroines are young artists in their thirties. She returns to this persona (an older version of Maggie Flood in *Expensive Habits*) in *The Rags of Time* (2009). Although some critics found the novel's many threads difficult to follow, they are easy to track if you've read her previous novels, for in this one she attempts to tie together all the loose ends. Moreover, Howard's criticisms of George W. Bush (referred to as "the Cheerleader") and her outrage over his wars in Iraq and Afghanistan remind us of her communal loyalty as well as Irish American women's roles as banshees.

Search for the word "war" in *The Rags of Time* and you will get ninety hits; search for "Iraq" and another dozen turn up. Read for pleasure and you find lines such as the following: "Today I am outraged by the use of camouflage in the desert. Disguises nothing, you've noticed? With sophisticated surveillance devices, there's no need for blotches simulating mud and sand. Camouflage of a sort is worn by the Cheerleader, his business suit, navy or gray. You've seen him bounce down the steps of Air Force One, sprightly, airy. Crossing the tarmac, he waves us off, the palm of his hand denying access as we watch the evening news. Thumbs-up, he gives us the finger; his tight-lipped smile, mum's the word" (Howard 2009, 6). Whether Howard is writing about *War and Peace*, the Civil War, Afghanistan or Iraq, her message is clear—young men and women are being maimed and dying for a lost cause—and it is the Cheerleader's fault.

The first decade of the twenty-first century was dominated by lying, greed, abuse, and betrayal. Given the misinformation about Weapons of Mass Destruction and yellow cake uranium, the torture of prisoners at Abu Ghraib, the betrayal of CIA agent Valerie Plame, the mishandling of disaster aid after Hurricane Katrina, rendition and the recession, Bernie Madoff and the Wall Street collapse, anger seems an obvious reaction. While this stance does not characterize all twenty-first-century Irish American women's novels, it is emblematic of the most extreme of third-wave feminists such as those by Colleen Curran,[10] Martha O'Connor, and Gillian Flynn. These writers reflect the views of second-wave radical feminists inasmuch

10. The Irish American Colleen Curran is not to be confused with her Irish Canadian doppelganger, Colleen Curran, a playwright.

as their characters rebel against being members of "the most fundamentally oppressed class within a misogynistic Western patriarchal culture; the view of gender as a system that operates to ensure continued male domination; . . . and the understanding of the diversity of male sexual violence against women as an institution within the power structure of patriarchy"—views originally espoused by Shulamith Firestone, Andrea Dworkin, Mary Daly, and Audre Lorde (Madsen 2000, 153), and updated by the gadfly Daly in *Welfare* (2010), which, like Evelyn Murphy's *Getting Even* (2006), cites the earnings gap, governmental family policies, and the ongoing division of labor as factors in women's poverty.

The novels of Curran and her peers expose a culture that "keep[s] women in a subordinate position where they are dominated by men" (Madsen 2000, 153). Equally important, these novels answer Dworkin's complaint that "the stories of female suffering, of the brutal violence that women experience, do not get told" (quoted in Madsen 2000, 162). In Dworkin's eyes, radical feminism provided an "accurate analysis" of women's conditions, an outlet for women to vent their frustrations against these constraints, and therefore a means of survival "not based on self-loathing, fear, and humiliation, but instead on self-determination, dignity, and authentic destiny" (Madsen 2000, 35). Third-wave Irish American novels get some of this right. Curran and O'Connor seem to echo Lorde's argument that "The Erotic [Is] Power": "To experience the erotic is to 'do that which is female and self-affirming in the face of a racist, patriarchal, and anti-erotic society'" (quoted in Madsen 2000, 168). This seems to work for the female characters in third-wave novels—until their partners reject them in yet another display of patriarchal power.

Third-wave feminists are generally defined as "women who were reared in the wake of the women's liberation movement of the seventies" (Baumgardner and Richards 2000, 15). These women did not have to fight their mothers' battles; they were raised to believe that "girls can do anything boys can," and thus possess a confidence often foreign to their mothers. Third-wave issues include child abuse, self-mutilation, eating disorders, and body image, as well as depression, rape, physical abuse, sexual agency, birth control, and abortion rights—major themes in twenty-first-century Irish American women's novels (Baumgardner and Richards 2000, 17–21).

Gillian Flynn's writing provides the antidote for the post-9/11 infantilization of women. As *Entertainment Weekly* writes, "Flynn coolly demolished the notion that little girls are made of sugar and spice in *Sharp Objects*, her sensuous and chilling first thriller" (Cruz 2006, n.p.). Published in 2006, *Sharp Objects* is the third of three closely related third-wave novels. It was preceded by Colleen Curran's *Whores on the Hill* and Martha O'Connor's *The Bitch Posse*.[11] These works share a number of disturbing parallels, which suggest they may be more representative of this generation than older readers are aware. Each novel features a trio of outcast teenage girls: Flynn's antagonists are Kylie, Kellsey, and Kellsey, all thirteen, led by Amma, also thirteen; Curran's girls—Astrid, Juli, and Thisbe—are fifteen; O'Connor's—Rennie, Cherry, and Amy—are high school seniors. All are alienated from their parents and their peers. They drink and take drugs, they are sexually active, and they are cutters. Although all profess "girl power," they are obviously depressed and—contrary to assertions that the slut is actually a rebel (Wolf 1990)—suffering from low self-esteem due to estrangement from their mothers.

In this regard, these works are clearly distinguishable from those of post-feminist writers, for "post-feminism dovetails closely with a heightened social and economic emphasis on showplace domesticity, virtuoso parenting, and technologies mobilized in the name of family cohesion. It may very well be one of the ideological connectors between a contemporary sense of unfettered material entitlement and a moral discourse of virtuous familialism" (Tasker and Negra 2007, 7).

While the distant matriarch is a familiar Irish American trope, with few exceptions the mothers in these twenty-first-century Irish American women's novels bear little resemblance to their predecessors. Juli's mother drinks to drown her guilt over the imminent death of her mentally challenged daughter. Amma's mother appears to be withdrawn because (like her foremothers) she mourns the death of a child; however, she actually caused her child's death in a case of Munchausen By Proxy gone wrong: "The caregiver, usually the mother, *almost always* the mother, makes her child ill to get attention

---

11. *The Bitch Posse* was first published as *The Bitch Goddess Diary* in 2005.

for herself. You got Munchausen, you make yourself sick to get attention. You got MBP, you make your child sick to show what a kind, doting mommy you are" (Flynn 2006, 228). There are no doting mommies in these books. Most are divorced, more interested in escaping reality or pursuing new loves than in raising their daughters.

Of course, a bad mother is no excuse to murder. In *Sharp Objects*, Amma and her gang of three torture and kill two of their classmates because Amma resents her mother's attention to them. The high school seniors in *The Bitch Posse* accidentally murder their lecherous drama teacher while trying to scare him into never seducing another underage girl. Amma is a psychopath so she feels no guilt. But the Bitch Posse—Rennie, Cherry, and Amy—are wracked.

Martha O'Connor's *The Bitch Posse* ostensibly alternates setting and point of view with individual chapters moving between Rennie, Cherry, and Amy's high school escapades in 1988, and attempts to deal with their unresolved guilt in 2003. This nonlinear strategy does not work—unless O'Connor's intent is to show that the girls' guilt has left them unable to mature. Colleen Curran's *Whores on the Hill* includes no murders, only a prank gone wrong. This comparatively tame novel is set in a Catholic girls' school (on a hill) in Milwaukee. The protagonists are called the "whores on the hill" because they manage to look like punks even while wearing their school uniforms—"Fishnet stockings under our uniform skirts, black combat boots, oxford shirts torn at the collar, at the cuffs . . . scapulas, rosaries, every single crucifix we owned" topped with razor-cut hair and kohl-rimmed eyes—while remaining on the honor roll (Curran 2005, 21). In true (third-wave) feminist style, the friendship of Astrid and Juli causes newcomer Thisbe—who had not spoken in "six months and seventeen days"—to regain her voice (12).

Whereas these girls would rank their counterparts in *The Bitch Posse* as "skanky ho[s]," they view their own behavior as empowering. Baumgardner and Richards maintain that "third wave women have been seen as non-feminist when they are actually living feminist lives" (2000, 48), accusations arising from the tendency of some third-wavers, particularly the above novelists, to depict apparently promiscuous young women. But third-wavers view sexuality quite differently. "You know there is power in promiscuity, but there's a trick to it," says one of the "whores" on the hill. "You know the difference between doing something for fun and doing something because you feel pressured. Own it. Love it. Live it. And tell the rest of the world to step the fuck off, pronto" (Curran 2005, 55). Not surprisingly, much of the novel revolves around the girls exploring their sexuality. They claim to hold the power, but repeatedly they are used, sometimes raped by boys they supposedly control. Their conversations include comments such as "I just couldn't believe he was going out with me" (101), and acting out that reveals their anger. Most telling is their fascination with self-mutilation. Juli burns herself with cigarettes and cuts her arms. The first time Thisbe does it, she "smil[es] through the sting, savoring it" (127).

These actions and reactions parallel those in the other third-wave novels. In *Sharp Objects*, the journalist Camille cuts words into her skin: *cook, cupcake, kitty, curls . . . baby-doll . . . harmful . . . petticoat . . . wicked*. Doing so gives her control (Flynn 2006, 60–61). In *The Bitch Posse*, Cherry explains that "one slice across with a knife or razor blade and pain and hatred and self-loathing melt away" (O'Connor 2003, 83). She justifies cutting by noting that Princess Diana—a touchstone for all the young women in these novels—was also a cutter. Later, she tells Amy, "It's just taking the pain inside and putting it outside where it's real." After Cherry cuts her arm, Rennie takes the razor blade and slices hers. "She opens her eyes as if shaken awake, and her tears have stopped. She doesn't look afraid anymore." So Amy takes it and draws blood: "It struck like a tuning fork and vibrated with life; I *do* feel better. I feel alive, and everything around me is crisper, cleaner, louder, more defined. The air rings with importance. I matter. I am. This is better than blanking out with vodka" (94–95). Similarly, when Rennie cuts herself, "Everything feels so clear, the horrible self-hating feelings are gone" (203). Rennie sums it up when she says, *You have to hurt if you want to feel anything at all* (71).

In the hierarchy of self-mutilation, these actions are considered moderate. In fact, most self-mutilation falls into this category. Cutting has become increasingly popular, reaching almost epidemic proportions and considered the twenty-first-century equivalent of anorexia both in usage and inducing a feeling of control (Focus 2009). It occurs mostly in girls ages thirteen to nineteen and, as the above quotations suggest, serves as a release from tension or stress. According to Mary Pipher, author of *Raising Ophelia*, when self-mutilation is widespread, it suggests "enormous cultural processes at work." Just as anorexia and bulimia reflected twentieth-century pressure on young women to be thin, self-mutilation "can be seen as a concrete interpretation of our culture's injunction to young women to carve themselves into culturally acceptable pieces." It may be viewed as an act of submission or, in the case of girls in these novels, a cry for help: "Stop me from hurting myself in the ways that the culture directs me to" or "I will hurt myself more than the culture can hurt me" (1994, 158).

Gradually these angry third-wave novels faded away as the country began to change. After the bungling of disaster relief for victims of Hurricane Katrina, the tide began to turn against the Bush administration and its post-9/11, anti-woman mindset. In 2006, the Democratic Party retook Congress; the following year Nancy Pelosi became the first female Speaker of the male-dominated House of Representatives. In 2008, even Republicans recognized the power of women's votes, as exemplified in the nomination of Sarah Palin as Republican vice-presidential candidate. Similarly, the desire for a different type of president led to Hillary Clinton's becoming the first female not only to win a presidential primary but also to receive 18 million votes in the presidential election. That same year, Ann Dunwoody became the first female to be promoted to four-star general; and following the election of Barack Obama, Sonia Sotomayor and Elena Kagan were appointed to the United States Supreme Court.

Popular culture reflected this changing mindset: the American public finally grew tired of movies about innocent young girls depicted in *Amelie* (2001), *Whale Rider* (2002), and *Little Miss Sunshine* (2006), and moved on to embrace more powerful women such as Lisbeth, *The Girl with the Dragon Tattoo* (2008), and Karen Clark, the U.S. Assistant Secretary of State for Diplomacy in the political satire *In the Loop* (2009), and messages about the dehumanization of the war in *The Hurt Locker* (2009), directed by Kathryn Bigelow, the first woman to win the Academy Award for best director.

Irish American women's prominence rose markedly during this period. In 2004, Nancy Keenan—listed by *Washingtonian Magazine* as among the one hundred most powerful women in America—was elected president of NARAL Pro-Choice America (Huffington Post 2012). Kathleen O'Toole served as Boston's commissioner of police until 2006, when she stepped down to become chief inspector of Garda Siochana, Ireland's twelve-thousand-member national police force (Slack 2006). In 2005, Joan Walsh, featured regularly on MSNBC, was named editor in chief of *Salon*. Doris Kearns Goodwin published two new books: *Team of Rivals* (2005), and *Lincoln* (2006). Likewise, Monica McGoldrick published *Ethnicity and Family Therapy* (2005) and co-edited *Revisioning Family Therapy: Race, Culture, and Gender* (2008).

Angry that women still earn 25 percent less than men, Evelyn Murphy, former lieutenant governor of Massachusetts, researched and wrote *Getting Even* (2006) and established WAGE—Women Are Getting Even—which began collaborating with groups around the country to offer salary negotiation workshops. In 2007, Kate Moira Ryan collaborated with Linda S. Chapman to turn Ann Bannon's "Beebo Brinker Chronicles" into a play produced by Lily Tomlin and Jane Wagner (Bannon 2011. The late Robert F. Kennedy's daughter, Kerry, published *Being Catholic Now*, featuring interviews with other famous Catholics, in 2008. Her sister Rory spent the decade producing and directing awardwinning political documentaries on topics such as AIDS, the dangers of nuclear power and Abu Ghraib, as well as a biography of the correspondent Helen Thomas. Not surprisingly, Kennedy cousin Maria Shriver was also politically active during this decade. In addition to serving as First Lady of California, in 2009 she produced an Emmy-winning HBO documentary on Alzheimer's disease, from which her father suffered, and "The Shriver Report," which examined the status of women in the workplace. This renewed respect for women was evident as Irish American women's novels began to change in tenor and theme. Rebecca Barry's *Later, at the Bar* (2007), a "novel in stories," provides a darkly humorous view of women as men's equals—in drinking and in failed relationships—a third-wave view of equality. Although the men's stories are as prominent as the women's, the men remain unmoored while the women persevere. The women may not be happier, but they are strong enough to carry on alone. Gillian Flynn's second novel, *Dark Places* (2009), tells the story of Libby Day, a young woman emotionally stunted by her family's murder. Libby gains agency—and a life—as she slowly deciphers who really committed the murders. Tess Callahan's *April and Oliver* (2009) also falls into this category. Like Libby Day, April has failed to mature because of a trauma in her life. Raped and molested by her uncle, she remains mired in physically abusive relationships believing she deserves no better. Despite her basic lack of self-esteem—and unlike heroines in the earlier third-wave novels—April is otherwise a generous, loving, and decent character. She laughs off the attentions of her cousin Al and fends off the advances of Oliver, who is engaged. As the novel closes, April has moved away from the city and has finally begun to attend college. But rather than tying up the plot with a neat bow, Callahan returns to the feminist practice of writing beyond the ending (Du Plessis 1985). April's fate is in her own hands; she will decide whether to spend it with Oliver or to continue independently.

The latter part of the first decade marked the return of errant feminists as well. Nora Hammond, heroine of Mary McGarry Morris's *The Last Secret* (2009), is the typical superwoman: she volunteers, works for the family newspaper with her husband, Ken, and keeps track of their teenagers. While Nora feels overworked, she senses that Ken is too, for he is rarely home—until he admits he's having an affair with her best friend. Although Nora is angry, she is determined to hold her family together regardless of Ken's infidelities. But ultimately, she allows a psychopath to beat her rival almost to death before she snaps back to reality and kills the man with a shovel, "hitting him. Again and again . . . sobbing with every blow after chopping blow" (Morris 2009, 264–65). Then she divorces her husband and starts law school.

On the lighter side is Caitlin Macy's second book, *Spoiled* (2009), a collection of short stories about rich young women in New York City. In content and tone, we find a twenty-first-century equal to Mary McCarthy's renowned Irish satire, for Macy skewers the lives of the pampered rich. In "Bait and Switch," Elspeth is vacationing with her sister Louise in Europe. "It was so nice, such a treat, in Europe, to ride Louise's long coattails; intolerable to have to cope on one's own, getting by, like any tourist, with foolish smiles and an ingratiating overuse of the formal 'you' form" (Macy 2009, 17). In "The Secret Vote," Alice feels no qualms about planning an abortion after amniocentesis reveals her baby has Down syndrome. "If one wanted to be honest, though, wasn't it better to admit that there was no choice to be made? Wasn't it, not unlike the upcoming election, the case that you'd always more or less known which way you would vote?" (45). Her attitude is further conveyed in disparaging comments about her mother giving change to the homeless: "Poor Maureen had never discovered that a new morality had overtaken the old, and the former was all about maintaining personal boundaries—talk to the hand, dump that addict friend, wash that problem person out of your hair, and congratulate yourself afterward on your inner growth" (50).

"Annabel's Mother" recounts the plight of a little girl raised by her nanny. After the narrator praises the nanny, "she seemed pleased by my hypothetical support, but it suddenly struck me as a foolish—nay, a total bullshit thing to have said—the kind of crap we privileged white mothers were probably spewing all the time, because talk was so very cheap" (80). Gossip is led by "Victoria and Marnie, best friends who lived at 48 West, and whose children—each had a pair of twins—were always being paraded into the park and then handed quickly off to the pair of specially trained twin nannies who attended them" (72). Gossip varies with the seasons, "such as the size of the husbands' bonuses or where people summered, not that you used that verb. And there was the year-round fodder, such as which park mother coming back from postpartum lockup had found her six-month-old calling the nanny 'Mama' and fired the woman on the spot sans severance; or who had had a shit fit and threatened the big D when she found her husband had supported her mother-in-law's feeding Carleton a banana (he was only allowed indigenous fruit)" (73).

This narrator quits the park after the humiliation of admitting that she and her husband do not own a summer house. Subsequent stories feature spoiled children, nasty actresses, and a jealous socialite who steals her house-keeper's beloved red coat—and then can't decide where to hide it since the woman cleans for her. In what may be a nod to Maureen Howard, "Bad Ghost" tells the story of the neglected child of the famed novelist Margery Flood (see chapter 4). Considering taking a job as the child's nanny, Stacey admits that "the idiocy of people amazed her. Or not the idiocy but the shortsightedness—the guilelessness; the fact that they didn't lead their lives looking for an opening" (165). *Spoiled* underscores the difference between feminist and post-feminist literature. Whereas post-feminism accepts duplicity by failing to recognize it, feminism exposes and critiques the characters' hypocrisy—and Irish American feminists satirize it.

For many people, 9/11 marked the end of an era. Gains in women's rights were either ignored—with the hope of abolishing women from the workplace—or readily accepted as complete. This mindset clearly affected the literature of the decade. Many younger writers accepted the status quo, churning out formulaic novels for entertainment and financial gain. While some second-wave feminists retreated into the safety of marriage, family, or the church, others remained true to their beliefs. This decade also saw the rise of third-wave Irish American feminists. Their novels reveal young women's battles with sexism, sexual abuse, depression, addiction, and low self-esteem, as well as the very obvious need to avoid complacency. In sum, these novels continue to reflect feminist literary history.

Contrary to assertions that apart from the works of Elizabeth Cullinan and Alice McDermott, Irish American literature "remains enshrouded and unrevealed" (Quinn 2006, 684), these novels continue to reflect, if not effect, change. They have revealed the sainted matriarch as human—loving, detached, hyper-religious, hypocritical, long-suffering, manipulative, secretive, triumphant, resentful, frustrated, lonely, and homicidal when necessary. In so doing, they created an abundance of realistic, unforgettable characters: Mrs. Holztman, Mrs. Keeley, Mrs. Devlin, and Flannery O'Connor's many controlling mothers. At the same time, these writers opened the bedroom doors to remind us that women have needs, that their desires can sometimes overcome society's strictures as well as their common sense. Who can forget Meg Sergant, Frankie Addams, Isabel Moore, Mary Agnes Keeley, Frannie Thorstin, and Eileen Myles, or their third-wave counterparts: Kylie, Kellsey, and Kellsey; Astrid, Juli, and Thisbe; Rennie, Cherry, and Amy? Irish American women have also created heroic figures like Marianne Mulvaney, who overcomes rape and abandonment and forgives her family, and Nora Hammond, who kills her rival and makes a new life. These women are survivors.

Despite some aberrations after 9/11, Irish American women writers have carried on their duties as banshees. Loud and strong, Maggie Flood, Nell Plat, and Eileen Finney defend women's independence. Angry and aggressive, their authors have scolded the government for its oxymoronic reification and mistreatment of mothers, faulted the church for its prejudice against women, and indicted society for its failure to heed the plight of depressed housewives, pregnant teens, abandoned daughters, and abused wives.

Mary Gordon has noted that "the Irish have managed to do these things no one else could do. . . . The English told them they couldn't learn to read, and they produced some of the best literature in the English language. Their church wasn't supposed to exist, and it became the strongest Catholic church in the world. A whole population is wiped out by famine, and they come here with no skills, no money, no family, and prosper beyond anyone's expectations" (quoted in Dezell 2001, 72).

While this statement applies to both males and females, it is particularly true of Irish American women writers. These women ignored traditional Irish feelings of humility and self-deprecation as well as the belief that they and their stories were not important enough to record (Dezell 2001). In addition to carrying on traditional Irish American themes and traits—religion, satire, alienation, ethnic doubleness, and stylistic experimentation—they drew on autobiographical experiences to make them true to life. Then they threw in a feminist twist, subverting the traditional by adding sexuality and sexual preference and raising consciousness through discussions of women's health, domestic violence, and self-mutilation. In doing so, they expanded the boundaries of Irish American literature by 50 percent: they included the women.

Works Cited

Index

Works Cited

Allison, Dorothy. 1992. *Bastard Out of Carolina*. New York: Plume.

———. 1998. *The Cave Dwellers*. New York: Plume.

———. 1995. "Introduction." In *The Redneck Way of Knowledge*. New York: Vintage.

Almeida, Linda Dowling. 2006. "Irish America, 1940–2000." In Lee and Casey, *Making the Irish American*, 548–74.

———. 2001. *Irish Immigrants in New York City, 1945–1995*. Bloomington: Indiana Univ. Press.

Andermahr, Sonya. 2000. "'A Person Positions Herself on Quicksand': The Postmodern Politics of Identity and Location in Sarah Schulman's *Empathy*." In *"Romancing the Margins"? Lesbian Writing in the 1990s*, edited by Gabriele Griffin, 7–20. London: Harrington Park Press.

Anonymous. 1835. *Six Months in a House of Correction; or, The Narrative of Dorah Mahoney, Who Was under the Influence of the Protestants about a Year, and an Inmate of the House of Correction in Leverett St., Boston, Mass., nearly Six Months*. Boston: Benjamin J. Mussey.

Anthony, Katherine. 1914. *Mothers Who Must Earn*. New York: Survey Associates.

Araujo, Susanna. 2008. "I'm Your Man: Irish American Masculinity in the Fiction of Joyce Carol Oates." In Ebest and McInerney, *Too Smart to Be Sentimental*, 157–70.

Atwood, Margaret. 1986. *The Handmaid's Tale*. New York: Random House.

Baehr, Ninia. 1990. *Abortion without Apology*. Boston: South End Press Collective.

Bagnel, Joan. 1974. *Gone the Rainbow, Gone the Dove*. New York: Penguin.

Banning, Margaret Culkin. 1976. *Country Club People*. New York: Lightyear Press.

———. 1935. *The First Woman*. New York: Harper & Bros.

———. 1942. *Women for Defense*. New York: Duell, Sloan, and Pearce.

———. 1926. *The Women of the Family*. New York: Harper & Bros.

Bannon, Ann. 2011. "Ann Bannon." www.annbannon.com.

Barr, Nevada. 1984. *Bittersweet*. New York: HarperCollins.

Barron, James. 2000. Obituary. "Mary Cantwell, 69, Author and *Times* Writer." *New York Times*, February 2. http://www.nytimes.com/2000/02/02/nyregion /mary-cantwell-69-author-and-times-writer.html.

Barry, Peter. 2009. *Beginning Theory: An Introduction to Literary Criticism*. 3d ed. Manchester: Manchester Univ. Press.

Barry, Rebecca. 2007. *Later, at the Bar*. New York: Simon & Schuster.

Baumgardner, Jennifer, and Amy Richards. 2000. *Manifesta: Young Women, Feminism, and the Future*. New York: Farrar, Strauss and Giroux.

Beattie, Ann. 1995. *Another You*. New York: Vintage.

———. 1976. *Chilly Scenes of Winter*. New York: Vintage.

———. 2002. *The Doctor's House*. New York: Scribner.

———. 1991. *Falling in Place*. New York: Vintage.

———. 1985. *Love Always*. New York: Vintage.

Bell, Rudolph. 1985. *Holy Anorexia*. Chicago: Univ. of Chicago Press.

Bender, Eileen T. 1987. "Autonomy and Influence: Joyce Carol Oates's *Marriages and Infidelities*." In *Joyce Carol Oates*, edited by Harold Bloom, 45–59. New York: Chelsea House.

———. 1987. *Joyce Carol Oates, Artist in Residence*. Bloomington: Indiana Univ. Press.

———. 1979. "'Paedomorphic' Art: Joyce Carol Oates' *Childwold*." In *Critical Essays on Joyce Carol Oates*, edited by Linda W. Wagner, 117–22. Boston: G. K. Hall.

Bennett, Alma. 2002. *Conversations with Mary Gordon*. Jackson: Univ. Press of Mississippi.

Berlin, Ellin. 1950. *Lace Curtain*. New York: Hammond.

Blais, Madeleine. 2001. *Uphill Walkers*. New York: Atlantic Monthly Press.

Bly, Nellie. 1890. *Around the World in 72 Days*. New York: Pictorial Weeklies.

———. 1888. *Six Months in Mexico*. New York: American.

———. 1887. *Ten Days in a Madhouse*. New York: Ian L. Munro.

Blythe, Will. 2009. "Men Behaving Oddly." *The New York Times Book Review*, July 19, 13.

Bogan, Louise, and Ruth Limmer. 1980. *Journey around My Room*. New York: Viking.

Bois, Danuta. 1997. "Margaret Bourke-White." *Distinguished Women of Past and Present*. http://www.distinguishedwomen.com/biographies/bourke-white.html.

Bolotin, S. 1982. "Voices from the Post-Feminist Generation." *New York Times Magazine*, October 17.

Bona, Mary Jo. 2004. "Gay and Lesbian Writing in Post–World War II America." In *A Concise Companion to Postwar American Literature and Culture*, edited by Josephine G. Hendin, 210–37. Malden, MA: Blackwell.

Bourke, Angela, ed. 2002. *The Field Day Anthology of Literature: Irish Women's Writing and Traditions*. Vols. 4 and 5. New York: New York Univ. Press.

———. 2004. *Maeve Brennan: Homesick at "The New Yorker."* New York: Counterpoint.

Boyd, Blanche McCrary. 1976. *Mourning the Death of Magic*. New York: MacMillan.

———. 1973. *Nerves*. Plainfield, VT: Daughters.

———. 1995. *The Redneck Way of Knowledge*. New York: Vintage.

———. 1992. *The Revolution of Little Girls*. New York: Vintage.

———. 1997. *Terminal Velocity*. New York: Knopf.

Boylan, Jennifer Finney. 2003. *She's Not There: A Life in Two Genders*. New York: Broadway Books.

Brady, Maureen. 1982. *Folly*. New York: Crossings Press.

———. 1979. *Give Me Your Good Ear*. Argyle, NY: Spinsters Ink.

Brennan, Maeve. 1962. "An Attack of Hunger." *The New Yorker*, January 6, 26+.

———. 1964. "The Carpet with the Big Pink Roses on It." *The New Yorker*, May 23, 47+.

———. 1974. *Christmas Eve*. New York: Scribner.

———. 1963. "The Drowned Man." *The New Yorker*, July 27, 26+.

———. 1969. *In and Out of Never-Never Land*. New York: Scribner.

———. 1965. "The Shadow of Kindness." *The New Yorker*, August 14, 30+.

———. 1968. "The Sofa." *The New Yorker*, March 2, 39+.

———. 1997. *The Springs of Affection*. Boston: Houghton Mifflin.

———. 1954. "Talk of the Town: Skunked." *The New Yorker*, January 23, 26+.

———. 1966. "The Twelfth Wedding Anniversary." *The New Yorker*, September 24, 60+.

Brightman, Carol. 1992. *Writing Dangerously*. New York: Harcourt Brace.

Brown, Helen Gurley. 1962. *Sex and the Single Girl*. New York: Random.

Brownmiller, Susan. 1999. *In Our Time: Memoir of a Revolution*. New York: Random House.

Brundson, Charlotte. 1991. "Pedagogies of the Feminine: Feminist Teaching and Women's Genres." *Screen* 32, no. 4: 364–81.

Cahill, Susan. 1976. *Earth Angels: Portraits from Childhood and Youth*. New York: Harper & Row.

Call, Cynthia E. 2002. "Marxism in Carson McCullers' 'Strangled South.'" http://www.scrye.com/~cynders/mccullers.html.

Callahan, Tess. 2009. *April and Oliver*. New York: Hatchette.

CARA (Center for Applied Research in the Apostolate). 2005. "Self-Reported Mass Attendance of U.S. Catholics Unchanged during Last Five Years." The Center for Applied Research in the Apostolate, Georgetown University. January 10. http://cara.georgetown.edu/AttendPR.pdf.

Carden, Mary Paniccia. 2003. "(Anti) Romance in Alice McDermott's *At Weddings and Wakes* and *Charming Billy*." In *Double Plots: Romance and History*, edited by Susan Strehel and Mary Paniccia Carden, 3–23. Jackson: Univ. of Mississippi Press.

Carey, Jacqueline. 2003. *The Crossley Baby*. New York: Ballantine.

———. 1992. *Good Gossip*. New York: Ballantine.

———. 2008. *It's a Crime*. New York: Ballantine.

———. 1996. *The Other Mother*. New York: Random House.

Carey, Lisa. 2006. *Every Visible Thing*. New York: HarperCollins.

———. 2000. *In the Country of the Young*. New York: HarperCollins.

———. 2004. *Love in the Asylum*. New York: HarperCollins/Perennial.

———. 1998. *The Mermaids Singing*. New York: HarperCollins.

Carpenter, Mary Wilson. 1996. "Female Grotesques in Academia: Ageism, Antifeminism, and Feminists on the Faculty." In Clark, Garner, Higonnet, and Katrak, *Antifeminism in the Academy*, 141–68.

Carr, Virginia Spencer. 1987. "Introduction." *Collected Stories of Carson McCullers*. Boston: Houghton Mifflin.

Carson, Rachel. 1962. *Silent Spring*. New York: Houghton Mifflin.

Casey, Daniel J., and Robert E. Rhodes. 2006. "The Tradition of Irish American Writers: The Twentieth Century." In Lee and Casey, *Making the Irish American*, 649–62.

Cervetti, Nancy. 2012. *S. Weir Mitchell, 1829–1914: Philadelphia's Literary Physician*. College Station: The Pennsylvania State Univ. Press.

Chafe, William. 1991. *The Unfinished Journey: America since World War II*. 2nd ed. New York: Oxford Univ. Press.

Chopin, Kate. 1890. *At Fault*. St. Louis: Nixon Jones.

———. 1899. *The Awakening*. Chicago: Herbert S. Stone.

Clark, VeVe, Shirley Nelson Garner, Margaret Higonnet, and Ketu H. Katrak, eds. 1996. *Antifeminism in the Academy*. London: Routledge.

Cleary, Kate. 1897. *Like a Gallant Lady*. Chicago: Way and Williams.

———. 1901. "The Stepmother." *McClure's Magazine*, September 17.

Cochrane, Fergus. 2010. *The End of Irish America?* Dublin: Irish Academic Press.

Cologne-Brooks, Gavin. 2005. *Dark Eyes on America: The Novels of Joyce Carol Oates*. Baton Rouge: Louisiana State Univ. Press.

Conway, Katherine. 1901. *Lalor's Maples*. Boston: Pilot.

———. 1900. *The Way of the World and Other Ways: A Story of Our Set*. Boston: Pilot.

———. 1909. *The Woman Who Never Did Wrong and Other Stories*. Boston: T. J. Blynn.

Cook, Karin. 1998. *What Girls Learn*. New York: Vintage.

Coppock, Vicki, Deena Haydon, and Ingrid Richter. 1995. *The Illusions of "Post-Feminism."* London: Taylor & Francis.

Corrigan, Kelly. 2008. *The Middle Place*. New York: Hyperion.

Coyle, Kathleen. 1930. *A Flock of Birds*. New York: E. P. Dutton.

Cruz, Gilbert. 2006. "Review of 'Sharp Objects.'" *Entertainment Weekly*, September 22. www.ew.com/ew/article/0,1537748.00.html.

Cullinan, Elizabeth. 1960. "The Ablutions." *The New Yorker*, February 6, 37+.

———. 1982. *A Change of Scene*. S. Yarmouth, MA: John Curley.

———. 1969. *House of Gold*. New York: Random House.

———. 1971. *In the Time of Adam*. Boston: Houghton Mifflin.

———. 1960. "Le Petit Dejeuner." *The New Yorker*, August 13, 32+.

———. 1961. "The Power of Prayer." *The New Yorker*, January 7, 28+.

———. 1961. "The Reunion." *The New Yorker*, February 18, 38+.

———. 1967. "A Sunday Like the Others." *The New Yorker*, August 26, 26+.

———. 1960. "The Time of Adam." *The New Yorker*, September 10, 42+.

———. 1960. "The Voices of the Dead." *The New Yorker*, April 16, 40+.

———. 1977. *Yellow Roses*. New York: Viking.

Culturenorthernireland.org. 2008. "Kathleen Coyle." http://www.culturenorthern ireland.org/article/506/kathleen-coyle.

Cummings, Kathleen Sprow. 2009. "Do Women Have Souls? Catholicism, Feminism, and the Council at Macon." *Commonweal*, September 11. http://www .thefreelibrary.com/_/print/PrintArticle.aspx?id=208508722.

Curran. Colleen. 2005. *Whores on the Hill*. New York: Vintage.

Curran, Mary Doyle. 1948. *The Parish and the Hill*. Boston: Houghton Mifflin.

Currie, Ellen. 1995. *Available Light*. New York: Scribner.

Daly, Brenda. 1996. *Lavish Self-Division: The Novels of Joyce Carol Oates*. Jackson: Univ. of Mississippi Press.

Daly, Mary. 1973. *Beyond God the Father*. Boston: Beacon Press.

———. 1968. *The Church and the Second Sex*. Boston: Beacon Press.

————. 1978. *Gyn/Ecology: The Metaethics of Radical Feminism*. Boston: Beacon Press.

————. 1998. *Pure Lust*. Boston: Women's Press.

————. 1998. *Quintessence: Realizing the Archaic Future: A Radical Elemental Feminist Manifesto*. Boston: Beacon Press.

————. 2011. *Welfare*. New York: Polity Press.

Daniel, Frank. 1962. "Flannery O'Connor Shapes Own Capital." *The Atlanta Journal and The Atlanta Constitution*, July 22, C2.

Davis, Flora. 1991. *Moving the Mountain: The Women's Movement in America since 1960*. New York: Simon & Schuster.

Day, Dorothy. 1924. *The Eleventh Virgin*. New York: Alfred and Charles Boni.

————. 1939. *House of Hospitality*. New York: Sheed and Ward.

————. 1952. *The Long Loneliness*. New York: Harper & Row.

————. 1999. *On Pilgrimage: The Sixties*. Grand Rapids, MI: William B. Eerdmans.

Day, Lincoln H. 1964. "Patterns of Divorce in Australia and the United States." *American Sociological Review* 29 (August): 509–22.

Deane, Seamus. 1991. *The Field Day Anthology of Irish Literature*. Vols. 1–3. Dublin: Field Day.

Deasy. Mary. 1948. *Hour of Spring*. New York: Arno, 1976.

De Lauretis, Teresa. 1989. "The Violence of Rhetoric: Considerations on Representation and Gender." In *The Violence of Representation*, edited by Nancy Armstrong and Leonard Tennenhouse, 239–56. New York: Routledge.

Del Rosso, Jeanna. 2005. *Writing Catholic Women: Contemporary International Catholic Girlhood Narratives*. New York: Palgrave.

Dezell, Maureen. 2001. *Irish America: Coming into Clover*. New York: Doubleday.

Dijkstra, Bram. 1986. *Idols of Perversity: Fantasies of Feminine Evil in Fin de Siècle Culture*. New York: Oxford Univ. Press.

Diner, Hasia. 1983. *Erin's Daughters in America: Irish Immigrant Women in the Nineteenth Century*. Baltimore: Johns Hopkins Univ. Press.

Dolan, Jay P. 2008. *The Irish Americans: A History*. New York: Bloomsbury Press.

Donnelly, Eleanor. 1897. *A Round Table of the Representative American Catholic Novelists, at Which Is Served a Feast of Excellent Stories*. New York: Benzinger Bros.

Donnelly, Gabrielle. 1998. *The Girl in the Photograph*. New York: Penguin Putnam.

Donnelly, Nisa. 1989. *The Bar Stories*. New York: St. Martin's Press.

Donner, Robert. 1961. "She Writes Powerful Fiction." *The Sign* 40 (March): 46–48.

Donoghue, Stacy. 1996. "The Reluctant Radical: The Irish-Catholic Element." In *Twenty-four Ways of Looking at Mary McCarthy*, edited by Eve Swertka and Margo Viscusi, 17–27. Westport, CT: Greenwood Press.

Donovan, Josephine. 1992. *Feminist Theory.* New York: Continuum International.

Dowd, Christopher. 2011. *The Construction of Irish Identity in American Literature.* New York: Routledge.

DuBois, Ellen Carol. 1987. *Feminist Scholarship.* Normal: Univ. of Illinois Press.

Du Plessis, Rebecca Blau. 1985. *Writing beyond the Ending.* Bloomington: Indiana Univ. Press.

Durso, Patricia Keefe. 2008. "Maureen Howard's 'Landscapes of Memory.'" In *Too Smart to Be Sentimental: Contemporary Irish American Women Writers*, edited by Sally Barr Ebest and Kathleen McInerney, 52–80. South Bend: Notre Dame Univ. Press.

Dworkin, Andrea. 1978. *Right-Wing Women: The Politics of Domesticated Females.* London: The Women's Press.

Ebest, Ron. 2005. *Private Histories: The Writing of Irish Americans, 1900–1935.* South Bend: Univ. of Notre Dame Press.

———. 1994. Review, "*The Next Parish Over*, edited by Patricia Monaghan." New York: New Rivers Press. [First published in *Eire Ireland* 29, no. 3: 180–82.]

Ebest, Sally Barr, and Ron Ebest. 2003. *Reconciling Catholicism and Feminism? Personal Reflections on Tradition and Change.* South Bend: Univ. of Notre Dame Press.

Ebest, Sally Barr, and Kathleen McInerney. 2008. *Too Smart to Be Sentimental.* South Bend: Univ. of Notre Dame Press.

Echols, Alice. 1989. *Daring to Be Bad: Radical Feminism in America, 1967–1975.* Minneapolis: Univ. of Minnesota Press.

Edgeworth, Maria. 1800. *Castle Rackrent.* London: Oxford Press, 1903.

Elie, Paul. 2008. "What Flannery Knew: Catholic Writing for a Critical Age." *Commonweal*, November 21, 12–17.

Encyclopedia of World Biography. 2005–2006. "Mary Daly." http://www.bookrags.com/biography/mary-Daly.

Ennis, Catherine. 1988. *To the Lightening.* New York: Naiad Press.

Evasdaughter, Elizabeth. 1996. *Catholic Girlhood Narratives.* Boston: Northeastern Univ. Press.

Ezekiel, Tish O'Dowd. 1984. *Floaters.* New York: Atheneum.

Faderman, Lillian. 1991. *Odd Girls and Twilight Lovers.* New York: Columbia Univ. Press.

Faludi, Susan. 1991. *Backlash: The Undeclared War against Women*. New York: Anchor Books.

————. 2007. *The Terror Dream: Fear and Fantasy in Post–9/11 America*. New York: Holt.

Fanning, Charles. 1997. *The Exiles of Erin: Nineteenth-Century Irish American Fiction*. 2nd ed. New York: Dufours Editions.

————. 1990; 2nd ed. 2001. *The Irish Voice in America*. Lexington: Univ. of Kentucky Press.

Farley, Lynn. 1978. *Sexual Shakedown*. New York: McGraw Hill.

Farnham, Marynia F., and Ferdinand Lundberg. 1947. *Modern Woman: The Lost Sex*. New York: Harper.

Felski, Rita. 1989. *Beyond Feminist Aesthetics: Feminist Literature and Social Change*. Cambridge: Harvard Univ. Press.

Ferguson, Moira, Ketu H. Katrak, and Valerie Miner. 1996. "Feminism and Antifeminism: From Civil Rights to Culture Wars." In Clark, Garner, Higonnet, and Katrak, *Antifeminism in the Academy*, 35–66.

Finlay, Barbara. 2006. *George W. Bush and the War on Women: Turning Back the Clock on Progress*. London: Zed Books.

Finneran, Kathleen. 2000. *The Tender Land*. New York: Houghton Mifflin.

Fiztgerald, Eileen. 1996. *You're So Beautiful*. New York: St. Martin's Press.

FitzGerald, Francis. 1972. *Fire in the Lake: The Vietnamese and the Americans in Vietnam*. New York: Little, Brown.

Fitzsimons, E. A. 1878. *The Joint Venture: A Tale in Two Lands*. New York: James Sheehy.

Flanagan, Thomas. 2004. *There You Are: Writings on Irish and American Literature and History*. New York: New York Review of Books.

Flynn, Gillian. 2009. *Dark Places*. New York: Random House.

————. 2006. *Sharp Objects*. New York: Three Rivers Press.

Focus Adolescent Services. 2009. "What Is Self-Injury?" http://www.focusas.com /SelfInjury.html#What_kinds_of_people_self-injure.

Ford, Elaine. 2007. *The American Wife*. Ann Arbor: Univ. of Michigan Press.

————. 1983. *Missed Connections*. New York: Dell.

————. 1980. *The Playhouse*. New York: McGraw Hill.

Ford, Kathleen. 1986. *Jeffrey County*. New York: St. Martin's Press.

————. 1968. *The Three-Cornered House*. New York: McGraw-Hill.

Foster, Jeannette Howard. 1958. *Sex Variant Women in Literature*. New York: F. Muller.

Frank, Louise. 1986. *Louise Bogan.* New York: Columbia Univ. Press.

Friedan, Betty. 1963. *The Feminine Mystique.* New York: W. W. Norton.

Fulton, Alice. 2008. *The Nightingales of Troy.* New York: Norton.

Gale, Robert L. 1999. "Kathleen Thompson Norris." In *American National Biography*, edited by John Garraty and Mark C. Cases, n.p. New York: Oxford Univ. Press.

Gallagher, Tess. 1997. *At the Owl Woman Saloon.* New York: Scribner's.

———. 1986. *The Lover of Horses.* New York: Harper & Row.

———. 2009. *Soul Barnacles.* Ann Arbor: Univ. of Michigan Press.

Gandolfo, Anita. 1992. *Testing the Faith: The New Catholic Fiction in America.* Westwood, CT: Greenwood Press.

Gerson, Kathleen. 1986. *Hard Choices: How Women Decide about Work, Career, and Motherhood.* Berkeley and Los Angeles: Univ. of California Press.

Getz, Lorene M. 1980. *Flannery O'Connor: Her Life, Library, and Book Reviews.* Studies in Women and Religion. New York: Edwin Mellen Press.

Gilbert, Sandra M., and Susan Gubar. 1996. "Fighting For Life." In *Critical Essays on Carson McCullers*, edited by Beverly Lyon Clark and Melvin J. Friedman, 147–54. New York: Hall.

———. 1994. *No Man's Land: Letters from the Front.* Vol. 3. New Haven: Yale Univ. Press.

———. 1989. *No Man's Land: Sexchanges.* Vol. 2. New Haven: Yale Univ. Press.

Gilligan, Carol. 2008. *Kyra.* New York: Random House.

Gilman, Richard. 1969. "On Flannery O'Connor." *The New York Times Review of Books*, August 21, 24–26.

Ginsberg, Elaine, and Sara Lennox. 1996. "Antifeminism in Scholarship and Publishing." In Clark, Garner, Higonnet, and Katrak, *Antifeminism in the Academy*, 169–200.

Glasgow, Ellen. 1945. *Barren Ground.* New York: Doubleday Doran.

———. 1911. *The Miller of Old Church.* New York: Macmillan, Doran.

———. 1922. *One Man in His Time.* New York: Doubleday.

———. 1909. *The Romance of a Plain Man.* New York: Macmillan.

———. 1928. "Some Literary Woman Myths." *New York Herald Tribune Books*, May 20, 1, 5–6.

———. 1939. *They Stooped to Folly.* New York: Literary Guild.

———. 1913. *Virginia.* New York: Grosset & Dunlap.

Gleason, Philip. 1985. *Contending with Modernity: Catholic Higher Education in the Twentieth Century.* New York: Oxford.

Goodwin, Doris Kearns. 1996. *Character Above All*. New York: Simon & Schuster.

———. 1987. *The Fitzgeralds and the Kennedys*. New York: Simon & Schuster.

———. 1976. *Lyndon Johnson and the American Dream*. New York: St. Martin's Press.

———. 1995. *No Ordinary Time*. New York: Simon & Schuster.

———. 2006. *Team of Rivals: The Political Genius of Abraham Lincoln*. New York: Simon & Schuster.

———. 1997. *Wait Till Next Year*. New York: Simon & Schuster Touchstone.

Gordon, Caroline. 1956. *The Malefactors*. New York: Harcourt Brace.

———. 1951. *The Strange Children*. New York: Scribners.

Gordon, Lois. 2011. "Ann Beattie Biography." http://biography.jrank.org/pages/4143/Beattie-Ann.html.

Gordon, Mary. 1991. "Abortion: How Do We Really Choose?" In *Good Boys and Dead Girls*. [Originally published in *The Atlantic Monthly*, 1980.]

———. 1991. "Abortion: How Do We Think about It?" In *Good Boys and Dead Girls*. [Originally published in *The New York Review of Books*, 1984.]

———. 2007. *Circling My Mother*. New York: Pantheon.

———. 1980. *The Company of Women*. New York: Ballantine.

———. 1978. *Final Payments*. New York: Anchor Books.

———. 1991. *Good Boys and Dead Girls: And Other Essays*. New York: Penguin.

———. 1994. *Men and Angels*. New York: Ballantine.

———. 1989. *The Other Side*. New York: Penguin.

———. 2005. *Pearl*. New York: Random House.

———. 2009. *Reading Jesus: A Writer's Encounter with the Gospels*. New York: Random House.

———. 1994. *The Rest of Life*. New York: Penguin.

———. 1996. *The Shadow Man*. New York: Vintage.

———. 1998. *Spending*. New York: Scribner.

Gott, Patricia. "Hardly Sentimental: The 'Bad Girls' and Lonely Men of Mary McGarry Morris's Fiction." In Ebest and McInerney, *Too Smart to Be Sentimental*, 171–88.

Grant, Stephanie. 2008. *Map of Ireland*. New York: Scribner's.

———. 1995. *The Passion of Alice*. New York: Bantam Books.

Grealy, Lucy. 1994. *Autobiography of a Face*. New York: Houghton Mifflin.

Greeley, Andrew. 1985. "The Success and Assimilation of Irish Protestants and Catholics in the United States." *Social Science Research* 72, no. 4: 229–35.

Greene, Gayle. 1993. "Looking at History." In *Changing Subjects: The Making of Feminist Literary Criticism*, 4–30. New York: Routledge.

Greer, Germaine. 1984. *Sex and Destiny*. New York: Harper & Row.

Griffin, Gabriele. 2000. "'Romancing the Margins'"? In *Lesbian Writing in the 1990s*, edited by Gabriele Griffin, 1–6. London: Harrington Park Press.

Grubgeld, Elizabeth. 2004. *Anglo-Irish Autobiography: Class, Gender, and the Forms of Narrative*. Syracuse: Syracuse Univ. Press.

Grumbach, Doris. 1982. "Maureen Howard's Understated Elegance." Review of Maureen Howard's *Grace Abounding*. *Washington Post*, October 10, 5.

———. 1975. "Things Happen, Seem to Mean Something, Then Disappear into Memory." Review of Maureen Howard's *Before My Time*. *New York Times*, January 19, n.p.

Guiney, Imogene. 1908. *Blessed Edmund Campion*. London: Macdonald and Evans.

———. 1892. *"Monsieur Henri": A Footnote to French History*. New York: Harper and Bros.

———. 1904. *Robert Emmet, A Survey of His Rebellion and of His Romance*. London: David Nutt.

Hagan, Edward A. 2010. *Goodbye Yeats and O'Neill: Farce in Contemporary Irish and Irish American Narratives*. Amsterdam: Rodopi Press.

Hall, Radclyffe. 1928. *The Well of Loneliness*. New York: Avon Books.

Halley, Anne. "An American Story: Mary Doyle Curran (1917–1981)." Unpublished ms.

Hamill, Pete. 2006. "Once We Were Kings." In Lee and Casey, *Making the Irish American*, 526–34.

Hardwick, Elizabeth. 1972. "Foreword." *Intellectual Memoirs: New York, 1936–1938*. New York: Harcourt, Brace, Jovanovich.

Harkins, Susan Lynn. 1991. "Morris Again Looks in on the World of the Weak." *Orlando Sentinel*, March 3, F8.

Harper's Magazine. 1982. "Margaret Culkin Banning (1891–1982)." http://harpers.org/subjects/MargaretCulkinBanning.

Harris, Bernice Kelly. 1943. *Sweet Beulah Land*. New York: Doubleday.

Hartmann, Susan. 1982. *The Home Front and Beyond: American Women in the 1940s*. Boston: Twayne.

Heilbrun, Carolyn. 1979. *Reinventing Womanhood*. New York: Norton.

Heilemann, John. 2006. "What If 9/11 Never Happened? A Counter-History." *New York Magazine*, August 14, n.p. http://nymag.com/news/features/19147/.

Hendin, Josephine. 1970. *The World of Flannery O'Connor.* Bloomington: Indiana Univ. Press.

Hennessey, James. 1981. *American Catholics: A History of the Roman Catholic Community in the United States.* New York: Galaxy.

Higgins, Marguerite. 1965. *Our Vietnam Nightmare.* New York: Harper & Row.

Hill, Kathleen. 2010. *Who Occupies This House?* New York: Triquarterly.

Hite, Molly. 1989. *The Other Side of the Story: Structures and Strategies of Contemporary Female Narrators.* Ithaca: Cornell Univ. Press.

Hoberek, Andrew. 2005. *The Twilight of the Middle Class.* Princeton: Princeton Univ. Press.

Hoeness-Krupsaw, Susanna. 2008. "The World of Mary Gordon: Writing from the 'Other Side.'" In Ebest and McInerney, *Too Smart to Be Sentimental,* 201–19.

Hoffman, Joyce. 2008. *On Their Own: Women Journalists and the American Experience in Vietnam.* Cambridge, MA: DeCapo Press.

Hornbacher, Marya. 2006. *Wasted.* New York: Harper Perennial.

Horgan, Goretti. 2001. "Women in Ireland: A Cross-Cultural Experience." http://www.centerforwomeninleadership.org/files/old-content/php/funding/documents/amyblue.pdf.

Horowitz, Daniel. 1998. *Betty Friedan and the Making of "The Feminine Mystique": The American Left, the Cold War, and Modern Feminism.* Amherst: Univ. of Massachusetts Press.

Howard, Maureen. 1971. *Before My Time.* New York: Penguin.

———. 2001. *Big as Life: Three Tales for Spring.* New York: Penguin.

———. 1965. *Bridgeport Bus.* New York: Penguin.

———. 1975. *Facts of Life.* Boston: Little, Brown.

———. 1982. *Grace Abounding.* New York: Penguin.

———. 1986. *Expensive Habits.* New York: Summit.

———. 1997. Foreword. In Kearns, *Cabbage and Bones,* xi–xiv.

———. 1998. *A Lover's Almanac.* New York: Viking.

———. 1992. *Natural History.* New York: Carroll & Graf.

———. 1962. *Not a Word about Nightingales.* New York: Atheneum.

———. 2009. *The Rags of Time.* New York: Penguin.

———. 1978. "Salvation in Queens: *Final Payments.*" *New York Times,* April 16, 1, 32.

———. 2004. *The Silver Screen.* New York: Penguin.

Huf, Linda. 1983. *A Portrait of the Artist as a Young Woman: The Writer as Heroine in American Literature.* New York: Ungar.

Huffington Post. 2012. "Nancy Keenan." http://www.huffingtonpost.com/nancy-keenan.

Jacobson, Beatrice. 2008. "Alice McDermott's Narrators." In Ebest and McInerney, *Too Smart to Be Sentimental*, 116–35.

Jiles, Paulette. 2009. "She Was Tall in the Saddle." Review of *Half-Broke Horses*, by Jeannette Walls. *The Globe and Mail*, November 6. http://www.theglobeandmail.com/news/arts/books/article1353695.ece.

Johnson, Toni O'Brien, and David Cairn. 1991. *Gender in Irish Writing*. Dublin: Open Univ. Press.

Jones, Ann T. 1992. *A Country Divorce*. New York: Delphinium Press.

Jones, Mary Harris. 1925. *The Autobiography of Mother Jones*. Chicago: Charles H. Kerr.

Kalven, Janet. 2003. "Feminism and Catholicism." In Ebest and Ebest, *Reconciling Catholicism and Feminism?*, 32–46.

Katzman, David M. 1981. *Seven Days a Week: Women and Domestic Service in Industrializing America*. Chicago: Univ. of Illinois Press.

Kauffman, Linda S. 1993. *American Feminist Thought at Century's End: A Reader*. Oxford, UK: Blackwell.

Kearns, Caledonia, ed. 1997. *Cabbage and Bones: An Anthology of Irish American Women's Fiction*. New York: Holt.

Kelly, Myra. 1910. *Little Aliens*. New York: Scribner's.

———. 1904. *Little Citizens, The Humors of School Life*. New York: McClure, Phillips.

———. 1907. *Wards of Liberty*. New York: McClure.

Kennedy, William. 1988. *Quinn's Book*. New York: Viking.

Kennelly, Karen, CSJ. 1977. "Mary Malloy: Women's College Founder." In *Women of Minnesota: Selected Biographical Essays*, edited by Barbara Stuhler and Gretchen Kreuter, 116–35. St. Paul: Minnesota Historical Society Press.

Kenny, Kevin. 2003. *New Directions in Irish American History*. Madison: Univ. of Wisconsin Press.

———. 2006. "Race, Violence, and Anti-Irish Sentiment in the Nineteenth Century." In Lee and Casey, *Making the Irish American*, 364–80.

Kenschaft, Lori J. 1996. "Homoerotics and Human Connections: Reading Carson McCullers as a 'Lesbian.'" *Critical Essays on Carson McCullers*, edited by Beverly Lyon Clark and Melvin J. Friedman, 220–34. New York: Hall.

Klein, Naomi. 1997. *Promiscuities*. New York: Random House.

Koch, John T. 2005. *Celtic Culture: A Historical Encyclopedia*. Vols. 1–5. Santa Barbara: ABC-CLIO.

Kolosky, Bernard. 1996. *Kate Chopin*. New York: Twayne.

Kroeger, Brooke. 1995. *Nellie Bly: Daredevil, Reporter, Feminist*. New York: Three Rivers Press.

Krug, Nora. 2012. "Nora Roberts' Three Decades of Writing Have Led to 200 Books." *Washington Post*, April 16. http.//articles.washingtonpost/2012-04-16 /lifestyle/35450849_1_romance_novels_first-book-new-book.

Labrie, Ross. 1997. *The Catholic Imagination in American Literature*. Columbia: Univ. of Missouri Press.

LaPerla, Ruth. 2009. "More Gumption, Less Gucci." *New York Times*, August 13, E1, 10.

Larkin, Emmet. 1972. "The Devotional Revolution." *American Historical Review* 77, no. 3: 625–52.

Laughlin, Clara E. 1902. *The Evolution of a Girl's Ideal: A Little Record of the Ripening of the Affections to the Time of Love's Coming*. New York: Revell.

———. 1907. *Felicity*. New York: Scribners.

———. 1910. *"Just Folks."* New York: Macmillan.

———. 1905. *When Joy Begins*. New York: Revell.

———. 1913. *The Work-a-Day Girl: A Study of Some Present Conditions*. In *Women in America from Colonial Times to the Twentieth Century*, edited by Leon Stein and Annette K. Baxter, n.p. New York: Arno, 1974.

Lear, Linda. 1997. *Rachel Carson: Witness for Nature*. New York: Holt.

Lee, Amy. 2008. "Sojourners between Dreams and Reality." In Ebest and McInerney, *Too Smart to Be Sentimental*, 220–32.

Lee, J. J., and Marion R. Casey, eds. 2006. *Making the Irish American*. New York: New York Univ. Press.

Lerner, Gerda. 1975. "Placing Women in History: A 1975 Perspective." *Feminist Studies* 3: 5–15.

Lewis, Jone Johnson. [n.d.] "Mary Daly." http://womenshistory.about.com/od /feministtheology/p/mary_daly.htm.

Liukkonen, Petri. 2008. "Author's Calendar: Flannery O'Connor (1935–1964)." http://www.kirjasto.sci.fi/flannery.htm.

Lordan, Beth. 1998. *And Both Shall Row*. New York: Picador.

———. 2004. *But Come Ye Back*. New York: HarperCollins.

Lynch, Lee. 1988. *The Amazon Trail*. New York: Naiad Press.

———. 1987. *Dusty's Queen of Hearts Diner*. New York: Naiad Press.

———. 1984. *Old Dyke Tales*. New York: Naiad Press.

———. 1983. *Toothpick House*. New York: Naiad Press.

Lysaght, Patricia. 1986. *The Banshee: The Irish Death Messenger*. 2nd ed. Boulder, CO: Roberts Rinehart.

Macy, Caitlin. 2000. *The Fundamentals of Play*. New York: Anchor.

———. 2009. *Spoiled*. New York: Random House.

Madsen, Deborah. 2000. *Feminist Theory and Literary Practice*. New York: Pluto Press.

Mageean, Deirdre. 1997. "Making Sense and Providing Structure: Irish-American Women in The Parish Neighborhood. In *Peasant Maids—City Women*, edited by Christiane Harzig, 223–60. Ithaca: Cornell Univ. Press.

Manning, Martha. 1994. *Undercurrents*. San Francisco: Harper Collins.

Martin, Bradford. 2011. *The Other Eighties: A Secret History of America in the Age of Reagan*. New York: Hill and Wang.

Maslin, Janet. 2009. "The Girls of Summer." *The New York Times*, June 12, 25, 27.

Mason, Bobbie Ann. 2005. *An Atomic Romance*. New York: Random House.

———. 1999. *Clear Springs*. New York: Harper Collins Perennial.

———. 1993. *Feather Crowns*. New York: HarperCollins.

———. 1985. *In Country*. New York: HarperCollins.

———. 2006. *Nancy Culpepper*. New York: Random House.

———. 1998. *Spence + Lila*. New York: Harper & Row.

Matthews, Pamela R. 1995. *Ellen Glasgow and a Woman's Traditions*. Blacksburg: Univ. of Virginia Press.

Maxwell, William. 1998. Foreword. *Springs of Affection*. Berkeley, CA: Counterpoint.

McCaffrey, Lawrence J. 1992. *Textures of Irish America*. Syracuse: Syracuse Univ. Press.

McCarthy, Mary. 1977. *Birds of America*. New York: Harcourt Brace.

———. 1979. *Cannibals and Missionaries*. New York: Harcourt Brace Jovanovich.

———. 1955. *A Charmed Life*. New York: Harcourt Brace.

———. 1942. *The Company She Keeps*. New York: Dell.

———. 1963. *The Group*. New York: Harcourt Brace.

———. 1952. *The Groves of Academe*. Orlando, FL: Harcourt.

———. 1968. *Hanoi*. New York: Harcourt Brace & World.

———. 1957. *Memories of a Catholic Girlhood*. New York: Harcourt Brace & World.

———. 1949. *The Oasis*. New York: Avon.

———. 1967. *Vietnam*. New York: Harcourt Brace & World.

McConnell, Vicki. 1982. *Mrs. Porter's Letter*. New York: Naiad Press.

———. 1984. *The Burnton Widows*. New York: Naiad Press.

McCullers, Carson. 1951. *The Ballad of the Sad Café*. New York: Houghton Mifflin.

———. 1940. *The Heart Is a Lonely Hunter*. New York: Bantam.

———. 1946. *The Member of the Wedding*. New York: Bantam.

———. 1941. *Reflections in a Golden Eye*. New York: Bantam.

McDermott, Alice. 2006. *After This*. New York: Farrar, Straus and Giroux.

———. 1982. *A Bigamist's Daughter*. New York: Random House/Dell.

———. 1992. *At Weddings and Wakes*. New York: Dell.

———. 1998. *Charming Billy*. New York: Farrar, Straus and Giroux.

———. 2002. *Child of My Heart*. New York: Farrar, Straus and Giroux.

———. 2000. "Confessions of a Reluctant Catholic." *Commonweal* 127, no. 2: 12–16.

———. 1987. *That Night*. New York: Random House/Dell.

McElroy, Wendy. [n.d.] "Gertrude Kelly: Forgotten Feminist." *The Memory Hole: Anarchism and Feminism: Restoring to Proper Place Department*. http://tmh .floonet.net/articles/gkelly.shtml.

McGarry, Jean. 1985. *Airs of Providence*. Baltimore: Johns Hopkins Univ. Press.

———. 2006. *A Bad and Stupid Girl*. Ann Arbor: Univ. of Michigan Press.

———. 1992. *The Courage of Girls*. New Brunswick: Rutgers Univ. Press.

———. 2002. *Dream Date*. Baltimore: Johns Hopkins Univ. Press.

———. 1997. *Gallagher's Travels*. Baltimore: Johns Hopkins Univ. Press.

———. 1994. *Home at Last*. Baltimore: Johns Hopkins Univ. Press.

———. 1986. *The Very Rich Hours*. Baltimore: Johns Hopkins Univ. Press.

McGoldrick, Monica. 1998. "Belonging and Liberation: Finding a Place Called 'Home.'" In *Re-Visioning Family Therapy*, edited by Monica McGoldrick, 215–28. New York: Guilford.

McGoldrick, Monica, Nydia Garcia-Preto, Paulette Moore Hines, and Evelyn Lee. 1989. "Ethnicity and Women." In *Women in Families*, edited by Monica McGoldrick, Carol M. Anderson, and Froma Walsh, 169–99. New York: Norton.

———. 1995. *You Can Go Home Again*. New York: Norton.

McGrath, Kristin. 1994. *House Work*. Bridgehampton, NY: Bridge Works.

McGraw, Erin. 2002. *The Baby Tree*. Ashland, OR: Story Line Press.

———. 1989. *Bodies at Sea*. Urbana: Univ. of Illinois Press.

———. 2004. *The Good Life*. Boston: Houghton Mifflin.

———. 1996. *Lies of the Saints*. San Francisco: Chronicle Books.

———. 2003. "Not from Here." In *In the Middle of the Middle West*, edited by Becky Bradway, 119–29. Bloomington: Indiana Univ. Press.

———. 2008. *The Seamstress of Hollywood Boulevard*. Boston: Houghton Mifflin.

McInerney, Kathleen. 2008. "Forget about Being Irish: Family, Transgression, and Identity in The Fiction of Elizabeth Cullinan." In Ebest and McInerney, *Too Smart to Be Sentimental*, 97–115.

McKinney, Ruth. 1938. *Industrial Valley*. New York: Harcourt Brace.

———. 1938. *My Sister Eileen*. New York: Harcourt Brace.

McRae, Diana. 1988. *All the Muscle You Need*. New York: Spinster's Ink.

McRobbie, Angela. 2007. "Post-feminism and Popular Culture." In Tasker and Negra, *Interrogating Post-feminism*, 27–39.

Meagher, Timothy J. 2005. *The Columbia Guide to Irish American History*. New York: Columbia Univ. Press.

———. 2006. "The Fireman on the Stairs: Communal Loyalties in the Making of Irish America." In Lee and Casey, *Making the Irish American*, 609–48.

Meany, Mary. 1865. *The Confessors of Connaught; or, The Tenants of a Lord Bishop*. Philadelphia: Peter Cunningham.

Menand, Louis. 2011. "Books as Bombs: Why the Women's Movement Needed *The Feminine Mystique*." *The New Yorker*, January 24. http://www.newyorker .com/arts/critics/books/2011/01/24/110124crbo_books_menand.

Millet, Kate Murray. 1982. *Going to Iran*. New York: Coward, McCann & Geoghagen, 1982.

———. 1969. *Sexual Politics*. New York: Doubleday.

Miner, Valerie. 1987. *All Good Women*. Crossing Press.

———. 1981. *Blood Sisters*. Ann Arbor: Michigan State Univ. Press.

———. 1982. *Movement*. New York: Methuen.

———. 1982. *Murder in the English Department*. New York: Mandarin.

———. 1985. *Winter's Edge*. New York: Feminist Press.

Minnesota Author's Biographies. [n.d.] "Margaret Culkin Banning." Minnesota Historical Society. http://collections.mnhs.org/mnauthors/index.php/10001316.

Minot, Susan. 1998. *Evening*. New York: Vintage.

———. 1992. *Folly*. New York: Washington Square Press.

———. 1986. *Monkeys*. New York: Random House.

Mitchell, Margaret. 1936. *Gone With the Wind*. New York: Macmillan.

Moloney, Catriona, and Helen Thompson, eds. 2003. *Irish Women Writers Speak Out: Voices from The Field*. Syracuse: Univ. of Syracuse Press.

Moloney, Mick. 2006. "Irish American Festivals." In Lee and Casey, *Making the Irish American*, 426–42.

Monaghan, Patricia. 1993. "Grandmothers and Rebel Lovers: Archetypes in Irish-American Women's Poetry." *MELUS: The Society for the Study of the Multi-Ethnic Literature of the United States* 18, no. 1: 83–94.

Monaghan, Patricia, and Robert E. Rhodes. 2004. "Irish American Writing: Political Men and Archetypal Women." In *A Concise Companion to Postwar American Literature and Culture*, edited by Josephine G. Hendin, 323–50. Malden, MA: Blackwell.

Moore, Susanna. 2007. *The Big Girls*. New York: Random House.

———. 2003. *I Myself Have Seen It*. New York: National Geographic.

———. 1999. *In the Cut*. New York: Plume.

———. 2009. *Light Years: A Girlhood in Hawaii*. New York: Grove.

———. 1982. *My Old Sweetheart*. New York: Random House.

———. 1993. *Sleeping Beauties*. New York: Vintage.

———. 1989. *The Whiteness of Bones*. New York: Doubleday.

Morgan, Marabel. 1973. *The Total Woman*. New York: Revell.

Morgan, Robin. 1989. *The Demon Lover: The Roots of Terrorism*. New York: Simon & Schuster.

———. 1984. *Sisterhood Is Global: The International Women's Movement Anthology*. New York: Feminist Press.

———. 1970. *Sisterhood Is Powerful*. New York: Random House.

Morgan, Susan. 2011. "Mother Modern: A Pioneering Historian of Twentieth-Century California Architecture." *New York Times Style Magazine* (Fall), 59–60.

Morris, Mary McGarry. 1991. *A Dangerous Woman*. New York: Penguin.

———. 2000. *Fiona Range*. New York: Viking.

———. 2004. *A Hole in the Universe*. New York: Viking.

———. 2009. *The Last Secret*. New York: Three Rivers Press.

———. 2005. *The Lost Mother*. New York: Viking.

———. 1995. *Songs in Ordinary Time*. New York: Penguin.

———. 1988. *Vanished*. New York: Penguin.

Motley, The. 1958. "Interview with Flannery O'Connor." [Spring Hill College, Mobile, AL] 9 (Spring): 29–31.

Moynihan, Daniel Patrick. 2006. "The Irish." In Lee and Casey, *Making the Irish American*, 525–75.

Mullins, C. Ross. 1963. "Flannery O'Connor: An Interview. *Jubilee* 11 (June): 32–35.

Murphy, Evelyn. 2006. *Getting Even: Why Women Don't Get Paid Like Men—and What to Do about It.* New York: Touchstone.

Murphy, Maureen. 1979. "Elizabeth Cullinan: Yellow and Gold." In *Irish American Fiction: Essays in Criticism*, edited by Daniel Casey and Robert Rhodes, 139–52. New York: AMS Press.

Murphy, Patricia A. 1987. *Searching for Spring.* New York: Naiad Press.

Myles, Eileen. 1994. *Chelsea Girls.* New York: Black Sparrow Press.

———. 2000. *Cool for You.* Berkeley, CA: Soft Skull Press.

Negra, Diane. 2006. "Irishness, Innocence, and American Identity Politics before and after September 11." In *The Irish in Us*, edited by Diane Negra, 354–71. Durham: Duke Univ. Press.

Nolan, Alice. 1870. *The Byrnes of Glengoulah: A True Tale.* New York: P. O'Shea.

Nolan, Janet. 2004. *Servants of the Poor.* South Bend: Univ. of Notre Dame Press.

Norris, Kathleen. 1911. *Mother.* New York: Macmillan.

Oates, Joyce Carol. 2009. *A Fair Maiden.* Orlando: Houghton Mifflin Harcourt.

———. 2006. *After the Wreck I Picked Myself Up, Spread My Wings, and Flew Away.* New York: HarperCollins.

———. 2006. "Afterword." *Expensive People.* New York: Modern Library.

———. 1975. *The Assassins.* New York: Vanguard.

———. 2002. *Beasts.* New York: Carroll & Graf.

———. 1980. *Bellefleur.* New York: Penguin.

———. 2006. *Black Girl, White Girl.* New York: HarperCollins.

———. 1999. *Black Water.* New York: Penguin.

———. 1999. *Blonde.* New York: HarperCollins.

———. 1982. *A Bloodsmoor Romance.* New York: Warner.

———. 1975b. *The Childwold.* New York: Fawcett.

———. 1981. *Contraries.* New York: Oxford Univ. Press.

———. 1979. *Cybele.* New York: Black Sparrow.

———. 1973. *Do with Me What You Will.* New York: Vanguard.

———. 1968. *Expensive People.* New York: Vanguard.

———. 2001. *Faithless.* New York: HarperCollins.

———. 1996. *First Love.* New York: Ecco.

———. 1993. *Foxfire.* New York: Macmillan.

———. 1967. *A Garden of Earthly Delights.* New York: Random House.

———. 2007. *The Gravedigger's Daughter.* New York: HarperCollins.

———. 2002. *I'll Take You There.* New York: HarperCollins.

———. 1997. *Man Crazy*. New York: Penguin Plume.

———. 1972. *Marriages and Infidelities*. New York: Vanguard.

———. 2005. *Mother, Missing*. New York: HarperCollins.

———. 2008. *My Sister, My Love*. New York: HarperCollins.

———. 1984. *Mysteries of Winterthurn*. Montreal: Ontario Review.

———. 2003. *Rape: A Love Story*. New York: Carroll and Graf.

———. 1991. *The Rise of Life on Earth*. New York: New Directions.

———. 1985. *Solstice*. New York: Dutton.

———. 1978. *Son of the Morning*. New York: Vanguard.

———. 2003. *Tatooed Girl*. New York: HarperCollins.

———. 1977. *The Triumph of the Spider Monkey*. New York: Black Sparrow.

———. 1969. *Them*. New York: Vanguard.

———. 1979. *Unholy Loves*. New York: Vanguard.

———. 1999. *We Were the Mulvaneys*. New York: Plume.

———. 1989. *(Woman) Writer*. New York: Plume.

———. 1971. *Wonderland*. New York: Random House.

———. 1987. *You Must Remember This*. New York: Putnam.

O'Connor, Flannery. 1965. *Everything That Rises Must Converge*. New York: Farrar, Strauss and Giroux.

———. 1955. *A Good Man Is Hard to Find*. San Diego, CA: Harcourt Brace.

———. 2008. *The Presence of Grace and Other Book Reviews*. Edited by Carter W. Martin. Athens: Univ. of Georgia Press.

———. 1952. *The Violent Bear It Away*. New York: Farrar, Strauss and Giroux.

———. 1952. *Wise Blood*. New York: Farrar, Strauss and Giroux.

O'Connor, Martha. 2005. *The Bitch Posse*. New York: St. Martin's Press.

O'Connor, Thomas H. 1995. *The Boston Irish: A Political History*. Boston: Northeastern Univ. Press.

O'Hagan, Anne. 1915. "The Doom of the Home. And What about the Cave Man? And Woman's Work? And Rubber-Plants?" *Vanity Fair* 4, no. 2: 49.

———. 1916. "The Four Ages of Women." *The Survey* 36 (April): 80.

———. 1907. "Some Compensations of Spinsterhood," "The Spinster's Men Friends," "The Married Woman and the Spinster," "What Becomes of Our Ideals?," "The Neurotic Spinster of Literature." *Harper's Bazaar* 41 (February, March, July, August, and October).

O'Hehir, Diana. 1988. *The Bride Who Ran Away*. New York: Washington Square Press.

———. 1984. *I Wish This War Were Over.* New York: Washington Square Press.

Ohman, Richard. 1984. "The Shaping of a Canon: U.S. Fiction, 1960–1975." In *Canons,* edited by Robert Von Hallberg, 377–402. Chicago: Univ. of Chicago Press.

O'Neill, Thomas, and William Novak. 1987. *Man of the House: The Life and Memoirs of Tip O'Neill.* New York: Random House.

O'Reilly, Augustine. 1880. *Strange Memories: Death Bed Scenes, Extraordinary Conversions, Incidents of Travel, etc.* New York: Sadlier.

Owenson, Sydney. 1999. *The Wild Irish Girl.* New York: Oxford.

Palko, Abigail L. 2007. "Out of Home in the Kitchen: Maeve Brennan's Herbert's Retreat Stories." *New Hibernia Review* 11, no. 4: 73–91.

Palmer, Paulina. 1993. *Contemporary Lesbian Writing: Dreams, Desire, Difference.* Buckingham, UK: Open Univ. Press.

Patchett, Ann. 2001. *Bel Canto.* New York: HarperCollins.

———. 1997. *The Magician's Assistant.* Orlando: Harcourt Brace.

———. 1992. *The Patron Saint of Liars.* New York: Harper's.

———. 2007. "P.S." Run. New York: HarperCollins.

———. 2007. *Run.* New York: HarperCollins.

———. 2004. *Truth & Beauty.* New York: Harper Collins.

Peters, Bruce. 2003. "Reconciling the Places Where Memory Resides." In Ebest and Ebest, *Reconciling Catholicism and Feminism?,* 177–89.

Pichardo, Ernesto, CLBA. 1998. "Santería in Contemporary Cuba: The Individual Life and Condition of the Priesthood." *CLBA Journal.* http://www.church ofthelukumi.com/santeria-in-contemporary-cuba.html.

Pipher, Mary. 1994. *Reviving Ophelia.* New York: Grosset/Putnam.

Pyron, Darden Asbury. 1992. *Southern Daughter: The Life of Margaret Mitchell.* New York: Perennial.

Quindlen, Anna. 1998. *Black and Blue.* New York: Random House.

———. 1991. *Object Lessons.* New York: Ivy.

———. 1994. *One True Thing.* New York: Dell.

———. 2006. *Rise and Shine.* New York: Random House.

Quinn, Peter. 1985. "William Kennedy: An Interview." *Recorder* 1, no. 1: 65–81.

Rahv, Phillip, and William Phillips, eds. 1946. *Partisan Review Reader: Ten Years of the Partisan Review, 1934–1944.* New York: Dial.

Reichardt, Mary, ed. 2010. *Between Human and Divine: The Catholic Vision in Contemporary Literature.* Washington: The Catholic Univ. of America Press.

Rich, Adrienne. 1979. "When We Dead Awaken: Writing as Re-Vision." In *On Lies, Secrets, and Silence*. New York: Norton.

Rivers, Caryl. 1973. *Aphrodite at Mid-Century: Growing Up Female and Catholic in Postwar America*. New York: Doubleday.

———. 1984. *Girls Forever Brave and True*. New York: St. Martin's Press.

———. 2003. "Knock. Knock. Who's There? Same Ol' Editor-Guys." *Women's e News*, April 9. http://www.womensenews.org/article/cfm/dyn/aid/1285/context/archive.

———. 1984. *Virgins*. New York: St. Martin's Press.

Robinson, B. A. 2008. "The Catholic Church and Homosexuality: Statements and Events Prior to 1997." Ontario Consultants on Religious Tolerance. ReligiousTolerance.org, http://www.religioustolerance.org/hom_rom6.htm (updated July 25, 2008).

Rohy, Valerie. 2000. *Impossible Women: Lesbian Figures and American Literature*. Ithaca: Cornell Univ. Press.

Ruether, Rosemary Radford. 2003. "American Catholic Feminism: A History." In Ebest and Ebest, *Reconciling Catholicism and Feminism?*, 3–12.

———. 1993. *Sexism and God-Talk: Toward a Feminist Theology*. Boston: Beacon.

Russo, Maria. 2009. "BFs Forever." *New York Times Sunday Book Review*, June 9. http://www.nytimes.com/2009/06/14/books/review/Russo-t.html.

Rustin, Susanna. 2011. "A Life in Writing: Ann Patchett." *The Guardian*, June 10. http://www.guardian.co.uk/culture/2011/jun/10/ann-patchett-life-writing -interview.

Ryan, Mary Ann. 2008. "Tess Gallagher: A Network of Sympathies and Distant Connections. In Ebest and McInerney, *Too Smart to Be Sentimental*, 139–56.

Sadlier, Mary Ann. 1866. *Aunt Honor's Keepsake*. New York: Sadlier.

———. 1861. *Bessy Conway; or, The Irish Girl in America*. New York: Sadlier.

———. 1864. *Con O'Regan; or, Immigrant Life in the New World*. New York: Sadlier.

———. 1862. *Old and New; or, Taste vs. Fashion*. New York: Sadlier.

———. 1850. *Willy Burke; or, The Irish Orphan in America*. Boston: Patrick Donahoe.

Savage, Elizabeth. 1975. *A Good Confession*. New York: Little, Brown.

Savigneau, Josyane. 1995. *Carson McCullers: Un coeur de jeunne fil*. Translated by Joan E. Hoard. New York: Houghton Mifflin.

Sayers, Valerie. 1994. *The Distance between Us*. New York: Doubleday.

———. 1987. *Due East*. New York: Doubleday.

———. 1988. *How I Got Him Back*. New York: Doubleday.

Scanlan, Anna. 1895. *Dervorgilla; or, The Downfall of Ireland*. Milwaukee: J. H. Yewdale.

Schneider, Herbert Wallace. 1952. *Religion in Twentieth-Century America*. Cambridge: Harvard Univ. Press.

Schuessler, Jennifer. 2011. "*The Glass Castle*." *New York Times Book Review*, July 17.

———. 2009. "Once More, With Feeling." *New York Times Book Review*, May 3, 18.

Schweikert, Patrocinio P. 1986. "Reading Ourselves: Toward a Feminist Theory of Reading." In *Gender and Reading*, edited by Elizabeth Flynn and Patrocinio Schweikert, 31–62. Baltimore: Johns Hopkins Univ. Press.

Scott, Bonnie Kime. 1979. "Women's Perspectives in Irish-American Fiction from Betty Smith To Mary McCarthy." In *Irish-American Fiction*, edited by Daniel J. Casey and Robert E. Rhodes, 87–104. New York: AMS.

Segal, Lynne. 1999. *Why Feminism?* New York: Columbia Univ. Press.

Seidler, John, and Katherine Meyer. 1989. *Conflict and Change in the Catholic Church*. New Brunswick: Rutgers Univ. Press.

Seyersted, Per. 1980. *Kate Chopin: A Critical Biography*. Baton Rouge: Louisiana State Univ. Press.

Shannon, William. 1990. *The American Irish: A Political and Social Portrait*. Amherst: Univ. of Massachussetts Press.

Sheehy, Gail. 1974. *Passages*. New York: Random House.

Shelley, Thomas J. 2006. "Twentieth-Century American Catholicism and Irish Americans." In Lee and Casey, *Making the Irish American*, 574–608.

Showalter, Elaine. 1997. *Hystories*. New York: Columbia Univ. Press.

———. 2001. *Inventing Herself: Claiming a Feminist Intellectual Heritage*. New York: Scribner's.

———. 2009. *A Jury of Her Peers: American Women Writers from Anne Bradstreet to Annie Proulx*. New York: Knopf.

———. 1990. *Sexual Anarchy: Gender and Culture at the Fin de Siècle*. New York: Viking.

Sifton, Elisabeth. 1962. "The Art of Fiction." *Paris Review* 27 (Winter-Spring): 6.

Simkin, John. [n.d.] "Women's Suffrage." Spartacus Educational Encyclopaedia. USA History. http://www.spartacus.schoolnet.co.uk/USAwomen.htm.

Sister X. 2009. "Cross Examination: Why Is Rome Investigating U.S. Nuns? *Commonweal*, October 9. http://www.commonwealmagazine.org/cross-examination.

Slack, Donovan. 2006. "O'Toole Stepping Down as Police Commissioner." *Boston Globe*, May 9. http://www.boston.com/news/local/massachusetts/articles/2006/05/09/otoole_stepping_down_as_boston_police_commissioner/.

Smith, Anthony Burke. 2010. *The Look of Catholics: Portrayals in Popular Culture from the Great Depression to the Cold War*. Lawrence: Univ. of Kansas Press.

Smith, Betty. 1963. *Joy in the Morning*. New York: Harper & Row.

———. 1958. *Maggie-Now*. New York: Harper & Brothers.

———. 1948. *Tomorrow Will Be Better*. New York: Harper & Brothers.

———. 1943. *A Tree Grows in Brooklyn*. New York: HarperCollins.

Smith, Norma. 2002. *Jeannette Rankin: America's Conscience*. Helena: Montana Historical Society Press.

Snell, Tracy. 1994. "Women in Prison." U.S. Department of Justice, Office of Justice Programs. Bureau of Justice Statistics. http://www.ojp.gov/bjs/pub/ascii/wopris/text.

Stanton, Maura. 1988. *The Country I Come From*. Minneapolis, MN: Milkweed.

———. 1979. *Molly Companion*. New York: Avon.

Stewart, Ramona. 1975. *Age of Consent*. New York: Signet.

———. 1973. *Apparition*. New York: Little, Brown.

———. 1970. *The Possession of Joel Delaney*. New York: Bantam.

———. 1978. *Seasons of the Heart*. New York: Putnam.

———. 1979. *The Sixth Sense*. New York: Delacourt.

Sullivan, J. Courtney. 2009. *Commencement*. New York: Farrar, Straus and Giroux.

Takaki, Ronald. 1993. *A Different Mirror: A History of Multicultural America*. New York: Little, Brown.

Tasker, Yvonne, and Diane Negra. 2007. "Introduction: Feminist Politics and Post-feminist Culture." In Tasker and Negra, *Interrogating Post-feminism*, 1–26.

———, eds. *Interrogating Post-feminism*. Durham: Duke Univ. Press.

Tessier, M. 2002. "Bush Appointments Include Fewer Women." *Women's e-News*, February 11. www.womensnews.org.

———. 2001. "Women's Appointments Plummet under Bush." *Women's e-News*, July 1 (revised October 1). www.womensnews.org/article-cfm/dyn/aid/600/context/archive.

Thompson, Dorothy. 1949. "Occupation: Housewife." *Ladies Home Journal*, March.

Thompson, Helen. 2003. "Emma Donoghue." In *Irish Women Writers Speak Out: Voices from the Field*, edited by Helen Thompson, 169–80. Syracuse: Syracuse Univ. Press.

Tobin, Kathleen. 2003. "Catholicism and the Contraceptive Debate." In Ebest and Ebest, *Reconciling Catholicism and Feminism?*, 202–26.

Trisco, Robert. 1976. *Catholics in America, 1776–1976*. Washington, DC: National Conference of Catholic Bishops.

Ulster History Circle. 2013. "Kathleen Coyle." http://www.ulsterhistory.co.uk /kathleencoyle.htm.

Vaid, Urvashi. 1994. "Foreword." In Sarah Schulman, *My American History: Lesbian and Gay Life During the Reagan/Bush Years*. New York: Routledge.

Vassar College Libraries. [n.d.] *Guide to the Margaret Culkin Banning Papers*. http://specialcollections.vassar.edu/findingaids/banning_margaret_culkin.html #d0e51.

Wachtel, Eleanor. 2002. "Mary Gordon." In *Conversations with Mary Gordon*, edited by Alma Bennett, 81–89. Jackson: Univ. Press of Mississippi.

Wadler, Joyce. 2007. "Dark Work in a Sunny Spot: At Home with Susanna Moore." *New York Times*, June 21, D1, 6.

Wald, Alan. 1996. "The Left Reconsidered." In *Twenty-four Ways of Looking at Mary McCarthy*, edited by Eve Swertka and Margo Viscusi, 69–76. Westport, CT: Greenwood Press.

Wall, Eamonn. 1999. *From the Sine-e Café to the Black Hills: Notes on the New Irish*. Madison: Univ. of Wisconsin Press.

Walls, Jeannette. 2006. *The Glass Castle*. New York: Scribner.

———. 2009. *Half-Broke Horses*. New York: Scribner.

Watanabe, Nancy Anne. 2010. "The Contemporary Catholic Bildungsroman: Passionate Conviction in Shusaku Enda's *The Samurai* and Mary Gordon's *Men and Angels*." In Richardt, *Between Human and Divine*, 189–206.

Waters, Maureen. 2001. *Crossing Highbridge: A Memoir of Irish America*. Syracuse: Syracuse Univ. Press.

Wearing, Sadie. 2007. "Subjects of Rejuvenation: Aging in Post-feminist Culture." In Tasker and Negra, *Interrogating Post-feminism*, 277–300.

Weaver, Mary Jo, ed. 1995. *Being Right: Conservative Catholics in America*. Bloomington: Indiana Univ. Press.

———. 1985. *New Catholic Women*. New York: Harper & Row.

———. 1993. *Springs of Water in a Dry Land: Catholic Women and Spiritual Survival Today*. Boston: Beacon Press.

———, ed. 1999. *What's Left?* Bloomington: Indiana Univ. Press.

Webb, Jim. 2004. *Born Fighting: How the Scots-Irish Shaped America*. New York: Random House.

Weekes, Anne Owens. 1993. *Unveiling Treasures: The Attic Guide to the Published Works of Irish Women Literary Writers.* London: Attic Press.

Wells, Joel. 1962. "Off the Cuff." *The Critic* 21 (August–September): 4–5, 71–72.

Wesley, Marilyn. 1993. *Refusal and Transgression in Joyce Carol Oates' Fiction.* New York: Greenwood.

Westling, Louise. 1996. "Tomboys and Revolting Femininity." In *Critical Essays on Carson Mccullers,* edited by Beverly Lyon Clark and Melvin J. Friedman, 155–65. New York: Hall.

Whelehan, Imelda. 1995. *Modern Feminist Thought: From the Second Wave to "Post-Feminism."* New York: New York Univ. Press.

Wilson, Cintra. 2009. "Critical Shopper." *The New York Times,* May 7, E4.

Wolf, Naomi. 1976. *The Beauty Myth.* London: Chatto & Windus.

"Women of the Year." 1976. *Time Magazine,* January 5.

Woods, Randall Bennett. 2005. *Quest for Identity: America since 1945.* Cambridge: Cambridge Univ. Press.

Young, Mallory, and Suzanne Ferris. 2005. *Chick-Lit.* New York: Routledge.

Yow, Valerie R. 1955. *Bernice Kelly Harris: Storyteller of Eastern Carolina.* Chapel Hill: Univ. of North Carolina Library.

Zelizer, Gerald. 2002. "Quick Dose of 9-11 Religion Soothes, Doesn't Change." *USAToday.com,* January 7. http://www.usatoday.com/news/opinion/2002/01/08/ncguest2.htm.

Zimmerman, Bonnie. 1990. *The Safe Sea of Women: Lesbian Fiction, 1969–1989.* Boston: Beacon.

Index

"Ablutions, The" (Cullinan), 82–83
abortion: in 1970s, 95–97; Army of
    Three and, 74; Catholic Church
    and, 75–77, 109, 112, 143, 165;
    characters' rejection of, 133n4;
    Jerry Falwell on, 193; Mary Gor-
    don on, 145, 145n8; hotlines for,
    152; in Italy, 86; Alice McDermott
    on, 202; Erin McGraw on, 203–4;
    Medicare/Medicaid for, 89; movies
    about, 156; Nixon and, 69; Oates
    on, 133; Sinead O'Connor, 178;
    Ann Patchett on, 180; protests
    against, 54, 134, 178; Reagan
    administration and, 118, 120–21,
    130–31, 132–33; *Roe v. Wade*,
    95–96, 109, 132, 133; third-wavers
    and, 215, 221
"Abortion: How Do We Really
    Choose?" (Gordon), 145n8
"Abortion: How Do We Think About
    It?" (Gordon), 145n8
Abzug, Bella, 98
Academy Award, 219
"Accepted Wisdom" (McGraw), 122
"Accident, An" (Cullinan), 113–14
ACIS (American Conference for Irish
    Studies), x, 65
Adam and Eve, 77
Adams, Gerry, 210, 211

Adams, Jane, 22
Adam's Rib (Herschberger), 53
adoption, 132, 180, 208
adultery, 19, 25, 56, 93, 164, 178
affirmative action, 66, 69
*After the Wreck I Picked Myself Up,
    Spread My Wings, and Flew Away*
    (Oates), 213
After This (McDermott), 202
Against Rape (Thompson), 96
Age of Consent (Stewart), 108
AIDS, 112, 134–35, 137 140, 152
    168, 220
Airs of Providence (McGarry), 147,
    148, 242
Albright, Madeleine, 153
alcoholism, 12, 14, 25, 41, 46, 70,
    174, 179, 211; Cullinan on, 147;
    lesbian literature and, 136; McDer-
    mott on, 181–84; Minot on, 149,
    178; Myles on, 12, 167–68, 167n1,
    200; O'Hehir on, 147
Alice Doesn't Live Here Anymore
    (movie), 88
Alien (movie), 138–39
Alien 3 (movie), 156
alienation, 107–9, 146–47, 160,
    163–64, 167, 176, 224
allegory, 205
All Good Women (Miner), 136

Catholic Family Movement (CFM), 74, 75

Catholic Girlhood Narratives (Evasdaughter), 169

Catholics, divorce by, 16, 45–46, 50, 60, 75, 112–13, 165, 177–78

Catholics for Free Choice (CFFC), 107, 165

Catholics in America 1776–1976 (Trisco), 2

Catholic themes, 14–15, 78, 85, 109–10, 149–50, 198, 205; in 1960s, 72; in 1970s, 16, 106–15; in 1980s, 16, 143–50; in 1990s, 154, 165; in autobiographical novels, 109–12; by Margaret Culkin Banning, 25; by Madelaine Blais, 40; by Maeve Brennan, 16, 39, 74–75; by Lisa Carey, 204–5; by Cullinan, 16, 35, 53, 82–84, 112–14, 115, 146; by Colleen Curran, 217–18; by Mary Daly, 16, 76–77, 107–8; by Eleanor Donnelly, 8; by Caroline Gordon, 37; by Mary Gordon, 16, 40, 90–94, 109, 143–45, 205; by Howard, 16, 38, 80–81, 115; of individualism, 143, 149–50; by Caitlin Macy, 200–201; by Mary McCarthy, 13, 36–37, 44, 72–73; by Alice McDermott, 85, 201–2; by Mary Meany, 7; by Susan Minot, 148–49; by Mary McGarry Morris, 164; by Eileen Myles, 168; by Oates, 175; by Flannery O'Connor, 37, 82; by O'Dowd, 147, 200; of reconciliation, 143–49; by Augustine O'Reilly, 8; post-9/11 period, 198–208; post–World War II period, 36–40; pre-Famine generation, 5; by Caryl Rivers,

39, 79, 86, 89, 114–15, 145; by Mary Ann Sadlier, 7; by Elizabeth Savage, 110–12; by Valerie Sayers, 75n4; Scots Irish, 99; sentimental vs. realistic, 78; by Maura Stanton, 149–50; by J. Courtney Sullivan, 190–93

Catholic Women (Weaver), 165

Catholic women's colleges, 22–23

Catholic Worker, The (newspaper), 29

Catholic Working Women's Retreat Movement, 144

Cavedweller (Allison), 168

CFFC (Catholics for Free Choice), 107, 165

CFM (Catholic Family Movement), 74, 75

Change of Scene, A (Cullinan), 145, 146

Changing Subjects, 64

Chao, Elaine, 188

Chapman, Linda S., 220

Character Above All: Ten President (Goodwin), 154

Charmed Life, A (McCarthy), 43–44

Charming Billy (McDermott), 12, 14, 154, 180, 182–84, 202

Chelsea Girls (Myles), 167–68, 167n1

Chicago Tribune (newspaper), 24, 148, 197

Chick Lit (Young and Ferris), 197–98

chick lit, 190, 197–98

Chieftans (group), 105

Child of My Heart (McDermott), 201–2, 213

child sexual abuse, 173

Childwold (Oates), 94, 95, 97–98

Chilly Scenes of Winter (Beattie), 102

Chopin, Katherine "Kate" O'Flaherty, 25–26

Stanton, Maura, 109, 149–50

Stanwyck, Barbara, 33

Star Wars (movie), 88

stay-at-home wives and mothers. *See* housewives and mothers tradition

Stein, Gertrude, 54

Steinem, Gloria, 191

"Stepmother, The" (Cleary), 24–25

stereotypes: Irish, 5–7, 30, 65–66, 83, 208–9; of women, 20, 89, 137n6

Stewart, Ramona: *Age of Consent*, 108; *Apparition*, 108; *Casey*, 63n2, 78; historical novels by, 63, 63n2, 78; *The Possession of Joel Delaney*, 108–9; *Seasons of the Heart*, 108; *The Sixth Sense*, 108, 109

Stir-Fry (Donoghue), 116

St. Mary's College, 23, 76

Stone, Sharon, 156

Stop ERA movement, 89

Stop Rape (Parrent et al.), 96

Strange Memories: Death Bed Scenes, Extraordinary Conversions, Incidents of Travel, etc. (O'Reilly), 8

stream of consciousness, 28, 81, 160

Streep, Meryl, 139

Streetcar Named Desire, A (Williams), 41

strikes, 6, 20

Struthers, Sally, 89

suburbs, 31, 39, 54, 66, 75, 102–4, 154, 161, 181

suffragists, 2, 7–8, 20–22. *See also* women's liberation movement; women's rights

Sullivan, J. Courtney, 190–93

Sullivan, Kathleen, 153

"Sunday Like the Others, A" (Cullinan), 62

superwomen, 127, 221

Supreme Court: on abortion funding, 89; *Corning v. Brennan*, 98; *Eisenstadt v. Baird*, 98; first female appointees to state courts, 87; Obama appointments to, 219; Reagan appointments to, 119, 131, 133; *Roe v. Wade*, 96, 132, 133; on sexual harassment, 139; *Taylor v. Louisiana*, 98; women appointed to, 131, 153

surnames, 10

Swallow, Jean, 167n1

Sweeney, Terence Mac, 20

Sweet Beulah Land (Harris), 28

Swift, Jonathan, 5

Tailhook scandal, 152

"Talk of the Town" (column), 53, 58–59, 84

Tattooed Girl, The (Oates), 213

Taylor v. Louisiana, 98

teachers, 15, 18, 22–23, 26, 37, 41, 50–51, 77, 143, 183, 199, 211

Team of Rivals (Goodwin), 220

teenagers: in 1950s, 49; abortion for, 132, 151; contraception for, 131; post-feminist novels and, 190; self-mutilation by, 218–19; third-wave feminism and, 216–18

television shows, 34, 66–67, 87, 89, 139, 153, 155

Ten Days in a Madhouse (Cochrane), 10

Tender Land, The (Finneran), 206

Terminal Velocity (Boyd), 171

Terminator, The (movie), 139

Terms of Endearment (movie), 139

Terror Dream, The (Faludi), 186, 187, 188, 193, 194, 195, 198, 198n6

215; women's studies programs and, 136–37, 137n6; working women and, 60–61, 62–72. *See also* feminism; feminist themes; women's rights

Women's Liberation Movement (WLM) (Ireland), 87

Women's Military Advisory Committee, 188

Women's One World festivals, 135

women's rights: Bush administration and, 186, 187–89, 189n2, 193–94; death of, 2; early advocates for, 25; *The Handmaid's Tale* (Atwood) on, 117; post-9/11 period, 17, 186, 187–89, 189n2, 193–94, 198n6, 223–24; Reagan administration and, 117–20. *See also* feminism; suffragists; women's liberation movement

women's role. *See* wives and mothers tradition

women's studies programs, 55, 87–88, 136–37, 137n6, 152, 171–72

Women's Two Roles (Myrdal and Klein), 53

Wonderland (Oates), 95

Woods, Randall Bennett, 31, 41, 44, 50, 52, 53, 63, 65, 68, 69, 86, 87, 89, 90, 102, 104, 106, 118–19, 120, 130

Work-a-Day Girl: A Study of Some Present Conditions, The (Laughlin), 26

working women: in 1960s, 63–64; in 1970s, 86–87, 90; in 1990s, 153; affirmative action and, 66, 69; assimilation and, 50–51; birth control and, 21, 72–73; Catholic Church and, 79; history of, 18–19; labor activists and, 21–22; largest

ethnic group of, 15; marriage by, 51; in media, 66–69; notable exceptions among, 64; post-9/11 novels, 207; post-9/11 period, 187–88, 219–20; post–World War II, 30–35; pre–World War II period, 24, 26; Reagan administration and, 131; as role models, 36; sex discrimination laws and, 66, 69; sexual harassment decision and, 139; as superwomen, 127, 221; in "women's jobs," 63–64; women's liberation movement and, 60–61, 62–72

Working Women's Retreat Movement, 40

World War II, 30–32

Wyatt, Addie, 87

Xavier, Francis, 76

X-Files, The (TV show), 155

Yeats, William Butler, 9

Yellow Roses (Cullinan), 105, 113, 146

"Yellow Wallpaper, The" (Gilman), 27, 27n2, 122

Yezierska, Anzia, 54

You Must Remember This (Oates), 133

Young, Mallory, 197–98

Young Men's Sodality, 12

You're So Beautiful (Fitzgerald), 179

"You Say You Want a Devolution?" (Anderson), 198n7

Zaretsky, Eli, 98n2

Zimmerman, Bonnie, 88, 99, 100, 101, 135, 136, 140, 170, 171, 200